AFFECTIVE SPACES
MIGRATION IN SCANDINAVIAN AND
GERMAN TRANSNATIONAL NARRATIVES

LEGENDA

LEGENDA is the Modern Humanities Research Association's book imprint for new research in the Humanities. Founded in 1995 by Malcolm Bowie and others within the University of Oxford, Legenda has always been a collaborative publishing enterprise, directly governed by scholars. The Modern Humanities Research Association (MHRA) joined this collaboration in 1998, became half-owner in 2004, in partnership with Maney Publishing and then Routledge, and has since 2016 been sole owner. Titles range from medieval texts to contemporary cinema and form a widely comparative view of the modern humanities, including works on Arabic, Catalan, English, French, German, Greek, Italian, Portuguese, Russian, Spanish, and Yiddish literature. Editorial boards and committees of more than 60 leading academic specialists work in collaboration with bodies such as the Society for French Studies, the British Comparative Literature Association and the Association of Hispanists of Great Britain & Ireland.

The MHRA encourages and promotes advanced study and research in the field of the modern humanities, especially modern European languages and literature, including English, and also cinema. It aims to break down the barriers between scholars working in different disciplines and to maintain the unity of humanistic scholarship. The Association fulfils this purpose through the publication of journals, bibliographies, monographs, critical editions, and the MHRA Style Guide, and by making grants in support of research. Membership is open to all who work in the Humanities, whether independent or in a University post, and the participation of younger colleagues entering the field is especially welcomed.

ALSO PUBLISHED BY THE ASSOCIATION

Critical Texts
Tudor and Stuart Translations • *New Translations* • *European Translations*
MHRA Library of Medieval Welsh Literature

MHRA Bibliographies
Publications of the Modern Humanities Research Association

The Annual Bibliography of English Language & Literature
Austrian Studies
Modern Language Review
Portuguese Studies
The Slavonic and East European Review
Working Papers in the Humanities
The Yearbook of English Studies

www.mhra.org.uk
www.legendabooks.com

GERMANIC LITERATURES

Germanic Literatures includes monographs and essay collections on literature originally written not only in German, but also in Dutch and the Scandinavian languages. Within the German-speaking area, it seeks also to publish studies of other national literatures such as those of Austria and Switzerland. The chronological scope of the series extends from the early Middle Ages down to the present day.

Managing Editor
Dr Graham Nelson, 41 Wellington Square, Oxford OX1 2JF, UK
www.legendabooks.com

Affective Spaces

Migration in Scandinavian and German Transnational Narratives

❖

Anja Tröger

l

LEGENDA

Germanic Literatures 24
Modern Humanities Research Association
2021

Published by Legenda
an imprint of the Modern Humanities Research Association
Salisbury House, Station Road, Cambridge CB1 2LA

ISBN 978-1-83954-013-4 (HB)
ISBN 978-1-83954-014-1 (PB)

First published 2021

Copy-Editor: Dr Nigel Hope

CONTENTS

❖

ACKNOWLEDGEMENTS

❖

I would like to express my sincere gratitude to Bjarne Thorup Thomsen, Guy Puzey and Frauke Matthes, the supervisors of my PhD thesis on which this study is based. Their excellent supervision and encouragement, their support, constructive feedback and kindness made all the difference. My research has been carried out with the financial support of the University of Edinburgh's Northern Scholars PhD scholarship and I am most grateful for this generous stipend, without which this project could not have been realised. I am indebted to Peter Davies, who committed to my work with advice and highly valuable feedback at key moments, and also to my examiners, Arne Kruse and Moritz Schramm, for their thorough reading of my thesis and an inspiring discussion, which motivated me to publish this study.

While I have been fortunate to be part of the vibrant community in the School of Literatures, Languages and Cultures at the University of Edinburgh, I am particularly grateful to all staff in the Scandinavian Studies section, as they assured that I never rested within my comfort zone.

My thanks also go to Graham Nelson, Ritchie Robertson and Nigel Hope at Legenda for their careful reading and productive feedback at any stage in the publication process.

I am deeply indebted to Sara Kristina Davies, who allowed me to use one of her wonderful art works on the cover of this book — I am delighted.

I am particularly grateful to my friends Valerie Goodman, Robert Fell, Ian Anderson, Erden Göktepe and Étienne Sharp. Who had the glorious idea to extend peer support to the pub, to meet on a regular basis and to discuss our projects over a pint (or two)? I am very lucky to have Trish McGarry, Lucy Gilroyd and Nina Jones in my life, who are always there, by my side, with wisdom, kindness and laughter.

Above all, I would like to thank Steven Forbes, for his unfailing love and support. Parts of the work presented in chapter 5 will be published in Anna Meera Gaonkar, Astrid Øst Hansen, Hans Christian Post and Moritz Schramm (eds), *Postmigration: Art, Culture and Politics in Contemporary Europe* (London: Transcript, 2021).

A.T., January 2021

NOTE ON TRANSLATIONS

❖

Unless otherwise stated, all translations from languages other than English are my own, for reference only. All titles of primary, though not secondary texts, which are not originally published in English are translated. I am very much indebted to Kari Dickson for her generous support with translations from the Norwegian texts *Tante Ulrikkes vei* and *Opphold*, and to Ian Giles for his equally generous help with translations from the Swedish texts *Araben* and *De fördrivna*.

INTRODUCTION

❖

In 2013, the Swedish writer Jonas Hassen Khemiri published an open letter to Beatrice Ask, the Swedish Minister for Justice at the time, in response to her remarks in relation to the REVA project. This project, which ran in Sweden between 2008 and 2014, was initiated by the government with the aim to expedite 'the number of executed deportations of illegal immigrants from Sweden', and it granted the police the legal means to question anyone on the suspicion of lacking the sufficient documentation that would prove their rightful residence in the country.[1] It transpired that the police, despite being instructed otherwise, were predominantly questioning people on the basis of appearance, and concerns were raised that they were actually conducting racial profiling, which soon led to a heated public debate about the lawfulness of the REVA project. In defence of the project, Ask, in a radio interview, dismissed accusations of reinforcing institutional racism, and she stated that instead, the issue was of a personal nature: 'Upplevelsen av varför någon har frågat mig kan ju vara väldigt personlig' [One's experience of 'why someone has questioned me' can of course be very personal].[2] In response to this statement, Khemiri makes Ask an offer: 'Jag vill att vi byter skinn och erfarenheter. Kom igen' [I want us to trade our skins and our experiences. Come on].[3] This body swap would enable Ask

> att förstå att när du kommer ut på gatan, ned i tunnelbanan, in i köpcentret och ser polismännen stå där, med Lagen på sin sida, med rätten att närma sig dig och be dig bevisa din oskuld så väcker det minnen till liv. Andra övergrepp, andra uniformer, andra blickar.

> [to understand that when you go out into the street, down into the subway, into the shopping center, and see the policeman [sic] standing there, with the Law on his side, with the right to approach you and ask you to prove your innocence, it brings back memories. Other abuses, other uniforms, other looks.] (131)

And, while Khemiri lists some of these memories of racialised abuse, marginalisation and violence that Ask would have the chance to experience vicariously, he also points out, in his imagination merging his body with that of Ask, that 'vår kropp är uppvuxen innanför tullarna [...] vår verklighet är ombonade kuddrum i jämförelse med det som händer de på riktigt maktlösa, resurslösa, papperslösa' [our body grew up on this side of customs [...] our reality is like a cozy room full of pillows in comparison with what happens to those who are truly without power, without resources, without papers] (139). Yet, despite the ostensible privilege to be born within Sweden's national boundaries, it is difficult, Khemiri states, to feel a sense of belonging when you are excluded from society: 'Och det är omöjligt att vara en del av gemenskapen när Makten ständigt förutsätter att en är en Annan' [And it's impossible to be part of a community when Power continually assumes that you are an Other] (138). Identifying that power relations are not only at the core of, but also sanction practices of othering, Khemiri further observes, 'Men ingen gör något. I stället fokuserar vi på att lokalisera människor som har flytt hit på jakt efter den trygghet som vi är så stolta över att kunna erbjuda (vissa av) våra medborgare' [But no one does anything. Instead we focus on locating people who have moved here in search of the security that we're so proud of being able to offer (some of) our citizens] (141). In Khemiri's view, safety in Sweden is guaranteed disparately, and, while some qualify for security, others are exposed to measures of securitisation, which creates a divide between 'us' and 'them'.

Khemiri's open letter, first published in *Dagens Nyheter* on 13 March 2013, is a polemic answer to the lived reality of a particular political constellation in Sweden at a particular time. The twelve novels which constitute the core subject matter of this book negotiate in fictional form those themes Khemiri addresses: policies and practices of exclusion, processes of othering, and the disparate distribution of precarity in the context of migration. However, considering that a general requirement of fiction is 'that we step outside of ourselves and into "the shoes" of a character', these twelve texts offer the reader a similar vicarious act of the imagination as proposed to Ask by Khemiri: for the duration of the reading experience, the reader is asked to trade skins and experiences, and is invited to feel what it is like to be marginalised or othered, or to be in a close encounter with someone culturally or ethnically different from oneself. In this respect, the reading of fiction entails a cognitive challenge in contrast to watching a film or seeing a staged play, as it asks us to convert 'marks on a page into meaningful thoughts, emotions, relationships, and actions'. This conversion is facilitated by a process of identification with 'an abstract other to whom I have no physical access', and the reader's engagement with this abstract other becomes an 'imaginative act' that 'demands that I view the world from an alternative perspective'.[4] Furthermore, as Suzanne Keen points out, the reading of fiction grants the reader a certain freedom to reflect on, and react to, characters and themes in different ways than in real life, because 'the perception of fictionality releases novel-readers from the normal state of alert suspicion of others', which means that 'the contract of fictionality offers a no-strings-attached opportunity for emotional transactions of great intensity'.[5]

With regard to the twelve texts this study is concerned with, this contract of fictionality allows us to view the world from the perspectives of the texts' characters, or, to borrow Wayne C. Booth's phrase, to 'travel with' or 'stand against' characters who are either exposed to, or the agents of, marginalisation and othering.[6] In Milan Kundera's words, the freedom implicit in this contract grants us the unique opportunity to ponder about 'the relativity and ambiguity of things human', and to engage affectively and intellectually with quandaries in the characters' lives which might be unthinkable in our own reality; and yet, as these texts follow the genre conventions of realism insofar as they position their characters in recognisable locations and clearly delimited time frames, this proximity to the real world can be understood as a proposition to make connections between the literary realm and our own reality.[7] However, while Keen draws attention to the notion that the relationship between text and reader is indeed affective, she also builds a caveat into her argument by stating that it would require extensive empirical study to gauge the actual impact of reading on the reader's real world, as readers bring their emotional engagement to fictional texts, but 'they alone have the capacity to convert their emotional fusion with the denizens of make-believe worlds into actions on behalf of real others'.[8] In light of this, I conceive of the political or ethical reach of these texts beyond the confines of the literary realm as a potential. While the contract of fictionality grants us the freedom to entertain an alternative perspective on those politics depicted as impinging upon the characters' life situations, I view the politics of the texts themselves as an invitation to take up their impulses and translate them into our own reality.

The twelve literary texts are symmetrically divided between Denmark, Germany, Norway and Sweden, with three texts of each country's literature, and their publication dates fall into the relatively narrow timeframe between 2011 and 2017. While this text selection reflects the topicality that the accelerated and cumulative immigration to Europe predominantly from the Greater Middle East and Africa gained in the second decade of the twenty-first century, the migratory histories referred to in the texts' contents span a much wider period. The characters who travel to the four countries do so from different points of departure and moments in the past, so acknowledging that migration, obviously, is not a phenomenon limited to the current day and age. Only some of the texts engage implicitly or explicitly with the challenges that contemporary developments pose to the whole of Europe, whereas all twelve texts reimagine poignant issues such as marginalisation, othering and racism, and can thus be viewed as contributing to the ongoing and intensified debate about immigration. The texts focus not solely on characters who themselves migrate, but also on their descendants, and on characters who encounter those they perceive or marginalise as migrants. This multiplicity of perspectives allows me to illuminate the different steps of the migratory journey, as the texts encapsulate lived migrant experiences in different contemporaneous contexts, and capture the experiences of migrants — or of their descendants — who, at some point in their lives, made the difficult decision to leave their homes and countries to escape political strife and economic hardship, and to search for a better and safer life elsewhere. In short, the texts depict individual journeys that are arduously challenging, and characters who are forced to migrate for economic or political reasons, along with characters who are exposed to processes of marginalisation and othering in their so-called host countries. The texts correlate thematically, as they, in similar ways to Khemiri in his open letter, describe processes of othering not only as discursive and reinforced by social and political power relations, but also as embodied; they further detail how difference is felt and negotiated on the level of the skin, and when someone is thus made to feel different, how it affects this person's life, body and self-understanding. Comparing these texts enables me to explore precisely these affects and how they are produced, and to illustrate the ways in which they influence the texts' characters, and how this affective impact is facilitated and reinforced by social and political structures.

The chapters of this study follow the migratory journey chronologically and therefore the first line of enquiry is concerned with the ways in which the twelve texts depict the different stages of migration, from departure and travel to an uncertain arrival, and how they negotiate and problematise a sense of belonging, or the notion of integration. Leading on from this, I shall map out those affects which are generated by precarious life situations, in embodied encounters, and through policies and practices of inclusion or exclusion, and illustrate how they bear upon the characters' self-understanding. This, to put it differently, implies a detailed analysis of the ways in which the texts' characters affect the world around them, and how they, in turn, are reciprocally affected by their surroundings. In my analysis of the societal and political climates into which the characters' lives and histories are embedded, it is Khemiri's question to Ask that will guide the critical reading of the texts: 'När blir en personlig upplevelse en rasistisk struktur? När blir den diskriminering, förtryck, våld?' [When does a personal experience become a structure of racism? When does it become discrimination, oppression, violence?] (130). Looking at the texts through Khemiri's question allows me to point out how they depict the power relations underpinning the characters' conflicts and struggles, and in which ways they hold them up to the reader for critical reflection.

Reading twelve texts within the scope of this book implies that the discussions of these texts are far from exhaustive; instead, my readings are highly selective, and do not discuss, or only touch upon briefly, other possible strands of enquiry. In favour of a strong focus on the ways that affect, and related subjective emotions, can grant insights into socio-political power structures, I utilise interpretations through the lens of class, economics and gender in order to support this focus and substantiate related points, but not comprehensively; and, while it is possible to point out the narrative techniques which invite the reader's affective engagement, an extensive analysis of the reader's affective relationship with these fictional texts would go beyond the scope of this study and dilute the actual textual analysis. However, the multiplicity of texts and perspectives is conducive to comparing the depictions of individual migrant and postmigrant characters and the societies in which they live, and to scrutinising the texts' own political stances.[9] Comparing texts which centre on asylum seekers and refugees with texts featuring native Scandinavian or German characters who encounter those they perceive as 'other' is a productive way to throw into sharp relief how processes of marginalisation and othering work affectively; moreover, the politics of the individual texts are brought into clearer focus when they are contrasted with each other.[10]

With three texts each from the literatures of Denmark, Norway and Sweden, this study has a clear focus on Scandinavian themes; yet, the inclusion of three texts from German literature promises to yield results beyond those an inter-Scandinavian comparison could produce. The Scandinavian countries themselves are often imagined and described as an entity not only on a geopolitical, but also on a cultural level. This perceived unity certainly has historical roots as well as practical political realities, and in addition, since their coming into existence after the Second World War, the Scandinavian welfare states 'assumed common sets of national values that varied only somewhat within the region as a whole', which suggests a certain sense of homogeneity between the different Scandinavian nations.[11] It is not only Scandinavians themselves, however, who contribute to constructing this notion of a homogeneous North, but this image is also reinforced from outside Scandinavia, as Elisabeth Oxfeldt, with reference to the Nordic countries, points out: 'I verdensperspektiv representerer vi "den nordiske modellen" karakterisert av lykke, velstand, tillit og likhet' [In a global perspective, we represent 'the Nordic model' characterised by happiness, prosperity, trust and equality].[12] This global perspective is substantiated by the fact that the Nordic countries regularly top the ranking lists of both the Human Development Index (HDI) and the Happiness Report, which credits them with being the happiest countries in the world in terms of gender equality, income per capita, working conditions and standard of living. In Oxfeldt's view, as a result of these unique conditions, 'blir samtidens globale kontraster mellom privilegerte og ikke-privilegerte nasjoner ekstra grelle i tilfelle Skandinavia' [contemporary global contrasts between privileged and non-privileged nations become particularly glaring in the case of Scandinavia].[13] This observation poses the question of what the texts can tell us about Scandinavian societies. Do they engage with this particularly stark contrast when they depict characters from non-privileged nations who arrive or live at the margins of Scandinavian societies, and who enter into encounters with ostensibly privileged Scandinavians? This Scandinavian privilege and the concomitant perceived happiness are closely related to the notion of Scandinavian exceptionalism, which means, as Oxfeldt explains from a postcolonial perspective, that Scandinavians absolve themselves from historical feelings of guilt on the basis of the idea 'at man som skandinav ikke i særlig grad deltok i kolonisering, imperialisme og slavehandel' [that as a Scandinavian, you did not participate to a significant degree in colonisation, imperialism and slave trade]. Oxfeldt exposes this view of history as biased, and, by making a connection with the present day, explains that it has led to a Scandinavian self-image that has a tendency 'mot å være nokså uskyldsrent, og man tenker ikke på sin egen nasjon som aggressiv, eller dens handlinger som skamfulle' [towards being rather innocent, and you do not think of your own nation as aggressive, or its actions as shameful].[14] In view of this, I shall examine whether the texts depict the popular Nordic model as applicable to those constructed as 'other', or in which ways they challenge the veracity of this perceived happiness. The incorporation of German-literature texts in contrast with novels from Scandinavia makes it possible to spotlight each society and its potential set of problems in its own right. However, carving out correlations between the German and Scandinavian texts allows for a more in-depth questioning of the supposed homogeneity of the Scandinavian countries, and for scrutinising the notion of Scandinavian exceptionalism from a transnational perspective.

For the critical reading of the twelve novels, I draw on insights from affect theory and associated theoretical studies of emotions as an interpretative framework, which allows for investigations into multiple directions. Not only can the migratory and transnational experiences of the texts' characters be read as existentially lived and embodied encounters, but when the texts' aesthetic choices are interpreted through the lens of affect, it sheds light on the ways that 'affect develops the narrative architecture of a literary text'. These affective textual strategies 'offer us windows on contextual configurations', and facilitate a critical understanding of those social and political structures in which the characters' lives become involved.[15] Furthermore, affect as an analytical tool makes it possible to establish connections between the texts beyond their linguistic boundaries when thematic similarities are identified across different temporal and spatial settings, and when the related emotions are brought into resonance with each other. In summary, affect supports an exploration of the texts' transnational subjectivities; an investigation of the novels' emotional and affective textual composition; an analysis of the social and political undercurrents encroaching upon the characters' life situations; and an interpretative reading of how the texts' themes resonate with each other affectively. From these four directions, a concluding question can be distilled that will bring them together and interlink them: 'What is our responsibility toward those we do not know, toward those who seem to test our sense of belonging or to defy available norms of likeness?' Judith Butler finds a tentative answer to the ethical question that she phrases so poignantly when she suggests, 'Perhaps such a responsibility can only begin to be realized through a critical reflection on those exclusionary norms by which fields of recognizability are constituted'.[16] I contend, however, that a sense of ethical responsibility can be achieved not only through critical reflection, but that responsiveness to others, and, consequently, responsibility and pro-social action, may be generated via affect in situated and embodied encounters. This means exploring the ways in which the twelve texts negotiate such exclusionary norms either implicitly or explicitly, and how they display the characters' sense of affective responsibility, or lack thereof. In this sense, this study seeks to provide precisely the kind of critical reflection Butler calls for, while attempting to answer the question of whether or not these texts can contribute to fostering a sense of affective responsibility 'toward those we do not know'.

In his acclaimed essay collection, *The World, the Text, and the Critic*, Edward Said 'affirms the connection between texts and the existential actualities of human life, politics, societies, and events'. When literary texts are thus part of the social world, and when 'a text in its actually *being* a text is a being in the world', it is equally embedded into the 'realities of power and authority', which, according to Said, 'should be taken account of by criticism and the critical consciousness'. In agreement with Said's proposition, I understand the twelve texts not as images of the social world, but as closely connected to this world, in conversation and intercommunion with this world, via the reader. Affect, then, is a particularly valuable tool to assess the texts, as it enables an investigation of the power structures they depict, and also how these depictions possibly resonate with the social world by affectively engaging the reader. Therefore, the following discussion elaborates on different conceptualisations of affect and the body, and how they will be brought together to serve the critical readings best. In addition, it elucidates, and expounds the problems of, those key terms and concepts that have so far been only mentioned in passing but will be recurrent throughout the textual analyses: transnational literature and the postmigrant research perspective; borders, boundaries and liminal zones; and affective responsibility. This assembly of complementary theories and concepts enhances the task of the critic, which, as I understand it, is to expose those realities of power depicted in the texts, and how they possibly correlate with the reader's social world. This is because 'criticism', as Said convincingly argues, 'must think of itself as life-enhancing and constitutively opposed to every form of tyranny, domination, and abuse; its social goals are noncoercive knowledge produced in the interests of human freedom'.[17]

Transnational Literature

In broad terms, transnationalism can be understood as 'the multiple activities — economic, political, cultural, personal — that require sustained contacts and travel across national borders', and it is mainly referred to in relation with, and as an effect of, globalisation as a phenomenon of our current day and age: 'Enhanced transnational connections between social groups represent a key manifestation of globalization'.[18] In celebratory readings of transnationalism, movement and rootless mobility are often regarded as 'the dominant form of social life and individual experience of the contemporary "global" world of "flows" and "liquidity"'.[19] From this perspective, borders between nations are presumed to be porous and permeable. For those neo-nomadic cosmopolitans with multiple cultural affiliations across national borders, the notion of belonging has become fluid and is not bound to a nation-state, and hence, it is seen in binary opposition to sedentary forms of belonging. While there is no doubt, with an accelerated increase in the quantity of people and products travelling transnationally, that 'certain kinds of relationships have been globally intensified', the presence and reality of national borders, together with the concomitant immigration laws and policies, cannot be neglected, because 'the phantasm of limitless mobility often rests on the power of border controls and policing of who does and does not belong'.[20] Steven Vertovec confirms this observation when he asserts that, 'Almost regardless of global economic flows, inter-state pacts and other sides of globalization, nation-states firmly retain the right [...] to control migration and membership'.[21] Vertovec argues further that particularly migrant transnationalism 'confronts "identities-borders-orders"',[22] suggesting that this confrontation questions and problematises the reinforcement of national borders, and the disparate allocation of national memberships. Therefore, the importance of the nation, and the particular significance of its borders and their regulations, remains relevant for a conceptualisation of the term transnationalism; however, with the ambition, implied by the prefix trans-, towards a transcendence of these very borders. This study is informed by this ambition in that it analyses texts that challenge the imperative of particular border policies and practices; moreover, this ambition is reflected in the selection of texts from four contiguous countries, and comparisons between and across these countries.

The term 'transnational literature' initially came to stand for a creative reflection on the global phenomena of increased mobility and flux, and critics, such as Azade Seyhan, usually conceived of transnational texts as 'the contemporary tales of migration, exile, and displacement'.[23] The migrant background of the authors was often perceived as one of the texts' defining features, which ostensibly excluded them from the canons of national literatures; or the multinational, multicultural affiliations of authors who lead a cosmopolitan mobile lifestyle made categorisations into national literatures difficult. In recent years, however, the conception of transnationalism has shifted away from exclusively pertaining to those who actually migrate, or cross borders, and towards an understanding in which transnationalism and its effects also concern those who are viewed as sedentary: 'the intensity and multidirectionality of transnationalism imply that *all* are impacted by the flows of people, products, and ideas across borders, including those who do not themselves move'. Consequently, in literary studies, the production of transnational texts becomes untied from the author's migrant biography, and 'the adjective "transnational" may be better applied to *texts* dealing with a contemporary phenomenon rather than solely to *authors* who happen to have a migration background'.[24] This suggests that transnational literature is not merely 'a genre of writing that operates outside the national canon, [and] addresses issues facing deterritorialized cultures', but as writing that operates within, and as part of, any national canon of literature, transnationalising this very canon.[25] This does not mean that transnational texts have superseded tales of migration and displacement, but that they are not limited to these themes, and, when the focus has shifted from 'the movement of *some* [...] across borders toward the implication of *all*', individual migratory tales can be read as incorporated into cultural, social and political structures.[26] This means that, while the whole of any so-called national culture undergoes processes of commingling, and, to a certain degree, amalgamation, the fact remains that for some migrants, the crossing of borders is marked with difficulties and uncertainties.

In light of this, the purpose of characterising the twelve texts as transnational literature is to make evident 'the urgency of issues of belonging, inclusion and exclusion, citizenship, forced and unforced movement, status and privilege' — independently from the background of the texts' authors.[27] This understanding of transnational literature allows for the inclusion of a multiplicity of perspectives on migration and postmigration: it grants the scope to encompass texts that depict migratory journeys directly; or capture the experiences of postmigrant characters who have not necessarily migrated themselves; or portray seemingly sedentary native Scandinavian or German characters who encounter those they perceive as strangers to themselves. Furthermore, this understanding of transnational literature allows for analysing the individual experiences of the texts' characters within the wider framework of the cultural, social and political structures into which these imagined subjectivities are embedded. The concept of a postmigrant perspective, as Moritz Schramm lays it out, is closely related to this conceptualisation of transnational literature, and will complement the textual analysis particularly in chapter 5. According to Schramm's definition, the term 'postmigrant' itself circumscribes 'einen spezifischen Erfahrungsraum von Nachkommen von Zugewanderten' [a specific experiential space of descendants of migrants] who have not travelled themselves, but who are nevertheless shaped by 'den verbreiteten Fremdzuschreibungen als "Ausländer" oder "Migrant"' [the prevalent ascriptions by others as 'foreigner' or 'migrant']. The postmigrant perspective in literary analysis can be understood as a critical tool which enables the assessment of such postmigrant characters and their subjectivities; but, more importantly, as a research perspective, it has as its aim, 'Migration als gesellschaftliche Grundbedingung sichtbar zu machen' [to make visible that migration is a fundamental condition of any society], and further, to bring to light 'die Dynamiken der Ein- und Ausgrenzung, der Verhandlung und der Auseinandersetzung mit den in der Gesellschaft vorliegenden Folgen von früheren und aktuellen Migrationsbewegungen' [the dynamics of inclusion and exclusion, of the negotiations and debates about the existing consequences of past and present migration movements in society].[28] Similar to transnational literature as I understand it, the postmigrant perspective allows for a widening of the scope from personal and individual realms of experience to the whole of society, with the ambition to expose the power relations at the root of the characters' individual struggles. Instead of focusing on a particular canon of literature that is predicated on the migrant background of its authors, which would inevitably lead to a bracketing of such authors and their texts and to a methodological constriction, the texts are selected independently from the authors' background, and the authors' background will not be discussed. The fact that the texts are written in the four national languages Danish, German, Norwegian and Swedish affiliates them to the national literatures of these four countries respectively. The choice of texts from these four literatures acknowledges that linguistic and national parameters are still relevant and in place when it comes to cultural production, but, as I draw comparisons and create interrelations across these national and linguistic determinants, this study is informed by the ambition to highlight the connectivity of themes and texts beyond national boundaries.

Borders, Boundaries and Liminal Zones

When national borders, and also social and cultural boundaries, still play a significant role for conceptualisations of transnational literature, it is necessary to say a few words on the very topic of borders and boundaries. Borders, as territorial and political dividing lines, are recognised in international law and circumscribe geographic space; they also define the limits of sovereign power and of state control over those subjects living within these borders, with the implication that these limits may be forcefully upheld and defended.[29] Hence, borders are those political lines of demarcation where it is drawn out, and, if considered necessary, contested, who is regarded as belonging within these borders and who is not. When the power to demarcate inclusion and exclusion is inherent in borders, it is these contestations that make the border, and, as Nevzat Soguk rightly points out, 'borders acquire their meanings always contingently' because they are 'consequential only where and when border practices are at work'.[30] This indicates that these political lines of separation are by no means neutral, considering that they, through these practices, 'authorize a distinction between norm and exception'.[31] The policies in place and the practices executed to distinguish between norm and exception do not only pertain to the physical border between one country and another, but when borders are 'camouflaged and concealed in other forms', they become '[c]ultural fences, class walls, and gender ditches', and hence, the idea of the border is reproduced 'in the multiple localities and spatialities of state and society'.[32] In a similar vein, Avtar Brah argues that borders can be viewed as metaphors 'for psychological, sexual, spiritual, cultural, class and racialised boundaries'. Instead of denying the political reality of actual land borders, these metaphors are 'part of the discursive materiality of power relations' and can 'serve as powerful inscriptions of the effects of political borders'.[33] In this respect, the border area itself represents a 'relational framework' within which the negotiations between self and other, own and different, are played out, and the political reality of such border areas, as well as the concomitant power relations, expand into social and cultural dimensions within the confines of the nation-state.[34]

When this border area, or 'borderscape', continues from the spatial boundaries of the nation-state into the cultural and social arena, it is 'recognizable not in a physical location but tangentially in struggles to clarify inclusion from exclusion'.[35] Since these areas are open to overlaps and clashes, to the conflicts between belonging and un-belonging, the known and the unknown, the meaning of the border as a point of contention, as a delimitation between inclusion and exclusion, is inherently contestable. This suggests that the border area is predominantly characterised by uncertainty — an uncertainty which applies to those crossing a national border, and also to those within national borders engaged in negotiations of inclusion or exclusion. I make use of the term 'liminal zone', as it allows for an analysis of all those areas where the twelve texts depict precisely such negotiations. The term 'liminal zone' grants the scope to encompass situations in which the texts' characters travel towards, arrive at, or cross a state border, and it enables the inclusion of spaces such as refugee camps or centres for asylum seekers, in which some of the characters are detained. In addition, the term 'liminal zone' can refer to all those spaces where the texts mediate notions of sameness and difference in social or cultural contexts, and in personal encounters.

In its literal meaning, 'liminality' — from the Latin word *limen* — denotes a threshold and thus stands for a place or a state in-between, one that is marked by transitoriness and indeterminacy.[36] According to Michel Agier, in the context of migration, 'the presence and scope of a liminality' is 'the most universal characteristic of the border'.[37] When migrants, and particularly refugees and asylum seekers, arrive at, or cross, a border as the threshold between one country and another, they enter a liminal zone, the aforementioned place of uncertainty, which is neither here nor there; they are not yet familiar with the laws and customs of the new place and might keenly feel a sense of being 'foreign' or 'other' precisely because of this indeterminate state. In addition, newcomers such as asylum seekers or refugees are placed on the margins of society and are only peripherally noticed by the citizens who belong to the society of the so-called host country. Agier points out that this form of marginalisation has social implications, as it is concomitant with a 'state of uncertainty about existing socially and being recognized by others'. This lack of recognition, as Agier goes on to say, is tantamount to a 'liminal condition [...] which does not have the status of a social category', and, through the combination of marginalisation and the absence of a social status, newcomers find themselves in 'a state hardly perceptible, hardly audible and "voiceless"'.[38] Addressing the notions of invisibility and inaudibility in a similar way, Zygmunt Bauman argues that refugees are 'not only un*touch*ables, but un*think*ables [...] they are the *unimaginables*'.[39] It is crucial to remember, however, that this invisibility and voicelessness does not just happen by itself; rather, 'it takes an act of some will, as well as a certain amount of institutional force, to effect [the] invisibility [of refugees] and erase their relation to the norm'.[40] Yet, some of the twelve texts implicitly or explicitly broach the issue of asylum seekers and refugees and, by way of imagining the journeys of individual migrants and presenting them to the reader, counteract the view that these migrants are made voiceless and invisible. By giving asylum seekers and refugees a voice and a platform, these texts refute the claim that they are, as Bauman suggests, unimaginables.

When it comes to the ways in which the twelve texts depict those liminal zones in which boundaries of sameness and difference are staked out in personal encounters, and in social and cultural contexts, Ahmed's concept of stranger fetishism offers itself as a constructive tool to think critically through these encounters. Ahmed argues that white Westerners tend to produce the stranger as a figure — or a fetish — by constructing the 'other' as unknown, different or strange to them, thus ontologising the stranger because their being is determined from the outside by their status as strangers. In the embodied encounter, the stranger is fixed in a juxtaposition of proximity and distance; a bodily image is created as different by means of 'practices and techniques of differentiation', and the body 'becomes imagined through being related to, and separated from, particular bodily others'. When, on the basis of outward appearances, someone is marked as a stranger, as 'other', or as out of place, this differentiation is felt on the skin, and affectively charged, 'For if the skin is a border, then it is *a border that feels*'. This marking of one body as stranger than other bodies also initiates 'relations of social and political antagonism' when the body is viewed as being part of, and inscribed within, political, social and cultural formations.[41] To put it differently, every encounter implies a potential conflict which is registered on the skin and initiated by the forces that move between bodies.

As this brief outline illustrates, Ahmed is coming from the assumption that encounters are always embodied not only as face-to-face meetings, but also on the level of the skin, and from this observation, she derives her concept of stranger fetishism. It is here, in the physical realm of an encounter, that boundaries are delimited: 'Difference is not only found in the body, but is established as a relation between bodies'.[42] Brah suggests that in some discourses, difference is perceived as positing 'fixed and immutable boundaries', whereas others conceive of it as 'relational, contingent and variable'; in other words, notions of difference are dependent on the context and the ways in which particular discourses of difference are constituted. This observation holds true for discursive, and also for embodied, conceptualisations of difference, and instead of always signifying 'hierarchy and oppression [...] it is a contextually contingent question whether difference pans out as inequity, exploitation and oppression *or as* egalitarianism, diversity and democratic forms of political agency'.[43] When the embodied encounter can be regarded as a negotiation of physical boundaries — a boundary as flexible, sensitive and feeling as the skin — which can either reinforce or transform notions of what is familiar or strange, it is not only the potential for conflict that is implicit in every encounter, but also the capacity for the transcendence of boundaries. Referring to Gilles Deleuze and Félix Guattari's 'principle of proximity or approximation', or 'the sense in which becoming is the process of desire', Brian Massumi, discussing his interpretation of this notion of becoming, states, 'The place of invention is a space of transformational encounter, a dynamic in-between'.[44] To put it another way, in an encounter in which difference turns into a trigger for the desire to come closer to the 'other', formerly rigid boundaries become porous, and new, or unknown, qualities can emerge in the space between individuals. This perspective allows me to point towards the ways in which notions of sameness and difference are mediated in the twelve texts, and whether difference, as it is played out in the characters' encounters, leads to antagonism and conflict, or opens up the possibility for new alliances. However, to be able to assess such embodied encounters critically, it is necessary to conceptualise not only the body itself, but also the forces, or affects, that move between and beyond bodies.

Affect and the Body

Since the affective turn in the mid-1990s, affect has been defined differently — and sometimes contradictorily — within and across a number of disciplines, and research on affect has taken diverging, although often intersecting, routes. Gregory J. Seigworth and Melissa Gregg discuss these diverging routes and selectively outline eight orientations, or research strands, for critical approaches to affect, ranging from Spinozan-Deleuzian interpretations to neuroscientific ones.[45] Across these different research strands, the divergences begin with the question of what affects actually are, and to what extent affects differ from emotions, which illustrates the ambiguity that is implicit in the term itself, and, therefore, the difficulty to define it accurately. In his seminal study, *Parables for the Virtual*, Brian Massumi argues for a clear distinction between affect and emotion. Affects, Massumi propounds, are autonomous forces of relation that can be conceived of as impersonal, non-subjective intensities that are constitutive of the body, but simultaneously escape it: 'Affect is autonomous to the degree to which it escapes confinement in the particular body whose vitality, or potential for interaction, it is'. In contrast, Massumi defines emotions as personal qualities that can be arranged in categories, and have particular functions and meanings; an emotion, according to Massumi, is 'a subjective content, the sociolinguistic fixing of the quality of an experience [...] It is intensity owned and recognized'.[46] Conversely, Ahmed does not make a clear distinction between affect and emotion, and, blurring the boundary between the two categories, treats them as interchangeable. In Ahmed's view, emotions are personal and of the body, and they 'circulate between bodies' and '"stick" as well as move'. When emotions are thus produced in dynamic encounters, they 'shape the very surfaces of bodies, which take shape through repetition over time, as well as through orientations towards and away from others'. In this sense, emotions regulate the relationship between an individual and a social body in that they 'produce the very surfaces and boundaries that allow the individual and the social to be delineated as if they are objects'.[47] Bypassing the intricacies with regard to definition, Ann Pellegrini and Jasbir Puar are 'less interested in delimiting the boundaries of what affect is or is not and more compelled by the generative and productive multiplicity of its deployment as an analytical and political frame'.[48] In other words, instead of attempting a precise definition of affect, Pellegrini and Puar intend to examine what affects do, which implies, in their interpretation, that affects, and analyses through the lens of affect, are politically charged, and can potentially inspire political action.

The notion that affect can inspire action harks back to Benedict de Spinoza's *Ethics* from 1677, where he defines affect as 'affections of the body by which the body's power of acting is increased or diminished, aided or restrained'.[49] In his reading of Spinoza, Michael Hardt describes affects as developing simultaneous correspondences between body and mind, reason and passion; in this regard, affects refer to two sets of parallels: firstly, 'the mind's power to think' and 'the body's power to act', and secondly, 'the power to act and the power to be affected'. Affects, then, can be seen as part of a complex causality, or rather, a two-sided causality, as Hardt points out, 'because the affects belong simultaneously to both sides of the causal relationship. They illuminate [...] both our power to affect the world around us and our power to be affected by it'.[50] In this sense, affects instigate a responsiveness, or receptivity, to the world; being defined as corporeal and intellectual at the same time, affects circumscribe our capacity to think through and feel, to act in and react to, this world and the encounters we have with others. The understanding of affect as capacity implies that affects have the immanent potential 'for extending further still: both into and out of the interstices of the inorganic and non-living, the intra-cellular divulgences of sinew, tissue, and gut economies, and the vaporous evanescences of the incorporeal (events, atmospheres, feeling-tones)'.[51] In this theorisation, affects are understood as corporeal and, simultaneously, as reaching beyond the physical boundaries of the skin, including the subtle and minute forces, or intensities, that pass between bodies. This suggests that through these intensities, situations and events become affectively charged. Frederik Tygstrup confirms this notion with a threefold approach to affect, in which he conceives of affects as 'relational, as situational and as corporeal'. Tygstrup goes on to argue that affects 'cannot be pinned down to one specific realm or layer of reality, but [they] seem to persist as a material/immaterial halo or sphere hovering indistinctly but nonetheless insistently above and within any field of human agency and interaction'.[52] In this light, human encounters become imbued with affects, and also the situations and spaces where these encounters take place, which highlights our connection with, or disconnection from, the world.

When affect is understood as corporeal, while simultaneously emphasising relationality, it indicates that the body should always be conceptualised in relation to others. Substantiating this notion in his interpretation of Spinoza's *Ethics*, Gilles Deleuze describes the body in two correlating ways: a body 'is composed of [...] the relations of movement and rest, of speeds and slowness between particles', and, at the same time, it is defined by its 'capacity for affecting and being affected'.[53] This conception of the body is somewhat abstract as it comprises the body's physical reality — flesh and blood — as well as the forces and intensities that go beyond the body's physical limit. David Hillman and Ulrika Maude endorse the difficulty of theorising this protean entity of the body, when they state that the body is 'mutable, in perpetual flux, different from day to day and resistant to conceptual definition';[54] or, as Maurice Merleau-Ponty puts it, the body's 'unity is always implicit and vague. It is always something other than what it is [...] never hermetically sealed and never left behind'.[55] In view of this, a conceptualisation of the body can be located 'on a spectrum between relative fixity and radical flux', and, when the body is thus conceived of as an open concept, this openness holds the potential which instigates the body's relations to others and the world, and, as Michael Richardson asserts, 'the vectors of that potential [...] are affects'.[56]

Obviously, this conceptualisation of the body as always affectively implicated in others and the world implies that the body is receptive to a multiplicity of impulses that can have positive or negative effects. A case in point is Richardson's study *Gestures of Testimony*, in which he utilises affect theory to analyse the effects of torture and trauma. Although it is an extreme example, it is an insightful source to shed light on these negative effects, particularly when considering that, 'Certain encounters can change bodies radically, can cause them to grow, enlighten, transform, strengthen them — or mutate, freeze, rupture, break, traumatize'.[57] To think critically through the ways in which some encounters rupture and break bodies, Butler's notion of, and differentiation between, precariousness and precarity is instructive. According to Butler, precariousness is a fundamental condition of human life, because every human life 'requires various social and economic conditions to be met in order to be sustained as a life'.[58] These life-sustaining conditions are 'pervasively social', and therefore, Butler argues for a 'social ontology' instead of a 'discrete ontology of the person' in order to acknowledge both the dependency of the individual on a social body, and the concomitant precariousness.[59] In contrast, Butler defines precarity as a 'politically induced condition in which certain populations suffer from failing social and economic networks of support and become differentially exposed to injury, violence, and death.[60] This condition of precarity is reminiscent of Michel Foucault's definition of biopower, a term that he describes as 'the set of mechanisms through which the basic biological features of the human species became the object of a political strategy, of a general strategy of power'.[61] When precarity is understood as politically effectuated, it can prove to be a direct result of a bio-politics of difference with disparate perceptions of which lives should be sustained to a greater or lesser degree.

Butler's conceptualisation of precariousness and precarity highlights, on the one hand, the inherent relationality of the human body, its connectedness to the world: 'That the body invariably comes up against the outside world is a sign of the general predicament of unwilled proximity to others and to circumstances beyond one's control'. On the other hand, and similar to Richardson, Butler emphasises the vulnerability this precariousness entails, because the body is always 'exposed to others, vulnerable by definition'.[62] Most of the characters portrayed in the twelve texts epitomise this vulnerability, and also the sense of precarity Butler discusses, because they are either separated from former social networks, or exposed to conditions that jeopardise the safety of the body and the sustainability of life itself. Bauman, in his sombre reflections on the influx of refugees to Europe in 2015, finds a tentative answer for the reasons why precarity is distributed disparately when he suggests that those seeking refuge in Europe 'remind us [...] of the (incurable?) vulnerability of our own position and of the endemic fragility of our hard-won well-being'. Migrants, and those perceived or constructed as migrants, thus come to stand for this reminder, which can explain the hostility often shown towards newcomers by populations that are 'already haunted by the existential frailty and precariousness of their social standing and prospects'.[63] Roger Bromley phrases the same disturbing circumstances in less cautious terms when he states, 'At a time when the "European" narrative is ceasing to make sense, cohere, motivate, or hold people together at the economic, social, or political level [...] it is being re-assembled symbolically/discursively on a negative construction of immigration'.[64] The texts considered here negotiate precisely those dynamics Bauman, and also Bromley, touch upon; and, when text-internal affective contents are analysed in combination with 'the emotional aesthetics of a text', we are offered 'windows on contextual configurations, be these social or political'.[65] Seen this way, and when the texts' fictional characters and their individual subjectivities are read in relation to social and political structures, affect facilitates an understanding of contextual configurations, of which particular discursive or symbolic constructions of immigration are a part.

This brief outline of varying approaches to affect illustrates the differences, or discontinuities, when it comes to terminology and conceptualisations of affect, and it demonstrates its conceptual unruliness, as it is difficult to bind affect in one single definition. Despite these differences, or distinctions, however, there is a commonality between these different approaches, as they all conceive of affect as 'the relational substance connecting body and world'.[66] On the basis of this commonality, this study brings varying interpretations of affect into productive tension with each other to illuminate how affect works in the twelve texts, and to facilitate the critical reading of these texts and their characters in relation to societal structures. This focus, together with a conceptualisation of the body as an open system, enables me to investigate the emotional and physical aspects of the characters' journeys; how their interpersonal encounters are lived and embodied;

and the ways in which economic precarity, unequal power relations and processes of othering result in emotional and corporeal manifestations. Harking back to Tygstrup's threefold approach, affect further facilitates a consideration of the spatial aspects of the characters' life situations from an affective angle, and, consequently, how the characters relate to their surroundings. These spaces — the previously discussed liminal zones — can be perceived as 'affective infrastructures' which are, moreover, inscribed with national and transnational power structures such as border politics and immigration policies. The inclusion of spatial aspects in conjunction with an affective reading allows for an examination of the spaces themselves, and also for a thorough investigation of how the characters and their bodies within these spaces develop and change — for better or worse — through 'receiving and processing affective impulses impinging on them'.[67] While my approach to affect holds the possibility that different conceptualisations of affect appear to contradict each other, it affords a detailed focus on 'the productive potential of affect conceptualized within, between, and around bodies', and, additionally, an exploration into contextual social, cultural and political frameworks.[68]

Affective Responsibility

Following on from this discussion of various aspects of affect and the body, I shall now return to Butler's ethical question to assess the concept of affective responsibility: 'What is our responsibility toward those we do not know, toward those who seem to test our sense of belonging or to defy available norms of likeness?'.[69] In answer to her own question, Butler considers it crucial that those interpretative frames that shape our affective responses and inform our decisions to include or exclude some bodies over others are critically questioned, so that the frames themselves may be transformed. In addition, Butler argues for a relational ontology, in which responsibility arises out of the recognition of vulnerability as a basic human condition, and of an affective responsiveness to this condition. Emily Beausoleil takes up Butler's notion of a relational ontology and develops it into what she calls 'a *dispositional ethics*'. As a political theorist, Beausoleil, in her conceptualisation of a dispositional ethics, combines affect, democratic theory, neuroscience and the performing arts to develop new ways of thinking about responsible practices in 'the moving and ever-opaque terrain of political life'.[70] I am borrowing Beausoleil's approach to politics and adapt it to the critical analysis of literature. While Beausoleil commends utilising a dispositional ethics in real-life situations of political negotiations, her concept appears also particularly well suited to analysing the micropolitics underpinning the embodied encounters as they are depicted in the twelve texts. Similar dynamics to those which Beausoleil identifies as hindering the development of a dispositional ethics in the political arena can be observed and investigated in the encounters described in the texts; therefore, I utilise her concept to point out the ways in which the texts' characters respond affectively to 'others', and to highlight those factors that either instigate or impede affective responsibility.

In resonance with the previously discussed conceptualisation of the body as an open system, always in relation with others and implicated in the world, Beausoleil conceives of a dispositional ethics as emerging out of embodied encounters in which the focus lies on the fine adjustment of attentiveness to others and their difference in a particular situation, instead of responding to others on the basis of established moral codes. Beausoleil identifies listening as a prerequisite for this attentiveness and, ultimately, for responsible acts, when she suggests that 'to act responsibly towards others is at core to learn to hear what is yet white noise'. In order to be able to hear and respond to what is as yet unheard or unknown, however, listening has to be a reciprocal process of listening out, and, with the same care, of listening in and paying attention to one's own affective disposition to be able 'to resist the mental distancing of rationalization, defensiveness, or projection'.[71]

When an ethical stance arises out of a situated, relational and embodied encounter where listening takes place with care and attention to yield an affective response, the notion of responsibility is shifted from metaphysical or epistemological conceptualisations to affective terms. This approach to responsibility entails challenges which, however, only put more emphasis on how 'deeply affective' such an ethical stance is, as 'one must remain open within uncomfortable moments and the uncertain ground they present, invite challenge, and risk transformation, to encounter difference as difference'. Beausoleil goes on to say that this form of encounter is only possible when the self is not understood as a clearly delimited, or 'coherent subject who encounters difference beyond its bounds' but as 'self-as-multitude', able 'to loosen the hold of one's particular narrative and personal agenda [...] to open oneself to what might exceed such bounds in productive ways'. Importantly, Beausoleil clarifies that this perception of the self as multiplicity does not obliterate the coherent self in the embodied, affective encounter when she suggests that 'in the absence of cohesive identity one is not effaced but multiplied with greater possibilities for thought and action'; for when the hold on identification is softened, attention to one's own complexity 'provides the means to remain receptive and responsive even in intense and challenging encounters'.[72] Seen this way, receptivity is not a quality that weakens one's agency, but, on the contrary, demands a form of agency based on one's own integral complexity in response to the manifold challenges that any form of encounter can pose.

While this brief outline of a dispositional ethics describes an ideal scenario despite its challenges, Beausoleil builds two caveats into her conceptualisation that are worth mentioning. Firstly, such 'an attention to the self-in-formation',[73] the listening to others and the capacity to respond appropriately, is nothing that happens overnight: the integration of embodied learning, as Beausoleil argues, takes time and intensive practice, although its impact on thought and behavioural patterns is profound. Secondly, Beausoleil points towards the limits regarding the application of her insights to 'charged political contexts', such as 'the calcified dynamics of race, class and sexual privilege': to avoid running the risk of 'reducing politics to physiology', affective embodied approaches to ethics should also be 'informed by rigorous interrogation of other contextual factors that structure encounters'.[74]

Endorsing Beausoleil's dispositional ethics, I conceive of affective responsibility not as a general demand for unconditional responsibility towards others, but as an ethical affective response, realised in the particular and finite; because, as Bauman poignantly argues, 'An absolute, unlimited and unexceptional responsibility might be a commandment made to the measure of saints'.[75] As if in answer to Bauman, Ahmed proposes, 'We need to recognise the infinite nature of responsibility, *but the finite and particular circumstances in which I am called on to respond to others*'.[76] This means that a sense of responsibility has to be pragmatically identifiable so that it can be practically enacted; otherwise, it would run the risk of becoming meaningless due to its sheer overwhelming scale. In the same vein, affective responsibility emerges out of situated embodied encounters, in which one listens to an other and lets oneself be affected by the encounter. This requires training one's attention on one's own pre-conditionings, and the courage to supersede them with qualities as yet unknown, so that the dynamic in-between can indeed become 'a space of transformational encounter'.[77] I view this definition of affective responsibility as an ambitious template against which the encounters, as they are portrayed in the texts, are mapped. The aim of this approach is twofold: on the one hand, it enables me to point towards those factors in the characters' personal lives that limit or enhance their affective responsibility. On the other hand, and when the notion of affective responsibility is contrasted with contextual aspects that structure encounters, it will bring to the fore the power dynamics that often underpin them. With shedding light on the ways in which the texts negotiate affective responsibility, or a lack thereof, I seek to make a case for affective responsibility, and for an ethics emerging out of the mindful listening to others.

Chapter Outline

The selection of texts for the individual chapters is informed by the intention to explore a different aspect of affect in each chapter, and to contrast Scandinavian and Scandinavian texts closely with each other in order to shed light on thematic concurrences and discrepancies. While the focus of chapters 3 and 4 is solely on novels from Scandinavian literature which feature Scandinavian characters, chapters 1, 2 and 5 include German-literature texts in comparison with texts from Scandinavia. This compositional choice allows for an in-depth analysis of Scandinavian particularities and, simultaneously, it grants the scope to assess German texts in their own right, and to critically challenge Scandinavian concepts such as Scandinavian exceptionalism by placing them in a transnational context. Chapter 1, which compares the German text *Der Weg der Wünsche* [*The Way of the Wishes*] (2016) by Akos Doma and the Swedish text *En storm kom från paradiset* [*A Storm Blew in from Paradise*] (2012) by Johannes Anyuru, is concerned with the beginning of the migratory journey; it seeks to examine the personal motivations of the texts' characters and the political circumstances that compel them to flee their countries of birth.[78] Additionally, chapter 1 will trace the ways in which different forms of violence affectively impinge upon the characters' bodies and lives while they are geographically transitory. Chapter 2 explores how border crossings and processes of seeking asylum are reflected upon in the Danish text *Enmandstelt* [*A Tent for One*] (2016) by Alen Mešković and the German text *Ohrfeige* [*A Slap in the Face*] (2016) by Abbas Khider.[79] By drawing parallels between these two texts, this chapter illuminates the ways in which liminal zones are inscribed with national and transnational power relations, and how these structures, together with an ambiguous welcome, affect the texts' characters and their sense of belonging. Chapter 3, which provides a close reading of the Norwegian novel *Snakk til meg* [*Talk to Me*] (2011) by Vigdis Hjorth and the Danish novel *Tilfældets gud* [*The God of Chance*] (2011) by Kirsten Thorup, constitutes a shift in focus, as the texts portray Scandinavian characters who encounter those whom they perceive as strangers, or 'other' to themselves.[80] Through the critical angle of affective economies and Ahmed's concept of stranger fetishism, this chapter will analyse how the encounters between the texts' characters are embodied, and the ways in which the fetishisation of those characters constructed as 'other' are negotiated in the texts. Chapter 4 focuses on the Norwegian novel *Opphold* [*Residence*] (2014) by Aasne Linnestå, the Swedish novel *De fördrivna* [*The Displaced*] (2016) by Negar Naseh, and the Danish novel *Politisk roman* [*Political Novel*] (2013) by Lone Aburas.[81] At the centre of every one of these three texts are Scandinavian characters who encounter asylum seekers and refugees, and who position themselves in one way or another to these 'others'. This perspective appears reminiscent of chapter 3; however, while in chapter 3 the contact between the Scandinavian characters and those constructed as 'other' is sought out and willed, chapter 4 analyses Scandinavian characters who find themselves in relations of 'unwilled proximity' with others, and who respond to this 'obtrusive alterity' affectively.[82] Starting from the conception of a particularly Scandinavian form of guilt, chapter 4 investigates the notion of affective responsibility and its limits by mapping out which affects contaminate, and potentially block, the Scandinavian characters' sense of responsibility towards those they do not know. Chapter 5 centres on the Norwegian text *Tante Ulrikkes vei* [*Our Street*] (2017) by Zeshan Shakar, the German text *Vor der Zunahme der Zeichen* [*Before the Increase of the Signs*] (2016) by Senthuran Varatharajah and the Swedish text *Araben* [*The Arab*] (2014) by Pooneh Rohi.[83] This final chapter focuses on the texts' postmigrant characters by first discussing, and subsequently adopting, a postmigrant perspective for the critical analysis. This perspective provides an effective framework with which to explore how the texts portray their postmigrant characters' perceptions of themselves in relation to the societies in which they live, and how their self-understanding and sense of belonging are influenced from the outside. With regard to affect, chapter 5 follows two vectors of enquiry: on the one hand, it seeks to trace the affects that emerge in the characters' processes of remembering with respect to their narrative present, and, on the other, it displays the characters' struggles and conflicts by viewing them as embedded in, as well as induced by, the societies in which they live. The conclusion will assemble the different aspects of affect, the analyses of what Khemiri calls 'Maktens rutin. Våldets praktik' [The routines of power. The practices of violence] (139), and the findings from the examination of the texts' emotional aesthetics. This will facilitate a final consideration of how these power relations and practices compare across Scandinavian and German borders, and how they are the reason why so many people are not included in 'denna helhet, denna samhällskropp, detta vi' [this whole, this societal body, this we] (141).

Notes to the Introduction

1. Stina Fredrika Wassen, 'Where Does Securitisation Begin? The Institutionalised Securitisation of Illegal Immigration in Sweden: REVA and the ICFs', *Contemporary Voices: St Andrews Journal of International Relations*, 1 (2018), 78–103. The acronym REVA stands for 'Rättssäkert och Effektivt Verkställighetsarbete', or 'Legally Secure and Efficient Enforcement' (p. 78).
2. Cited in Jonas Hassen Khemiri, 'Bästa Beatrice', in *Jag ringer mina bröder* (Stockholm: Bonnier, 2013), pp. 129–41 (p. 130). Further references to Khemiri's text are given after quotations in the text.
3. Khemiri, p. 131, and Jonas Hassen Khemiri, 'An Open Letter to Beatrice Ask', *Asymptote*, trans. by Rachel Willson-Broyles, <http://www.asymptotejournal.com/nonfiction/jonas-hassen-khemiri-an-open-letter-to-beatrice-ask> [accessed 26 March 2019].
4. Thomas Blake, 'Affective Aversion, Ethics, and Fiction', in *The Palgrave Handbook of Affect Studies and Textual Criticism*, ed. by Donald R. Wehrs and Thomas Blake (Basingstoke: Palgrave Macmillan, 2017), pp. 207–34 (pp. 224, 225, 226).
5. Suzanne Keen, *Empathy and the Novel* (Oxford: Oxford University Press, 2007), p. 168.
6. Wayne C. Booth, *The Rhetoric of Fiction*, 2nd edn (Chicago: University of Chicago Press, 1983), p. 245.
7. Milan Kundera, *The Art of the Novel*, trans. by Linda Asher (New York: Perennial-Harper, 1988), p. 13.
8. Keen, p. 168.
9. The term 'postmigrant' can be understood as a temporal phrase when it is viewed as pertaining to individuals whose migratory journeys have come to an end because the destination has been reached, or as referring to descendants of immigrants who have never migrated themselves. While the term is only mentioned briefly here, I shall pay more critical attention to it in my discussion on transnational literature, and in chapter 5.
10. The term 'refugee' can either denote a person who has been forced to leave their home and seek refuge elsewhere, or a person who has been granted refugee status in the so-called host country. I use the term with reference to both meanings, assuming that it will be clear from the context which meaning is implied.
11. Jenny Björklund and Ursula Lindqvist, 'Introduction', in *New Dimensions of Diversity in Nordic Culture and Society*, ed. by Björklund and Lindqvist (Newcastle upon Tyne: Cambridge Scholars Publishing, 2016), pp. viii–xx (p. x).
12. Elisabeth Oxfeldt, 'Innledning', in *Skandinaviske fortellinger om skyld og privilegier i en globaliseringstid*, ed. by Oxfeldt (Oslo: Universitetsforlaget, 2016), pp. 9–31 (p. 12).
13. Ibid.
14. Ibid., p. 14.
15. Carrie Smith-Prei, 'Affect, Aesthetics, Biopower, and Technology: Political Interventions into Transnationalism', in *Transnationalism in Contemporary German-Language Literature*, ed. by Elisabeth Herrmann and others (Rochester: Camden House, 2015), pp. 65–85 (p. 70).
16. Judith Butler, *Frames of War: When Is Life Grievable?* (London: Verso, 2009), p. 36.
17. Edward Said, *The World, the Text, and the Critic* (New York: Vintage Books, 1991), pp. 5, 33, italics in original, 29.
18. Steven Vertovec, *Transnationalism* (London: Routledge, 2008), p. 2.
19. Sara Ahmed and others, 'Introduction', in *Uprootings/Regroundings: Questions of Home and Migration*, ed. by Ahmed and others (Oxford: Berg, 2003), pp. 1–20 (p. 3)
20. Vertovec p. 3; Ahmed and others, p. 5.

21. Vertovec, p. 89.

22. Ibid., p. 87.

23. Azade Seyhan, *Writing Outside the Nation* (Princeton: Princeton University Press, 2001), p. 4.

24. Elisabeth Herrmann and others, 'Introduction', in *Transnationalism in Contemporary German-Language Literature*, ed. by Herrmann and others (Rochester: Camden House, 2015), pp. 1–16 (pp. 4, 8, italics in original).

25. Seyhan, p. 10.

26. Herrmann and others, p. 4, italics in original.

27. Ibid.

28. Moritz Schramm, 'Jenseits der binären Logik', in *Postmigrantische Perspektiven: Ordnungssysteme, Repräsentationen, Kritik*, ed. by Naika Foroutan and others (Frankfurt a.M.: Campus, 2018), pp. 83–96 (pp. 83, 84, 91).

29. Hastings Donnan, 'Borders, Anthropology of', in *International Encyclopedia of the Social and Behavioral Sciences*, ed. by James D. Wright (Amsterdam: Elsevier, 2015), pp. 760–64 (p. 761).

30. Nevzat Soguk, 'Border's Capture: Insurrectional Politics, Border-Crossing Humans, and the New Political', in *Borderscapes: Hidden Geographies and Politics at Territory's Edge*, ed. by Prem Kumar Rajaram and Carl Grundy-Warr (Minneapolis: University of Minnesota Press, 2007), pp. 283–308 (p. 284).

31. Prem Kumar Rajaram and Carl Grundy-Warr, 'Introduction', in *Borderscapes: Hidden Geographies and Politics at Territory's Edge*, ed. by Rajaram and Grundy-Warr (Minnesota: University of Minnesota Press, 2007), pp. ix–xl (p. ix).

32. Soguk, pp. 284–85; Rajaram and Grundy-Warr, p. x.

33. Avtar Brah, *Cartographies of Diaspora: Contesting Identities* (London: Routledge, 1996), p. 198.

34. Michel Agier, *Borderlands*, trans. by David Fernbach (Cambridge: Polity Press, 2016), p. 19.

35. Rajaram and Grundy-Warr, p. xxviii.

36. 'Limen, n', in *Oxford English Dictionary Online* (Oxford: Oxford University Press, June 2019) <http://www.oed.com/view/Entry/108451> [accessed 16 August 2019].

37. Agier, *Borderlands*, p. 36.

38. Ibid., pp. 35, 36.

39. Zygmunt Bauman, *Liquid Times: Living in an Age of Uncertainty* (Cambridge: Polity Press, 2007), p. 45, italics in original.

40. Rajaram and Grundy-Warr, p. xvii.

41. Sara Ahmed, *Strange Encounters: Embodied Others in Post-Coloniality* (London: Routledge, 2000), pp. 44, 45, 25, italics in original.

42. Ibid., p. 44.

43. Brah, p. 126, italics in original.

44. Gilles Deleuze and Félix Guattari, *A Thousand Plateaus*, trans. by Brian Massumi (London: Bloomsbury, 2013), p. 318; Brian Massumi, *A User's Guide to Capitalism and Schizophrenia: Deviations from Deleuze and Guattari* (London: MIT Press, 1992), p. 106.

45. Melissa Gregg and Gregory J. Seigworth, 'An Inventory of Shimmers', in *The Affect Theory Reader*, ed. by Gregg and Seigworth (Durham, NC: Duke University Press, 2010), pp. 1–26 (pp. 6–8).

46. Brian Massumi, *Parables for the Virtual: Movement, Affect, Sensation* (Durham, NC: Duke University Press, 2002). pp. 35, 28.

47. Sara Ahmed, *The Cultural Politics of Emotion* (Edinburgh: Edinburgh University Press, 2004), pp. 4, 10.

48. Ann Pellegrini and Jasbir Puar, 'Affect', *Social Text*, 27 (2009), 35–38 (p. 37).

49. Benedict de Spinoza, *Ethics*, ed. and trans. by Edwin Curley (London: Penguin, 1996), p. 70.

50. Michael Hardt, 'What Affects are Good For', in *The Affective Turn: Theorizing the Social*, ed. by Patricia Ticineto Clough and Jean Halley (Durham, NC: Duke University Press, 2007), pp. ix–xiii (pp. ix, x, viii).

51. Gregg and Seigworth, p. 2.

52. Frederik Tygstrup, 'Affective Spaces', in *Panic and Mourning: The Cultural Work of Trauma*, ed. by Daniela Agosthino and others (Berlin: De Gruyter, 2012), pp. 195–210 (p. 201).

53. Gilles Deleuze, *Spinoza: Practical Philosophy*, trans. by Robert Hurley (San Francisco: City Lights Books, 1988), p. 123.
54. David Hillman and Ulrika Maude, 'Introduction', in *The Cambridge Companion to the Body in Literature*, ed. by Hillman and Maude (Cambridge: Cambridge University Press, 2015), pp. 1–9 (p. 1).
55. Maurice Merleau-Ponty, *Phenomenology of Perception*, trans. by Colin Smith (London: Routledge & Kegan Paul, 1962), p. 198.
56. Michael Richardson, *Gestures of Testimony: Torture, Trauma and Affect in Literature* (London: Bloomsbury, 2016), pp. 34, 35.
57. Ibid., p. 35.
58. Butler, p. 14.
59. Ibid., p. 19.
60. Ibid., p. 25.
61. Michel Foucault, *Security, Territory, Population: Lectures at the Collège de France, 1977–78*, ed. by Michel Senellart, trans. by Graham Burchell (Basingstoke: Palgrave Macmillan, 2007), p. 1.
62. Butler, p. 34.
63. Zygmunt Bauman, *Strangers at Our Door* (Cambridge: Polity Press, 2016), pp. 16, 4.
64. Roger Bromley, 'The Politics of Displacement: The Far Right Narrative of Europe and its "Others"', *From the European South*, 3 (2018) 13–26 (pp. 16–17).
65. Smith-Prei, p. 70.
66. Richardson, p. 36.
67. Frederik Tygstrup, 'Notes on Affect', in *Literatura e espaços afetivos*, ed. by Heidru Krieger Olinto and Viveiro de Castro (Rio de Janeiro: 7 Letras, 2014), pp. 147–57 (p. 156).
68. Richardson, p. 37.
69. Butler, p. 36.
70. Emily Beausoleil, 'Responsibility as Responsiveness: Enacting a Dispositional Ethics of Encounter', *Political Theory* 45 (2017) 291–318 (pp. 292, italics in original, 314).
71. Ibid., pp. 294, 308.
72. Ibid., pp. 295, 305, italics in original, 312, 306.
73. Ibid., p. 309.
74. Ibid., p. 312–13.
75. Bauman, *Strangers*, p. 82.
76. Ahmed, *Strange Encounters*, p. 147, italics in original.
77. Massumi, *User's Guide*, p. 106.
78. Akos Doma, *Der Weg der Wünsche* (Hamburg: Rowohlt, 2016); Johannes Anyuru, *En storm kom från paradiset* (Stockholm: Norstedts, 2011); Johannes Anyuru, *A Storm Blew in from Paradise*, trans. by Rachel Willson-Broyles (London: World Editions, 2015).
79. Alen Mešković, *Enmandstelt* (Copenhagen: Gyldendal, 2016); Abbas Khider, *Ohrfeige* (Munich: Hanser, 2016); Abbas Khider, *A Slap in the Face*, trans. by Simon Pare (London: Seagull Books, 2018).
80. Vigdis Hjorth, *Snakk til meg* (Oslo: Cappelen Damm, 2010); Kirsten Thorup, *Tilfældets gud* (Copenhagen: Gyldendal, 2011); Kirsten Thorup, *The God of Chance*, trans. by Janet Garton (London: Norvik Press, 2013).
81. Aase Linnestå, *Opphold* (Oslo: Aschehoug, 2014); Negar Naseh, *De fördrivna* (Stockholm: Natur & Kultur, 2016; Lone Aburas, *Politisk roman* (Copenhagen: Gyldendal, 2013).
82. Butler, p. 34.
83. Zeshan Shakar, *Tante Ulrikkes vei* (Oslo: Gyldendal, 2017); Senthuran Varatharajah, *Vor der Zunahme der Zeichen* (Frankfurt a.M.: Fischer, 2016); Pooneh Rohi, *Araben* (Stockholm: Ordfront, 2015). Further references to the primary texts are given after quotations in the text.

CHAPTER 1

❖

Departure, or
The Affective Concatenation of Violence in Akos Doma's *Der Weg der Wünsche* and Johannes Anyuru's *En storm kom från paradiset*

In his discussion regarding camps for asylum seekers and refugees, Zygmunt Bauman argues that these places are temporary arrangements that have been made permanent, and that those detained in these camps are forcefully held in a liminal zone, as their migratory journeys have been arrested, and the pathways back or forward blocked. Therefore, asylum seekers and refugees find themselves in a double bind, because they are 'expelled by force or frightened into fleeing their native countries, but refused entry into any other. They do not *change* places; they *lose* their place on earth and are catapulted into a nowhere.'[1] The German novel *Der Weg der Wünsche* (2016) by Akos Doma and the Swedish text *En storm kom från paradiset* (2012) by Johannes Anyuru have Bauman's 'nowhere' as one of their central themes and, moreover, they illuminate not only the spaces themselves, but also how the living conditions in these spaces affect their protagonists: looking back on political histories intertwined with personal trajectories of migration and displacement in the late 1960s and early 1970s, both texts depict protagonists who have lost their place on earth. In *Der Weg der Wünsche*, the married couple Teréz and Károly Kallay, together with their two children, the seven-year-old Misi and the fifteen-year-old Bori, flee their home country Hungary in 1972 to escape the oppression of the communist regime with the aim to reach Germany via Italy and Switzerland. The legal path to their destination requires a transit visa for Switzerland, an entry permit for Germany, and the family's recognition as political refugees; but when the acquisition of this paperwork becomes implicated in corrupt politics in the Italian transit camp for asylum seekers where the family are held, the obstacles in the way of reaching their destination appear almost insurmountable. P, the protagonist in Anyuru's novel and a Ugandan of the Langi tribe, trains as a fighter pilot in Greece, but returns to Zambia following a job offer as the pilot of a crop duster. Unaware of the political tensions between Tanzania and Uganda after Idi Amin's seizure of power in Uganda in 1971, P is arrested in the airport of Lusaka on his arrival, and flown out to Dar es Salaam in Tanzania, where he is detained and interrogated. Subsequently, he is placed in a succession of refugee camps in

Tanzania until he flees to Nairobi in Kenya to seek recognition as a political refugee by the UN, to finally make his way to Sweden.

With this study following the trajectory of migration chronologically, the present chapter is concerned with the beginning of the journey. I am looking at the protagonists' motivations in relation to the political circumstances that compel them to flee their countries of birth to highlight critically those forces and processes that lead to the loss of their place on earth. Despite their different geographies and political histories, there are obvious parallels between the two texts which can be brought into resonance with each other: the protagonists' personal histories, as well as their journeys, are pervaded by violence, and the two protagonists in focus, P in *En storm kom från paradiset*, and Teréz in *Der Weg der Wünsche*, are strongly affected by their violent experiences. Considering the significance of violence in these two texts, I explore precisely those spaces Bauman calls 'a nowhere', to illuminate the ways in which these spaces are permeated with violence, and to shed light on how the lives and bodies of the protagonists change when traumatic and violent experiences, and the related affects, concatenate.

I am using the term 'traumatic', or 'trauma', with caution, and with the awareness that it is usually inscribed within clinical — medical, psychological, psychoanalytical — discourses, or that it is, beyond personal damages, more often applied to catastrophic events with national or international dimensions. With the term 'trauma', I do not refer to the latter notion of collective trauma, but use it for the protagonists' personal experiences; for 'those "lesser" shatterings that nonetheless shake not the world, but the inner workings of an individual body and psyche'. I call the violent incidents in the protagonists' lives traumatic, because the term trauma 'gives name and shape to a form of experience that is a rupturing of the capacity to make sense of the world'.[2] Since these traumatic ruptures are brought about by violence, the term itself deserves some critical attention. However, physical violence is somewhat resistant to conceptual definition, as it encompasses, and allows for, a complex set of meanings, and can be used 'for both physical force and systemic or conceptual mistreatment'.[3] Bruce B. Lawrence and Aisha Karim confirm the complexity inherent in the term when they observe, 'There is no general theory of violence apart from its practices', and propound that therefore, theories of violence 'must be as varied as the practices within which they occur'.[4] Bringing different practices and contexts into relation with each other across time and space, and intersecting these aspects with affect, allows me to illustrate the extent to which violence can be understood as process, and it facilitates a fluid, dynamic and relational understanding of violence. When it comes to the effects of violence on the inner workings of the individual protagonists, I make use of the concept of traumatic affect, as it is laid out by Meera Atkinson and Michael Richardson, to point out the affective qualities of trauma. Traumatic affect can be understood as an open, non-prescriptive concept that circumscribes 'the mode, substance and dynamics of relation through which trauma is experienced, transmitted, conveyed, and represented'.[5] Reading the two texts through the concept of traumatic affect helps to visualise the 'affective operations, aftershocks and echoes of a traumatic encounter', and hence, to emphasise the relationality of both trauma and violence.

Assuming that the texts' protagonists are exposed to violence that is, at least in part, made possible by national or transnational power structures, the present chapter is an exploration into the intersections of violence, trauma, affect and power in the context of migration.

Violence that Makes and Unmakes Childhood, or the Unspeakability of Trauma

As mentioned before, Judith Butler argues that the body should be conceptualised in its relation to others, because it is always 'exposed to others, vulnerable by definition'. When Butler further states that, 'There is no life without the conditions of life that variably sustain life', she conceives of precariousness as a fundamental quality of the human body, as the body's existence is recognised through its vulnerability and mortality.[6] This notion is particularly urgent when it comes to children, as they are indeed dependent on their social surroundings and caregivers, and, without a sustaining environment, can neither survive nor flourish. This sense of precariousness, however, exposes children differentially to violence, particularly when the perpetrator is a caregiver on whom the child is dependent. As a child, P, in *En storm kom från paradiset*, is dependent on his older brother, because their father is dead, and their mother has left them. While P is detained in a refugee camp in Tanzania as an adult, he has a dream of his brother who is ready to beat him: 'Mannen i drömmen tar ett steg ut på savannen. Bältet i hans hand ringlar sig som en orm' [The man in the dream takes a step out onto the savannah. The belt in his hand coils like a snake] (126–27; 130). This dream, in turn, triggers P's memories of his childhood:

> Han minns den natten. När han väl kom hem efter att ha suttit och huttrat ute i mörkret och gräset i flera timmar slog hans bror honom med bältet så att han inte kunde gå på flera dagar. Det fortsatte. Det var hans barndom, hans uppväxt [...] Han minns skammen över de nerpissade madrasserna [...] Han blev slagen med knytnävar, med skor, med böcker, han kastades ner på det hårda trägolvet med sprucken läpp, med blåtiror, med ett brutet finger, näsblod. Han haltade hemifrån med låren randiga av piskrapp i den stora, nakna gryningen. Han kom hem från skolan och lagade mat. Dagarna gick. Skräcken avtog aldrig. Den var hans liv.

> [He remembers that night. Once he came home after sitting and shivering in the darkness and the grass for several hours, his brother beat him with the belt so hard that he couldn't walk for several days. It continued. That was his childhood, his upbringing. [...] He remembers his shame over the mattresses he wet. [...] He was beaten with fists, with shoes, with books; he was thrown onto the hard wooden floor with a burst lip, with black eyes, with a broken finger, a bloody nose. He limped away from home with his thighs striped with whiplashes in the great, naked dawn. He came home from school and prepared food. The days went by. The fear never lessened. This was his life.] (127–28; 131–32)

First and foremost, and without any extenuation, this scene depicts the domestic violence P is subjected to as a child, and it describes the immediate effects of this violence on the child's body. It also depicts accurately the psychological impact this violence has on P: hiding and bedwetting are common reactions of children exposed to domestic violence, and because the trust between the child and the person it is dependent on is broken, a hiding place seems to grant more safety than being close to a person.[7] Moreover, this scene portrays how violence is embedded in, and part of, daily life: it appears on the same level as going to school and preparing food, and, in all its horror, violence has almost become something 'normal'. Stylistically, this scene highlights the extent to which violence dominates and overshadows P's life. It begins with one particular event, *den natten* [that night], then underscores the continuation of violence with *det fortsatte* [it continued] and *dagarna gick* [the days went by], and gradually widens the scope from *hans barndom, hans uppväxt* [his childhood, his upbringing], to finally *hans liv* [his life]. This accumulation and progression of terms related to P's biography indicate the cyclical nature of violence, and also the way that violence has become part of his life.

With dissociating from the pain, P reacts to violence with a common response of abused children. In his imagination, he wishes he could be a bird and fly away from it: 'Han ville vara en fågel' [He wanted to be a bird] (30; 34). Eventually, P's coping mechanism from childhood manifests itself as a determining force in vital decisions in his life as an adult, and his migrations are inspired by his former wish to be able to fly: 'Han ville flyga' [He wanted to fly] (34; 38). This sentence, reiterated multiple times throughout the text, explains P's motivation to train as a fighter pilot in Greece, and his reasoning to return to Africa to fly a crop duster. The dominant presence of this wish to fly, however, seems to render P ignorant of any circumstances that might hinder this wish. Although it enables him to escape his brother's violence, it gains such a strong impetus in his life that it blinds him to the political situation — and, ultimately, the violence — he is returning to. P's interrogators in Tanzania reflect upon his political naivety with regard to the political tensions ensuing Idi Amin's seizure of power when they, disbelievingly, ask him: 'En utbildad ugandisk stridspilot reser från Rom till Zambia för att flyga besprutningsflygplan över fruktodlingar?' [A Ugandan fighter pilot travels from Rome to Zambia to fly a crop duster over fruit plantations?] (10; 13). P's answer, 'Jag ville bara flyga' [I just wanted to fly] (11; 15), is the only phrase he reiterates in his defence. The violence P's older brother subjected him to is reminiscent of Michael Richardson's assertion that some encounters 'can change bodies radically' in positive ways, whereas others 'rupture, break, traumatize':[8] instead of being supportive or strengthening, P's relationship with his brother ruptured his childhood, and traumatised him in such a way that he, consciously or not, is solely focused on flying away from the pain, and fleeing his brother's violence, even if this violence has long ceased in his adult life.

While these far-reaching repercussions of violence are rooted in traumatic experiences that continued over a long period of time, the violence that Teréz, in *Der Weg der Wünsche*, is exposed to is an isolated incident in her childhood, yet with similarly far-reaching consequences. Towards the end of the Second World War, when Teréz is fifteen, she flees with her mother and younger sister from Budapest and the approaching Red Army in the hope of crossing the border into Austria. Leaving the two others behind, Teréz sets out to try and find or buy some food, and, on the way back, is raped multiple times by American soldiers:

> Hände griffen nach ihr, sie streifte sie ab, stieß sie weg, schlüpfte zwischen zwei Schatten hindurch, eine Hand riss sie zurück. [...] ein Schlag traf sie ins Gesicht. [...] Alles wurde schwarz. Blut floss in ihre Kehle, sie schluckte. Sie lag auf dem Rücken, im Schnee, sie hielten sie fest, sie versuchte sich zu wehren, aber die Hände waren stärker. Sie packten ihre Beine und bogen sie über ihre Schultern, ihr Rückgrat knackte, sie brüllte auf, ihr Kopf fiel in den Schnee zurück. "Mama ..." [...] Sie kamen über sie, einer nach dem anderen, sie wusste nicht, wie viele es waren [...] Sie spürte den Schmerz nicht mehr, ihr Körper war taub, er war nicht mehr da.

> [Hands grabbed her, she brushed them off, pushed them away, slipped through between two shadows, a hand pulled her back. [...] a blow hit her in the face. [...] all went black. Blood flowed into her throat, she swallowed. She lay on her back, in the snow, they held her down, she tried to fight back, but their hands were stronger. They grabbed her legs and bent them over her shoulders, her spine cracked, she screamed, her head fell back into the snow. "Mum ..." [...] They came over her, one after the other, she didn't know how many there were [...] She didn't feel the pain any more, her body was numb, it was no longer there.] (329)

Psychologically, Teréz reacts to this brutal violation of her body in similar ways to P: she dissociates from the pain and her body. Instinctively, she cries out for her mother, because, 'In situations of terror, people spontaneously seek their first source of comfort and protection', but, 'When this cry is not answered, the sense of basic trust is shattered'.[9] Teréz confirms this assertion when she, alone again, feels 'ein nie gekanntes Gefühl von Leere' [an unfamiliar feeling of emptiness] and reflects that 'Gut und Böse, dass alles was Erwachsene sagten, eine Lüge war' [good and evil, that everything adults said, was a lie] (331). Judith Lewis Herman elucidates that traumatised people 'feel utterly abandoned, utterly alone, cast out of the human and divine systems of care and protection that sustain life'.[10] Herman's psychological observations reflect accurately how Teréz feels after she has been raped. She is alone in her suffering over this violent incident, as there is, in her view, no-one she can trust, or share it with, and she is forced to bear it in silence.

The two violent scenes quoted at length are memories that are embedded into the main dieglesis of these two texts as analepses, providing us with the contexts for a better understanding of the protagonists' affective and emotional conditionings. Both Teréz and P cannot find the right words to express themselves after the actual violent events, because they have experienced 'a horror so great that words are inadequate to it'.[11] When their respective traumatic experiences are cast in silence, the traumas themselves become unspeakable events, and the protagonists' silences distance them from the people around them, which, in turn, renders Teréz, and P too, lonely and isolated. When P, in Anyuru's novel, tells his girlfriend in Greece about his childhood, he mentions that his brother beat him, but 'han kunde inte säga allt som mannen hade gjort, han kunde inte sätta ord på det' [he couldn't say everything that the man had done; he couldn't put it in words] (41; 45). Nonetheless, the narrator knows: 'Men han vill berätta. Han behöver berätta historien för någon' [But he wants to tell. He needs to tell the story to someone] (85; 89). This conflict between unspeakable atrocities, and the refusal of these atrocities to be denied and buried, is what Herman calls 'the central dialectic of psychological trauma' (1): under the blanketing silence, it is discernible that there is a conflict between something terrible that wants to be told, but which is denied at the same time.

This central dialectic of trauma is similarly palpable in Doma's novel. Bori is told that her mother was very ill after the war, but, 'Die Eltern sprachen nie darüber' [The parents never talked about it] (20); Bori also notices that her mother has difficulties watching anything war-related on TV, but 'Sprechen wollte ihre Mutter darüber nie' [Her mother never wanted to talk about it] (95). When she returns to Budapest after the Second World War, Teréz 'sprach nicht, aß nicht, schlief schlecht, und wenn sie doch einschlief, schreckte sie bald schreiend wieder auf' [didn't talk, didn't eat, slept badly, and when she fell asleep after all she soon started up screaming] (62), which is explained with: 'Der Hunger, die Luftangriffe, das Leid und Sterben um sie hätten ihr die Kräfte geraubt und ihre Nerven zerrüttet, hieß es später' [The hunger, the air raids, the suffering and dying around her robbed her of her strength and shattered her nerves, it was said later] (61). With regard to the real reasons for Teréz's breakdown, this explanation simultaneously seeks to divert and attract the reader's attention. The fact that the narrator references an anonymous source casts doubt over the veracity of this explanation, while it, at the same time, invokes an undercurrent of terror and uncertainty which is keenly felt, particularly as Teréz's reactions are described in detail. The reader, and Bori too, know that something terrible happened, but it is denied, as it is not spoken about.

Affective Narrative Voices and Emotional Aesthetics

In his aforementioned study on torture, Richardson asserts, 'When trauma emerges it does so with violence, not just on the body but in and on language' (148). The fact that neither Teréz, in Doma's novel, nor P, in Anyuru's text, find the right words to articulate what happens to them confirms this and illustrates how unspeakability is one of the immediate results of trauma. The unspeakability of trauma, as Anna Gibbs argues, poses 'a problem for the generation afterwards', that is, 'how to translate what has not happened, at least not directly to them, but what is nevertheless transmitted as affect and an empty place where representation ought to be' (133). With regard to the narrative representation of the unspeakability of trauma, the same problem arises, and with it the question of how the narrators translate to the reader the empty spaces that trauma has left in Teréz's and P's lives. In Anyuru's novel, it transpires only some seventy pages into the text, with a narrative voice in the first person interrupting the main diegesis, that the third-person narrator is actually P's son, and that P possibly stands for *pappa*. The main narrative — P's story until he comes to Sweden — is framed in a meta-fictional manner by P's son, who, in six brief interspersions into the text, reflects on his relationship with his father, and, simultaneously, on the process of writing and researching his father's story. The narratological position from which P's story is told, is thus one of present-day Sweden, and it is mediated by a young man, born in Sweden, who tries to understand and come closer to his father, before it is too late, as P suffers from lung cancer and does not have long to live. In Doma's text, the story of the Hungarian family is told by an omniscient third-person narrator whose perspective nevertheless shifts ever so subtly between the four family members, selectively focalising the individual characters. In particular, when some of the events are seen through the eyes of the two children Misi and Bori, the text leaves gaps and ambiguities, because the children often lack understanding for, or knowledge of, the circumstances that affected, or still affect, their parents. Considering the different positions of these two narrators in the texts, I shall map out how the narrators' voices and their affective orientation shape the composition of the texts, and how these aesthetic strategies invite the reader to engage affectively with the protagonists.

As previously mentioned, Bori, in *Der Weg der Wünsche*, knows that something terrible has happened, but when her questions remain unanswered, she is left with precisely these empty spaces where representation ought to be. Teréz's silence is extended to the whole family and to the narrator, who, at least until the ending of the novel, does not fill these gaps with information. Instead, these empty spaces are filled with affect: the focalisation on Bori creates voids in which, for both Bori and the reader, the undercurrent of terror produced by silence becomes perceptible. This undercurrent of terror is further emphasised when Misi asks Teréz for a particular bedtime story, namely 'wie die Großmama über Nacht weiße Haare bekommen hat' [how grandma got white hair overnight] (251). Teréz, in the only interruption of the third-person narrator's voice, tells it as 'ein wundersames Abenteuer' [a wondrous adventure] (253), while she actually recounts her flight during the Second World War leading up to her rape. The writerly device that keeps Teréz from telling the story in its entirety is that Misi falls asleep, and only much later, and not in Teréz's own voice, is the end of the story revealed. The undercurrent of terror is transmitted affectively in the discrepancy between Misi's innocence and the reader's knowledge that hair usually turns white overnight as a reaction to shock; and in the contradiction between the actual contents and the way in which Teréz transforms them into a bedtime story suitable for children. In this way, the reader is held in suspense with regard to the ending, while simultaneously anticipating that this ending might be traumatic. These instances illustrate the ways in which the text's composition is built on the affects and effects of violence and trauma, and how narrative techniques such as selective focalisation, and a narrator who leaves gaps and ambiguities, translate the underlying threat and terror affectively. The reader learns about the ruptures in Teréz's psyche and her relation to the world, while the reasons for them are temporally displaced, which complicates the reader's spontaneous engagement with Teréz, and, simultaneously, reflects the effect that trauma has on language and the human psyche. When the silence is finally lifted and the missing information given, the reader is presented with the anticipated shock, produced by the scene in which Teréz is raped, and has now all the reasons to understand Teréz and empathize with her.

While the narrative composition in *En storm kom från paradiset* differs from that in *Der Weg der Wünsche*, it is similarly built on affects produced by violence. The narrator, P's son, references a plethora of meta-texts that he presents as his source material, or his archive: he rereads Franz Fanon's *The Wretched of the Earth*, and states, 'Jag har läst langis historia denna vinter' [I've been reading the history of the Langi this winter] (78; 82); he asks his father 'att få titta på hans fotografier på nytt' [to look at his photographs again] (120; 124) and references his father's diary in which P 'ville skriva ner vad han mindes av sitt liv' [wanted to write down what he remembered of his life] (80; 84). While the son highlights the seriousness of his research into his father's life, he underscores simultaneously how unreliable his source material is: 'Allt är så oformligt när det kommer till honom, allt viker undan när jag griper efter det, allt är skuggor' [Everything is so formless when it comes to him; everything darts away when I grasp for it, everything is shadows] (121; 125). Since the son fills the voids in his father's history with his own imagination in an attempt to make sense of these shadows of the past, he presents his father's story as self-consciously fictitious, which undermines the veracity his research seemingly implies. This notion is further substantiated when the son reveals that he altered his father's report considerably. Rereading his father's diary, the son notices 'att mer än en tredjedel eller kanske till och med så mycket som hälften utgörs av hans minnen från det halvårs värnplikt som han genomgick i Uganda innan han sändes till Aten' [that more than a third of it, or maybe even as much as half of it, is made up of his memories from the six months of military service he did in Uganda before he was sent to Athens] (81; 84–85). In the son's narrative, however, these memories are only mentioned in passing, whereas more than a third of his own text is taken up by P's imprisonment and interrogation in Tanzania, and the rest with P's time in the camps and his flight to Nairobi. The son therefore manages and manipulates the temporality in the narrative; he puts emphasis on and prioritises those areas in P's life that are most obscure to him because they were cast in silence, while he accelerates the narrative time in areas that are less interesting to him or already known, for instance when his father meets his Swedish mother in Nairobi, and when he dedicates less than five pages to this event and the following two years, in which P marries his mother and the couple eventually move to Sweden.

P's son refers to his father's diary as 'en text som sårar mig med sin längtan efter att göra livet begripligt' [a text that hurts me with its longing to understand life] (174; 178); however, while the father's desperate search for meaning pains the son, the son's reimagination of his father's story appears to be driven by the same motivation, a longing to make sense of events that, so far, have only been transmitted to him affectively. As P's history is so opaque, it is as if 'pappa kommer ur ingenting. Ur en väldig ensamhet som är som himlen' [Dad comes from nothing. From a great solitude that is like the sky] (119; 123). This loneliness creates an emotional distance between father and son, and hence, the affective traces of violence and trauma slide between generations. This generational slide is further highlighted when the son narrates one of his own dreams in which P appears metaphorically as the bird he always wanted to be: 'På nätterna, i den återkommande drömmen, håller jag en fågel mellan händerna, hårt, med de ryttlande vingarna in mot den lilla kroppen. Hela mitt liv denna ensamhet och känsla av ofrånkomlighet' [At night, in the recurring dream, I hold a bird in my hands, tightly, its hovering wings close to its little body. My whole life, this loneliness and sense of inevitability] (119–20; 123). As it is not clear if the son refers to his own loneliness or his father's, this dream reveals the cyclical nature of trauma, since the effects of violence work across generations; and, in addition, it illustrates the son's tenderness and empathy for his father's vulnerability. This empathy can be understood as the son's narratorial position from which he tries to make sense of P's history, and in this way, the son's interspersions into the main diegesis serve as an affective frame which may deepen the reader's understanding for P.

Both texts make subtle connections between their respective protagonists' childhood experiences, their consequences, and the time periods in which the texts are mainly set. In *Der Weg der Wünsche*, one of those connections is made by the title of the concluding part of the narrative, 'Im Schnee' [In the snow], consisting of the final nine chapters of the novel. Leading up to this part is the description of how the family fails to cross the Gotthard Pass in Switzerland on their way to Germany, because their car becomes stuck in snow when night falls; the family have nothing to eat, and they are not sure if they can stay warm enough to survive the night. The desperation of this situation, and the helplessness, together with similar weather conditions, trigger the memory of when Teréz was raped as a child in the snow. It appears that for Teréz, snow will always be associated with terror. Out of context, and therefore incomprehensible at first, this memory is pre-empted in the last sentence before the chapter containing the analepsis begins: '[Teréz] war allein, allein wie in allen den anderen durchwachten Nächten ihres Lebens, allein mit den Schritten, die lautlos und doch lauter als das Brausen und Tosen des Windes waren und näher kamen und kamen und kamen' [[Teréz] was alone, alone as in all the other nights of her life she spent waking, alone with the footsteps that were silent yet louder than the roaring of the wind, and came closer and closer and closer] (319). This sentence consolidates the connection between past and present, as it illustrates, with the nightmarish reiteration of *kamen und kamen* like threat and terror continuously approaching, how the repercussions of the past invade Teréz's present. The isolation, suggested by this sentence, is similar to the loneliness P experiences as an effect of violence, and is possibly owed to 'a sense of alienation, of disconnection, [which] pervades every relationship', and, together with silence, is a common effect of trauma.[12] Like Teréz, in *Der Weg der Wünsche*, P, in *En storm kom från paradiset*, is haunted by the memories of his past, or, more precisely, by a recurring image that is burned into his consciousness, and that he sees every time he closes his eyes: 'Det finns bara bröder, bröder som står i gräset och skriker' [There are only brothers, brothers who stand in the grass, screaming] (126; 130). This image has manifested itself in P's memory in such a way that his brother becomes universalised in the plural. In the same way that Teréz, in her mind, hears the footsteps of the soldiers approaching, P hears the screams of his brother; both sounds signify the terror of their respective childhoods, which haunts them and renders them silent and lonely, and overshadows their lives and relationships in the present.

The Nowhere: Violence Revisited

While, in Anyuru's novel, P's motivation to flee his country of birth is to escape the subjective violence of his brother, Teréz, in Doma's text, describes a different form of violence as their incentive to flee Hungary. When she is interrogated in the Italian camp, Teréz tells the official, 'Politischer Verfolgung seien sie nicht ausgesetzt gewesen, nicht direkt, nur in Form von Schikanen und Benachteiligungen, das schon seit Jahren' [They were not exposed to political persecution, not directly, only in the form of harassment and discrimination, for years] (93). This harassment entails Teréz's degradation at work, her transfer to the countryside without further notice, and the fact that the family of four is forced to live 'auf sechzehn Quadratmetern [...] ohne Küche, mit einem winzigen Badezimmer, das man mit den Nachbarn teilen musste' [on sixteen square metres [...] without a kitchen, with a tiny bathroom that you had to share with the neighbours] (27–28). The only explanation Teréz has is her political stance, 'ihre Weigerung, der Partei beizutreten' [her refusal to join the party] (16), because otherwise there is no justification other than the corruption of the political system: 'Bei jeder Zwangsaussiedlung wurde eine Wohnung, ein Haus enteignet, wurden Geld und Eigentum konfisziert. [...] es war legalisierter Diebstahl. Eine anonyme Anzeige genügte, und plötzlich war man ein "Feind des Volkes"' [With each forced eviction, a flat, a house was expropriated, money and property were confiscated. [...] it was legalised theft. An anonymous report was enough, and suddenly you were an 'enemy of the people'] (152). Here, Teréz describes what she calls 'dieses ganze System von Gefälligkeiten und Gegengefälligkeiten' [this whole system of one hand washing the other] (34): the workings of a corrupt power centre and its micro-textures which, with its structural violence, generates advantages for some, while it exposes others such as the Kallay family differentially to precarity. In the tension between the individual and corrupt state power, an atmosphere of oppression is generated that affects Teréz and her husband Károly in such a way that they feel suffocated; they are missing 'die Luft zum atmen' [the air to breathe] (71). Due to this systemic corruption, the social and economic conditions that ostensibly perpetuate their lives are deteriorating, so that the couple do not see their lives as sustainable any more. Thus, flight appears as the only solution: 'Wir gingen, weil uns nichts anderes übrig blieb, nicht einfach so [...] Wir wollten nie weggehen, man liebt doch seine Heimat, man hat nur die eine' [We left because we had no other choice, not just like that [...] We never wanted to leave, surely, you love your homeland, you've only got the one] (161). Teréz expresses here the personal pain and sense of loss concomitant with the difficulty to make the decision to leave your home.

After the Kallay family cross the border into Italy, they are hopeful that things will change for the better. This is, at least, what Teréz conveys to her children when she reassures them that, 'jetzt würde alles gut werden, jetzt seien sie *draußen*' [now everything would be alright, now they were *outside*] (87, italics in original). However, as they are detained in a transit camp that resembles a prison, they, instead of being outside, find themselves in a restrictive inside; in a liminal zone that dampens their optimism quickly, as the family are forced into inaction: 'Die Vormittage über warteten sie, warteten mit den anderen Flüchtlingen [...] warteten auf Antwort auf ihre Anträge und Briefe an die Behörden, deren Entscheidungen über ihr Schicksal bestimmen sollten' [In the mornings they waited, waited with all the other refugees [...] waited for answers to their claims and letters to the authorities, whose decisions would determine their fate] (141). The reiteration of the verb *warten* [to wait], together with Teréz and Károly's dependence on the authority's decisions, substantiates David Farrier's observation that asylum seekers are, while their claims are being processed, condemned to 'a condition of waiting, uncertainty and dependency that frustrates any chance for self-creation' (6).[13] In addition to this politically effectuated liminal status, the Kallay family lack 'a social category' because of their geographical, economic and social marginalisation:[14] 'Es war eine neue Welt für sie, aber keine zum Anfassen, die Glaswand ihrer Mittellosigkeit trennte sie von ihr. [...] Sie hatten Ungarn hinter sich gelassen, waren *draußen* [...] aber noch nirgendwo drinnen, sie lebten [...] im Niemandsland' [It was a new world for them, but they couldn't touch it, the glass wall of their indigence separated them from it. [...] They had left Hungary behind, were *outside* [...] but nowhere inside yet, they lived [...] in a no man's land] (97, italics in original). As if in direct reference to Bauman's notion of the nowhere, the narrator describes accurately how this nowhere is inscribed with a social, geographical and political liminality that renders the Kallay family 'hardly perceptible, hardly audible and "voiceless"'.[15] In addition to the silence that surrounds Teréz's traumatic childhood experiences, all members of the Kallay family are further silenced by immigration politics, which indefinitely delay their chances of reaching their destination.

Butler's definitions come to mind when the narrator makes the connection between a politically induced precarity and precariousness, and discloses:

> Sie saßen in der Falle, allein, am Ende der Welt. Sie waren aus allem herausgefallen, hatten alle Bande zu ihrer Heimat [...] gekappt, eine Rückkehr gab es nicht, sie lagen am Boden wie gefallenes Laub, jedem Windstoß und jeder Stiefelsohle ausgesetzt.
>
> [They were trapped, alone, at the end of the world. They had dropped out of everything, had cut all ties to their homeland, there was no return, they were lying on the ground like fallen leaves, exposed to every gust of wind and kick of the boot.] (215)

The Kallay family are deprived of the social and economic conditions that would make their lives fully sustainable, yet they cannot go back to where they came from; they have indeed lost their place on earth. From a gender perspective, this precariousness renders especially the female body, Teréz's body, vulnerable to sexual exploitation. Teréz becomes entangled in a system of abusive power relations, represented by the manager of the camp in Italy, Signor Monte, when he, in no unclear terms, offers a shortcut for their paperwork to be processed, and informs her, 'ob Sie morgen aus Capua fortkommen oder in einem Jahr oder in zehn Jahren oder nie wieder, hängt von mir ab' [whether you get away from Capua tomorrow, or in a year, or in ten years, or never again, depends on me] (166). Insinuating that this short cut only works via Teréz's body, Signor Monte advises her: 'Sie müssen Ihre Haut auf den Markt tragen, es ist nicht halb so schlimm, wie es klingt' [you have to sell your own skin, it's not half as bad as it sounds] (231), and, to make the extortion complete, he tells her, 'Sie wissen, dass Sie keine Wahl haben' [you know that you have no choice] (167). The affirmation of Signor Monte's superior position of power is facilitated by a system that allows him to reduce Teréz to her bare life — her body. Within this system of immigration politics and policies, it is possible for Signor Monte to exercise a biopower in which 'the basic biological features of the human species' — in this case Teréz's sexuality — become the object of a corrupt strategy that enables Signor Monte to violate Teréz's body with impunity.[16] This violation of her body foreshadows the end of the narrative when the narrator reveals that Teréz was raped in her childhood; for the reader, however, the ways in which these traumatic encounters and their aftershocks echo each other become clear only from the vantage point of the text's ending.

The two scenes in which Teréz's body is violated are told very differently, but these diverging narrative strategies have the same effect: both depictions equally evoke 'the very intensity that brings catastrophic trauma into being affectively'.[17] The forms and practices of violence, sly and coercive in the case of Signor Monte, and shockingly brutal in the case of the American soldiers, are mirrored in the styles in which these events are told, and thus language, instead of representing these events authentically, translates and transmits the emergence of trauma in these events affectively. The scene in which Teréz is raped by the soldiers is in sharp focus, as if the narrator does not allow the reader — as the only witness — to look away. This activates the reader's affective-empathetic engagement with Teréz: we are invited to feel with Teréz because we know that she cannot talk about the event, and that we are her only confidantes to share her loneliness and pain in the wake of being raped. The lengthy process in which Signor Monte convinces Teréz that it is inevitable that she surrenders her body is described in great detail, and yet the scene itself is only indirectly visible for the reader. Misi, who secretly follows his mother to Signor Monte's office, looks through the keyhole, and the narrator, focalising Misi, states: 'er sah [...] weiße Wände und weiße Laken' [he saw [...] white walls and white sheets] (238). The narrator, and also the reader, know only too well what is taking place, but as the scene is witnessed by a child who cannot gauge what is really happening, this distancing device leaves a gap for the reader to fill with their own imagination.

In *En storm kom från paradiset*, P, like Teréz, is interrogated and subjected to violence when he is detained by police in Tanzania on his return to Africa. Although the nature of the interrogation and the forms and practices of violence differ from those depicted in Doma's novel, both texts make similar connections between violence and language, and, by implication, silence. While Teréz's interrogation in Italy seems to follow standard procedures and effectively consists of questions and answers, the narrator in Anyuru's text, from the outset, makes the link between violence and interrogation, or potential physical pain and language: 'Han har inte blivit misshandlad, men våldet hänger i luften' [He hasn't been beaten, but violence is hanging in the air (11; 14). The Oxford English Dictionary's definition of torture confirms and strengthens this close link between pain and language by delineating torture as, 'The infliction of severe bodily pain, as punishment or a means of persuasion'.[18] This definition is problematic insofar as it omits psychological or emotional forms of torture, and as it is generally difficult to measure pain, or to decide what counts as severe pain, and what does not, because, as Elaine Scarry argues, pain not only resists language, but is also deeply personal. For the person suffering physical or emotional pain, it cannot be denied, but for the person witnessing someone else's pain, it creates doubt, as the witness cannot know the extent of the other person's pain. Scarry, however, acknowledges the conjunction of pain and language, when she defines torture as consisting of two components: 'a primary physical act, the infliction of pain, and a primary verbal act, the interrogation'. The verbal act is broken up into two elements, question and answer, and the questioning provides the torturer with a justification for their cruelty, as if the answer really mattered, whereas the answer connotes a betrayal to the truth for the detainee. According to Scarry, it is fundamentally wrong to understand the structure of torture in this way, because it reverses the ethical implications of torture, and it blurs 'the lines of moral responsibility': 'as soon as the focus of attention shifts to the *verbal* aspect of torture, those lines [...] change their shape in the direction of accommodating and crediting the torturers'.[19]

What I consider important with regard to P's interrogation is not to measure the severity of pain and violence inflicted to decide whether his treatment counts as torture or not, but rather the implicit structure of torture, the intimate connection between violence and language, and what it does to the protagonist subjected to it. From an affective angle on torture, Richardson argues that through violence, 'Specific and bodily affects are provoked and incited, amplified and modulated in the in-between of bodies in relation', and that violence is thus both physical and affective, because 'it assaults the very ways in which the body relates to others, to itself, and the world'. In view of this, it is pertinent to analyse the affects that are provoked in P's interrogation, and how they alter and mutate his relations to the world and to himself. Scarry suggests that in moments of acute pain, the prisoner's world is annihilated, and, as the torturer denies the physical reality of the prisoner's pain, the torturer's world expands, because it is contrasted with the prisoner's shrinking world: for the torturer, 'the absence of pain is a presence of world', whereas for the prisoner, 'the presence of pain is the absence of world'.[20] Accordingly, when the torturer's world grows with the prisoner's pain, and when their physical difference is so closely linked with the verbal reality of question and answer, pain is translated into power; the prisoner's pain becomes the torturer's power. In this sense, I read P's interrogation as the intersection of language, violence and power, to uncover how these intersecting forces affectively impinge upon his body and life.

The power relations are set out clearly for P when the interrogator tells him: 'Du finns inte längre. Det är dags att du börjar svara på våra frågor' [You no longer exist. It's time you start answering our questions] (11; 14). The interrogator denies P's existence in the figurative sense, but this denial implies a real threat to his life, since the interrogator suggests that no-one would miss him if they actually killed him. In this regard, the interrogator confers upon P 'the status of *living dead*', and, as the power to end P's life rests with the interrogator, he exercises what Achille Mbembe calls a 'necropolitics': the 'subjugation of life to the power of death'.[21] This potentially lethal threat of violence is linked to language, and makes P's life dependent on a confession, or the divulgement of the information the interrogator wants to hear: 'Du stödde Amins kupp och du stödjer honom nu. Du var på väg tillbaka till Uganda när vi gensköt dig i Zambia. Stämmer det?' [You supported Amin's coup, and you support him now. You were on your way back to Uganda when we intercepted you in Zambia. Is that right?] (65; 68–69). This incrimination is particularly preposterous considering that P is of the Langi tribe, and that Idi Amin, shortly after he seized power in Uganda, conducted brutal purges amongst Acholi and Langi soldiers, whom Amin thought to be favoured by his predecessor, Milton Obote.[22] In addition, P's memories, embedded as analepses into the linear narrative of the interrogation, reveal the absurdity of the interrogator's reiterated request that he should '[b]erätta sanningen' [tell the truth] (65; 69). To recapitulate, P's incentive to train as a fighter pilot, rather than being motivated by politics or patriotism, is exclusively rooted in his wish to fly and to flee his brother's violence: 'Han tänkte inte på politik' [He didn't think about politics] (19; 23). The interrogator's insistence on his particular version of the 'truth' suggests that his questions, '*as though* they motivated the cruelty, *as if* the answers to them were crucial',[23] are instead meant to reaffirm the position of power of Tanzania and its Prime Minister Julius Nyerere against the colonial powers, Idi Amin, and, by implication, P: 'Vi bekämpar imperialisterna. Det är tack vare imperialisterna som Amin har kommit till makten. [...] Dina vänner. [...] De erkänner hans regim som legitim, det gör inte vi' [We oppose the imperialists. It is thanks to the imperialists that Amin has come to power. [...] Your friends. [...] They have recognized his regime as legitimate; we don't] (50; 54). The interrogator speaks for the Tanzanian regime when he uses the first-person plural, and, in his rhetoric, makes P a synecdoche for everything this regime is opposed to.

The interrogator's opening question, 'Varför återvände du?' [Why did you come back?] (9; 13), is reiterated with nerve-racking frequency, which, in itself, is a form of torture and meant to 'break' the person who is interrogated. The question is, however, unchangingly answered by P with, 'Jag ville flyga' [I wanted to fly] (11; 15). When no other information is forthcoming, the methods are exacerbated: 'Vakten slog honom i bakhuvudet med ett tillhygge, antagligen med sin pistolkolv' [The guard hit him in the back of the head with a weapon, probably the butt of his pistol]. In this instance of intense pain, language is extinguished, because it loses all meaning: 'Han hör förhörsledaren tala men orden har ingen mening, de är bara läten, ljud' [He hears the interrogator speaking but the words have no meaning;

they're just sounds, noises] (26; 30); and, in the same moment, the connection is made between P's childhood and his present situation. He 'kletar runt med tummen i blodet en stund, i en sorts chockad fascination. Han minns sin barndom. Han minns en man som inte var hans far' [smears the blood around with his thumb for a moment, in a sort of shocked fascination. He remembers his childhood. He remembers a man who wasn't his father] (27; 31). Ahmed argues that 'the process of *recognition* [of pain] [...] is bound up with what we *already know*', and she elaborates that 'the sensation of pain is deeply affected by memories: one can feel pain when reminded of past trauma by an encounter with another'.[24] P's reaction to pain confirms Ahmed's point, and in a similar way as snow is always associated with terror for Teréz as it reminds her of the rape in her childhood, the pain P feels in the interrogation triggers memories of his brother's abusive violence. In this sense, both texts produce affective resonances between seemingly unrelated events, and the reader is granted insight into the 'complex circuitry' of violence, 'in which the effects of events concatenate'.[25] When these different events are thus linked, one traumatic event echoes another, and the texts illustrate how violence and its effects live on in the bodies that are subjected to it.

To add humiliation to pain, the interrogator demands, 'Ta av dig skorna och ta av dig kläderna' [Take off your shoes and take off your clothes] (27; 31), and P is forced to continue the interrogation in his underpants. When he repeatedly requests to have his clothes returned to him, he is told: 'När du berättar sanningen får du dina kläder' [You'll get your clothes back when you tell the truth] (65; 69). Violence, now exercised in the form of humiliation and physical deprivation, is once again linked to language, and P's treatment, as well as his reactions to it, confirm Richardson's observation that 'trauma emerges [...] with violence, not just on the body but in and on language' (148). When we first learn, 'Han är inte denna nakna, kliande, hostande, gråtande kropp' [He is not this naked, itching, coughing, crying body] (45; 49), and then, 'Förhören har gjort något med orden, slagit sönder dem och visat upp dem nakna som stenar' [The interrogations have done something to words, smashed them to bits and displayed them as naked as stones] (84; 88), it illustrates how the effects of violence on P's body and on language correlate. In the same way that P's body changes through violence, language is altered, and the words themselves become similarly broken and naked as P himself. Another echo of his violent childhood experiences is invoked when P, in the narrative present, dissociates himself from the pain and reproduces the same mechanism of self-protection that served him as a child when his brother beat him: 'Pojken gled ner från sin stol. [...] Det var inte han' [The boy slid down from his chair. [...] It wasn't him] (32; 36). Richardson states, 'It is what the pain *does* that is its affective quality', and precisely this affective quality separates P from his body and his self in the past, and also in the narrative now.[26] When P negates his body in this scene in the same way as he did when he was a child, it highlights the extent to which violence shatters the individual body and self, and it emphasises the relationality of trauma and violence.

Aftershocks: The Effects of Violence

While both texts make connections between seemingly unrelated violent events and bring to light how violence, despite being inflicted by one individual upon the other, is embedded in political structures, they also illustrate how the affective qualities of violence and trauma pervade the protagonists' lives long after the actual violence has ceased. In *Der Weg der Wünsche*, Teréz's coerced sexual encounter with Signor Monte has, notwithstanding its horror, the desired effect, and not long after Signor Monte raped Teréz, the Kallay family receive what they are waiting for so desperately: their entry documents for Germany. In a scene in which the narrator focalises Károly, Károly names every single document, and enthusiastically exclaims: 'Es ist vorbei, wir haben es geschafft, geschafft! Habe ich es nicht gesagt? Man muss nur geduldig sein' [It's over, we made it, we made it! Didn't I tell you? You just have to be patient], while Teréz stirs the soup in silence, seemingly 'ungerührt' [unstirred] (243). Unlike Károly, the reader knows what Teréz had to do to procure these documents, and Károly's naïve joy throws the systemic and physical violence Teréz was subjected to into sharp relief. Moreover, the contrast between Károly's exuberance and Teréz's silence highlights how alone Teréz is with the burden of knowledge, as it is only shared with the reader. Effectuated by focalisation, this gap of knowledge between Károly and Teréz, and also between Károly and the reader, grants us an understanding of Teréz's situation that Károly lacks, and, once again, invites us to feel with Teréz. This loneliness, together with her silence, is reminiscent of Teréz's past: in the same way that she could not talk about having been raped as a child, it is now impossible for her to share with her husband what Signor Monte coerced her into doing, and she becomes disconnected and alienated from her most intimate companion. When Teréz is thus propelled into isolation, her loneliness resonates with the sadness and emptiness she experienced as a child, and the two violent episodes concatenate through their affective qualities.

The affective relation between these two events is further strengthened, for shame emerges as Teréz's immediate affective reaction in both cases, and is, according to Herman, a common 'response to helplessness, the violation of bodily integrity' (53). When, as a girl, Teréz returns to her mother and sister without food, the reader learns, 'Sie [...] schämte sich' [she [...] was ashamed] (331); and, while Signor Monte harasses Teréz, the narrator reveals, 'sie schämte sich so' [she was so ashamed] (229). When affect is at once corporeal and intellectual, shame is felt intensely and painfully 'by and on the body', and it influences the way that 'the self feels about itself', namely, bad. At first, the subject turns to itself and away from what causes the shame in order to expel 'the badness', but 'the subject's movement back into itself is simultaneously a turning away from itself'. In other words, the self tries to expel itself from itself, and the problem is that with shame, 'the subject might have nowhere to turn'.[27] As a girl, Teréz had at least her uncle Barnabás, who granted her refuge and comfort on her return to Budapest; as an adult, Teréz has nowhere to turn, and because her capacity to make sense of the world is ruptured, she turns against herself. In another common response to rape, Teréz, in an attempt to purge the shameful experience from her body, slips into the ice-cold water of a nearby river and 'ließ sich von dessen trüber Reinheit waschen, reinigen' [let herself be washed, cleansed by its turbid purity]. When she states, 'die Kälte tat gut' [the cold was good] (240), the cold water counterpoises the intense feeling of shame, and helps to expel the badness. The impact of cold water, however, cannot change the way Teréz feels and thinks about herself, and, while she sits shivering on the riverbank, her reflections intensify the shame, particularly when she recalls, 'Imponiert, gefallen hatte er ihr damals, der Direttore' [he impressed her, she liked him, the Direttore] (241), which refers to a time when Teréz naively believed that Signor Monte had a genuine interest in helping her family. She takes a gun out of her handbag which she had found earlier in the camp, and fires, but shoots into the air, and we learn that it was time 'nach den Kindern zu sehen' [to check on the children] (242). For the time being, the responsibility for her family holds Teréz back from committing suicide despite the overwhelming shame that violence produces in her.

In P's case, the violence ends when the interrogator eventually realises that P cannot provide any information at all. When P is asked if he wants to seek asylum in Tanzania, he answers in the affirmative, reasoning with himself that 'ett flyktingläger måste vara bättre än burarna i källaren' [a refugee camp must be better than the cages in the cellar] (104; 109); however, the destitution continues after P is detained in a refugee camp in Tabora. The Kallay family in the Italian camp wait for their paperwork, whereas P has nothing to wait for; he is detained in a nowhere where linear time ceases to exist: 'Han har en liksom tidlös känsla i huvudet, en känsla av evighet som har med denna plats att göra' [He has a kind of timeless feeling in his head, a sense of eternity that has something to do with this place] (111; 116). The impersonal wording of 'Man sover, vaknar. Dagar går, och veckor' [One sleeps, wakes up. Days go by, and weeks] (133; 137) places further emphasis on the circularity and repetitive quality of time in this liminal zone. In addition, the physical deprivation in the camp affects P in similar ways as does the violence during the interrogation: 'Han blir allt magrare. Det är som att hans kropp tillhör någon annan. Han är genomströmmad av sorg, av utmattning' [He is getting thinner and thinner. It's as though his body belonged to someone else. He is flooded with sorrow, with exhaustion] (126; 130). P's self-perception does not correlate with the embodied reality in this situation, and therefore, he becomes alienated from his self and body, and, again, negates his body by dissociating himself from it.

The relations between Uganda and Tanzania became worse when Julius Nyerere offered Obote exile in Tanzania and granted him the right to work towards returning to Uganda. This work included the building of a guerrilla army of Ugandan refugees to free Uganda from Amin's rule and resulted in the attempt to invade Uganda in 1972.[28] It transpires that the person in charge of the camp where P is detained is Tito Okello, the former Ugandan army commander, also in exile in Tanzania, who actively recruits refugees in an army, and who plans to make P part of it: 'Vi kommer att störta Amin. [...] Ni kommer att få vapen innan vi går over gränsen. Håll dig beredd' [We're going to overthrow Amin. [...] You will be armed before we cross the border. Be prepared] (148; 152). Despite P's apolitical stance, he becomes entangled in these political tensions, and, should he be forced to fight in Okello's army, his life would be differentially jeopardised, as one of P's fellow refugees points out to him: 'Ingen langi kommer att överleva i Uganda. [...] Du är död så fort vi har korsat gränsen, pilot' [No Langi will survive in Uganda. [...] You're dead as soon as we cross the border, pilot] (155; 159). Discussing the affectivity of threat, Brian Massumi states that, 'The uncertainty of the potential next is never consumed in any given event. There is always a remainder of uncertainty, an unconsummated surplus of danger'.[29] In this sense, threat always points towards the future, but has an actual affective reality in the present, which is fear. This life-threatening uncertainty instigates fear in P, and, in turn, motivates him to flee the camp to make his way to Nairobi in Kenya where he hopes to be recognised as a political refugee by the UN, and so he runs, walks, and literally sells his last shirt to pay for the bus and train fares. In a concatenation of several violent events in P's life, his childhood urge to 'flyga bort' [fly away] (31; 34) changes to, 'Han är pilot. Han ska flyga igen' [He is a pilot. He will fly again] (77; 81), and finally to 'Han måste fly' [He has to run away] (126; 130). Flight, with the connotations of fleeing and flying merged in the English noun, has become the theme and motivation of P's life, triggered affectively by the experience of violence, and the ever-present unconsummated surplus of more violence.

When P flees across the nowhere, his flight is accompanied by a feeling of uprootedness that reinforces his alienation from his self and body, so much so that he loses his sense of self altogether, and his personal history, at least momentarily, becomes erased: 'Han mindes inte vem han var. Han mindes inte var han kom ifrån' [He doesn't remember who he was. He doesn't remember where he came from] (190; 194), as if the interrogator's remark that he does not exist has come true. Flight, which was once P's hope to escape violence, is now solely associated with fear, and when fear and flight coalesce, P's past and future affectively fold into an endless present in the anticipation that 'han aldrig kommer att stanna någonstans, aldrig, aldrig. Att han lämnade sitt hem en natt när han var pojke. Att han saknar det med varje ben i kroppen' [he will never get to stay somewhere, never, never. Because he left his home one night when he was a boy. Because he misses it with every bone in his body] (168; 172). When Herman discusses the effects of captivity on prisoners of war, she observes that the experience of time as circular and infinite, and as pervaded by violence and coercion, causes a 'rupture between present and past' that 'frequently persists even after the prisoner is released'. Because of this rupture and violence, '[t]he past, like the future, becomes too painful to bear, for memory, like hope, brings back the yearning for all that has been lost' (89).[30] These observations capture accurately how P feels: he expresses a sense of loss that resembles the way in which Teréz mourns the only *Heimat* one has got; and, in addition, he gives voice to his dread that the effects of violence may have destroyed his future. When P reaches Nairobi, he lacks the confidence and know-how to register as a refugee with the UN; he sleeps rough, works casual jobs, drinks and lives in a perpetual present 'trots att det är omöjligt [...] naket som en bit slaktavfall på gatan' [even though it is impossible [...] naked like a piece of offal on the street] (223; 227–28). The reader further learns that, 'Han slutar drömma om att flyga och istället invaderar lägret hans nätter' [He stops dreaming of flying and instead the camp invades his nights] (219; 223), and eventually, P considers ending his own life: 'Han plockar upp en glasskärva, håller den vassa kanten mot handledens hud. Han har ingen framtid. Ingen framtid' [He picks up a shard of glass, holds the sharp edge against the skin of his wrist. He has no future. No future] (222; 226). The immediate present in which P lives is pervaded by the nightmarish resonances of past trauma, and the hope of flying which was his former motivation in his life decisions, has been destroyed. P's future prospects become unbearable, as they would only entail his yearning for the dreams that have been shattered, and thus, the only solution he can think of is to commit suicide.

When trauma, as an effect of violence, ruptures the capacity to make sense of the world, P's wish to commit suicide is reminiscent of Teréz's reaction to shame in *Der Weg der Wünsche*: neither P nor Teréz have anywhere to turn to, and so they turn against themselves. However, while P does not commit suicide after all and at last manages to change his circumstances by marrying a Swedish woman and relocating to Sweden, Teréz's desperate situation intensifies when the family are stuck in the snow in Switzerland. Triggered by the snow, Teréz remembers how she was raped as a girl, and, with the memory of Signor Monte still at the forefront of her mind, these violent past experiences become linked with the present in a palimpsestic pattern in which, as Max Silverman elucidates, 'The relationship between present and past [...] takes the form of a superimposition and interaction of different temporal traces to constitute a sort of composite structure'.[31] Within this composite structure, the experiences from different time segments in Teréz's life become superimposed and thus interlinked; and, in addition, when viewed from the angle of affect, the affects that these experiences have produced are brought into contact, and resonate with each other. Teréz, feeling the desperation of her present situation in the snow, relives the desperation of the past; her past silence permeates the burden of her present silence, and when she remembers her past loneliness, the present isolation becomes amplified. When Teréz is thus doubly cast out of systems of protection both in the past and in the present, now merged, she commits suicide. This, at least, is one of the possibilities that the text's ambiguous ending suggests: Bori is focalised in the last chapter, and when she realises in the morning that her mother has disappeared, she follows Teréz's footsteps in the snow until they end at the edge of the abyss. Even if it is not merely Bori's wishful thinking when she, back in the car and clutching her talisman, hears footsteps and urges, 'Das musste ihre Mutter sein. [...] Sie musste es sein' [This had to be her mother. [...] It had to be her] (333), the fate of the Kallay family remains unknown. For all we know, the family have truly lost their place on earth, and whether they arrive at their destination — with or without Teréz — is left to our imagination.

Although P, in Anyuru's novel, outwardly manages to alter his desperate situation, he never settles in Sweden; his marriage breaks apart, he is unable to hold down a job, and the fear that inscribes the itinerary of his flight until he reaches Sweden has become all-encompassing: 'Han fruktar världen. Han fruktar de dunkla krafter som gång på gång har slagit sönder hans liv' [He is afraid of the world. He is afraid of the dim forces that have torn apart his life time and again] (229; 233). The actuality of these dim forces belongs to P's past, and yet, they persist affectively in his present in the form of an unrealised threat, so that for P, an unconsummated surplus of danger always remains: he 'blir aldrig en trygg varelse' [never becomes a calm, secure person] (118; 122). When the protective mechanism of P's childhood — his wish to fly — is replaced with a never-ending flight, the notion of flight turns into the overarching narrative of P's life: 'Han flydde från dödens fält. Det var hans liv' [He fled the fields of death. That was his life] (241; 245). Considering the reiteration of this notion in phrases such as, 'Han undkom dödens fält' [He escaped the fields of death] (245; 250), it is only apt that Walter Benjamin's discussion of Paul Klee's painting 'Angelus Novus' gives the text its title, is referenced several times in the text itself, and, in an altered version, serves as the last line of the text: 'En storm kom från paradiset. Stormen var livet' [A storm blew in from paradise. The storm was life] (248; 252); life, not progress, as Benjamin has it. When this storm is life, or rather P's life, the image of the angel merges with the son's image of P, and the angel's wings come to symbolise P's wish to fly. The storm, however, blows with such violent force that it becomes caught in the angel's wings, so 'daß der Engel sie nicht mehr schließen kann' [that the angel can no longer close them], in the same way that P can no longer fly. And, although this storm propels him 'unaufhaltsam in die Zukunft' [irresistibly [...] into the future], P, like the angel, has his back turned to it, looking back into the past. 'Wo eine Kette von Begebenheiten vor *uns* erscheint' [Where *we* can see a chain of events], writes Benjamin, 'da sieht *er* eine einzige Katastrophe, die unablässig Trümmer auf Trümmer häuft und sie ihm vor die Füße schleudert' [*he* sees one single catastrophe which keeps piling wreckage upon wreckage and hurls it in front of his feet].[32] This poetic imagery succinctly summarises the far-reaching consequences of violence and flight for P's life; instead of time developing in a linear way, P's violent experiences concatenate, and echo each other, until they blur into one single force that shatters his life. Simultaneously, this imagery illustrates the effect on P's son: therein lies a sadness about the loss of a father he never really had.

★   ★   ★   ★   ★

We have seen how, in the nexus between violence, trauma and power, various forms and practices of violence shape and twist the protagonists' relations to themselves and the world: in P's case, ongoing domestic violence when he was a child, and later mistreatment and privation in the context of interrogation, detention and flight. In Teréz's case, multiple rape when she was fifteen, the oppressive violence bound up with the corrupt political system in Hungary, and, once in Italy, sexual coercion facilitated by the unequal power structures embedded in the political microcosm of the transit camp. Although the personal and political circumstances in which these various forms of violence are exercised differ, the affective impact on the protagonists, and their reactions to violence, are similar: dissociation, loneliness, isolation, and, as their trust in the world and the future shatters in moments of intense distress, the protagonists' wish to take their own lives. Moreover, more recent violent experiences trigger the protagonists' memories of earlier ones, and therefore, those apparently unrelated separate incidents become connected. When concatenation can be understood as 'a word with a connection to circuitry, evoking linkages, patterns, a chain, and chain-reactions', it is the affective qualities of violence that resonate across time and space, linking not only different people, places and times, but also various forms of violence.[33] The affects produced by violence, and their embodiment and aftershocks, show that violence is not only relational, but also boundless, as its effects reach far beyond the immediate violent incident.

Furthermore, we have seen that violence and its concomitant affective qualities help to build the narrative composition of both texts. In Doma's novel, the narrator leaves gaps and ambiguities, which acknowledges Teréz's silences and the difficulty to put violence and trauma into words. These gaps are further emphasised through selective focalisation on the respective four members of the Kallay family. In Anyuru's novel, P's son fills the gaps which his father's silence leaves with his own imagination, and he presents the reader with a fictionalisation of his father's intimate thoughts, fears and dreams. To gain a better understanding for his father, the son, in writing his father's story, slips into his father's skin and experiences and imagines what it must be like to lose one's place on earth. The son assumes a narratorial position of empathy insofar as he feels for his father. With regard to the ways in which the combination of affective contents and aesthetics offer a window into contextual constellations, Ahmed's insights are instructive when she argues that '"feeling" [is] crucial to the struggle against injustice', and further, that, 'We need to respond to injustice in a way that shows rather than erases the complexity of the relation between violence, power and emotion'. Anyuru's and Doma's texts visualise how violence shapes and mutates migrating bodies, while they, simultaneously, bring to the fore how power relations, social norms and political practices facilitate and sustain those different forms of violence which impinge on the protagonists' lives. From this perspective, the texts address precisely the complex relationship between violence, power and emotion discussed by Ahmed, and the protagonists' pain and suffering are depicted as 'effects rather than origins' of violence.[34] While the writerly devices employed in both texts throw the effects of violence and trauma into sharp relief, the texts themselves invite us to reflect critically not only on these effects of violence, but also on their causes, or origins.

Notes to Chapter 1

1. Bauman, *Liquid Times*, pp. 44–45, italics in original.
2. Meera Atkinson and Michael Richardson, 'At the Nexus', in *Traumatic Affect*, ed. by Atkinson and Richardson (Newcastle upon Tyne: Cambridge Scholars Publishing, 2013), pp. 1–21 (pp. 2, 4).
3. Peter Fifield, 'The Body, Pain and Violence', in *The Cambridge Companion to the Body in Literature*, ed. by David Hillman and Ulrika Maude (Cambridge: Cambridge University Press, 2015), pp. 116–31 (p. 116).
4. Bruce B. Lawrence and Aisha Karim, 'Introduction', in *On Violence: A Reader*, ed. by Lawrence and Karim (Durham, NC: Duke University Press, 2007), pp. 1–15 (p. 7).
5. Atkinson and Richardson, p. 12.

6. Butler, pp. 33, 19.

7. Judith Lewis Herman, *Trauma and Recovery* (London: Pandora, 1997), pp. 100–08.

8. Richardson, p. 35.

9. Herman, p. 52.

10. Ibid.

11. Anna Gibbs, 'Apparently Unrelated: Affective Resonance, Concatenation and Traumatic Circuitry in the Terrain of the Everyday', in *Traumatic Affect*, ed. by Meera Atkinson and Michael Richardson (Newcastle upon Tyne: Cambridge Scholars Publishing, 2013) pp. 129–47 (p. 133).

12. Herman, p. 52.

13. David Farrier, *Postcolonial Asylum: Seeking Sanctuary before the Law* (Liverpool: Liverpool University Press, 2011), p. 6.

14. Agier, *Borderlands*, p. 35.

15. Ibid., p. 36.

16. Foucault, p. 1.

17. Richardson, pp. 119–20.

18. 'Torture', in *Oxford English Dictionary Online* (Oxford: Oxford University Press, June 2019) <http://www.oed.com/view/Entry/203700> [accessed 16 August 2019].

19. Elaine Scarry, *The Body in Pain: The Making and Unmaking of the World* (Oxford: Oxford University Press, 1985), pp. 28, 35, italics in original.

20. Ibid., pp. 40, 47, 37.

21. Achille Mbembe, 'Necropolitics', *Public Culture*, 15, (2003), 1–40 (pp. 39–40), italics in original.

22. George Roberts, 'The Uganda–Tanzania War, the Fall of Idi Amin, and the Failure of African Diplomacy, 1978–1979', *Journal of Eastern African Studies*, 4 (2014), 692–709 (p. 694).

23. Scarry, pp. 28–29, italics in original.

24. Ahmed, *Cultural Politics*, p. 25, italics in original.

25. Gibbs, p. 129.

26. Richardson, p. 144, italics in original.

27. Ahmed, *Cultural Politics*, pp. 103, 104.

28. Holger Bernt Hansen, 'Uganda in the 1970s: A Decade of Paradoxes and Ambiguities', *Journal of Eastern African Studies*, 1 (2013), 83–103 (p. 92).

29. Brian Massumi, 'The Future Birth of the Affective Fact: The Political Ontology of Threat', in *The Affect Theory Reader*, ed. by Melissa Gregg and Gregory J. Seigworth (Durham, NC: Duke University Press, 2010), pp. 52–70 (p. 53).

30. Herman, p. 89.

31. Maxim Silverman, *Palimpsestic Memory: The Holocaust and Colonialism in French and Francophone Fiction and Film* (New York: Berghahn, 2015), p. 3.

32. Walter Benjamin, *Gesammelte Schriften*, ed. by Rolf Tiedemann and Hermann Schweppenhäuser, I.2 (Frankfurt a.M.: Suhrkamp, 1972), pp. 697–698, italics in original; Walter Benjamin, *Illuminations*, ed. and intro. by Hannah Arendt, trans. by Harry Zohn (London: Fontana, 1973), p. 249, italics in original.

33. Atkinson and Richardson, p. 13.

34. Ahmed, *Cultural Politics*, p. 196.

CHAPTER 2

❖

Arrival in Liminality:
Seeking Asylum in Abbas Khider's *Ohrfeige*
and Alen Mešković's *Enmandstelt*

In his astute discussion on asylum, and the political implications of processes of seeking asylum on asylum seekers and on the respective nations where asylum is sought, David Farrier argues:

> Where it is granted, asylum is designed to confer on individuals the capacity to remake their lives free from threat and limitation. To seek asylum, however, refers to their induction into a condition of waiting, uncertainty and dependency that frustrates any chance for self-creation; it is a period of especially fraught relations with the host nation, and with the law.[1]

In the previous chapter, we have already seen how, when P and Teréz are detained in camps for refugees or asylum seekers before they even reach their destinations, their lives become interrupted, as they fall into a form of abeyance that, indeed, denies them the possibility to realise their personal aspirations. The power relations and political practices which govern these camps allow for different forms of violence to be sustained, which has far-reaching consequences for their lives. While chapter 1 focused on the protagonists' journeys and how they are ruptured, diverted and temporarily suspended in erratic and often violent ways, and on how a politically effectuated liminality permeates their lives when their journeys are halted, I shall now turn to a similar sense of liminality, but in the context of arrival and seeking asylum in the so-called host nation.

Two texts which illuminate processes of seeking asylum, and the restrictive conditions of being forced to live in liminality, are the Danish novel *Enmandstelt* (2016) by Alen Mešković and the German novel *Ohrfeige* (2016) by Abbas Khider. From the perspectives of asylum seekers themselves, they depict flight, arrival, seeking asylum and temporary habitation in various centres for asylum seekers in Denmark and Germany respectively. *Ohrfeige* relates Karim Mensy's flight from Iraq, his arrival in rural Bavaria in the winter of 2000, and his ensuing struggle for recognition as a political refugee; *Enmandstelt* captures the story of the Bosnian Muslim Emir Pozder, called Miki, who leaves a refugee camp in Croatia and arrives in Denmark in December 1994. Despite the obvious dissimilarities between Miki and Karim setting out from different points of departure and moments in time, and arriving at different destinations, there are commonalities between these two protagonists, their migratory journeys and narrative voices that make them directly comparable. Karim is nineteen when he arrives in Germany, and Miki is seventeen on arrival in Denmark, and, in addition to this similarity in age, Karim, like Miki, embarks on his journey alone and without a passport; he travels by the same means as Miki (by paying people smugglers); and, like Miki, arrives in a country other than he had intended: for arbitrary reasons, Karim ends up in Germany instead of France, and Miki in Denmark instead of Sweden. Moreover, the stories in both texts are told from a first-person narrative perspective, and hence, we are granted insight into the protagonists' subjective experiences of crossing borders, seeking asylum, and tackling the hurdles concomitant with restrictive immigration policies and practices in particular places and moments in time.[2]

While the protagonists' applications for asylum are processed, they are forcefully held in a state of geographical, social and political liminality which impedes any chance for self-realisation. When liminality is conceived of as an affective quality that is produced by national and transnational power relations such as border politics and asylum policies, this suggests, with reference to Farrier's earlier quoted observation, that the protagonists' relations with the law, and also with the host nations, are fraught while they are detained in these liminal zones. In this regard, I am looking at the factors that cause a strain in the protagonists' relations with the law, and at how the protagonists' lives and self-understanding change through the effects of this affective liminality. Miki, and also Karim, have to make their claims for asylum convincing enough to be granted refugee status. To think critically through the mechanisms that dominate the processing of the protagonists' asylum applications, I am drawing on Terry Tomsky's notion of a 'trauma economy'. On the premise that there is a marketable value in particular kinds of trauma, Tomsky conceives of a trauma economy as 'a circuit of movement and exchange where traumatic memories "travel" and are valued and revalued along the way'. Hence, traumatic memory is transformed into a currency whose value within the trauma economy depends on the 'economic, cultural, discursive and political structures that guide, enable and ultimately institutionalize the representation, travel and attention to certain traumas'.[3] Focusing on precisely those structures, it is not my aim to assess whether or not the protagonists' memories qualify as traumatic, but to point out how these structures bear upon Miki's and Karim's representations of their pasts in the context of seeking asylum. Tomsky explicates that within the framework of the trauma economy, there is a tendency for audiences to value one trauma as more significant than another, and when the term 'audiences' is extended to those officials, such as case workers or judges, who decide whether or not asylum is granted, I can use the concept of a trauma economy to highlight those dynamics that compel the protagonists to adapt their pasts to the currents of the trauma economy, and strain their relations with the law.

According to Farrier, it is, from a political perspective, only once asylum is granted that individuals regain the opportunity to shape their own lives, which suggests that the political agency of asylum seekers is limited while their applications are being processed. Looking at whether the texts depict the protagonists' opportunities to change their lives positively as having increased once they are granted asylum, or whether they suggest that gaining refugee status alone is not sufficient to end the protagonists' fraught relations with the law, will allow me to assess whether the texts confirm or complicate Farrier's assertion. This will also shed light on the ways in which the texts negotiate their protagonists' political agency while they are seeking asylum, and after they gain refugee status. Michel Agier argues that asylum seekers find themselves in 'a state hardly perceptible, hardly audible and "voiceless"', which suggests that they lack the political agency to resist exclusionary politics and policies that render them invisible and inaudible.[4] However, *Enmandstelt* and *Ohrfeige* contest the protagonists' voicelessness and invisibility a priori in that they reimagine those whom Zygmunt Bauman calls 'the *unimaginables*', and make the fictional voices of asylum seekers themselves heard.[5] Do the texts, however, employ aesthetic strategies beyond that, which can be viewed as counteracting the protagonists' politically effectuated sense of liminality?

While I am drawing on an understanding of key terms such as borders and liminality as I have discussed them previously, the term 'asylum seeker' also deserves some critical attention. From the outset, the term 'asylum seeker' is difficult to grasp, as the act of seeking asylum in itself implies a paradox. The Universal Declaration of Human Rights states that, 'Everyone has the right to seek and to enjoy in other countries asylum from persecution'; and yet, those states which signed up to the 1951 United Nations Convention for Refugees reserve their sovereign right to control and police who is granted asylum and who is not, whereby asylum seekers are often construed as a 'problem' or as 'illegal' despite the fact that the 1951 Convention highlights that asylum seekers can enter any territory without legal documentation.[6] The paradox lies in the very articulation of the asylum claim, because, as Farrier argues, the plea for admittance 'affirms sovereign power to exclude, but also undermines this by presupposing a right to sanctuary that supersedes the nation's founding prescriptions'. In this light, the articulation of the asylum claim can be seen as 'a kind of split statement' or a 'double-voiced discourse', and the claim to asylum can be regarded as a subordination to sovereign state power, while simultaneously disrupting this power and territorial order.[7] When asylum seekers are constructed as a threat through exclusionary asylum politics, their wish to find a new place of belonging after having spent time in displacement, or placelessness, is seen as a disruption of territorial, and of social, order. Asylum seekers are, as Roger Bromley argues, 'mapped against an already existing, fixed and (so the story goes) socially cohesive national culture'. Hence, they become misappropriated to reassert a national imaginary by way of juxtaposing the supposed completeness of the nation with a construction of asylum seekers as 'the figure of lack, indicating an absence and an aberration'.[8] When asylum seekers are viewed as an aberration even before they cross national borders, they are, as Ahmed points out, 'read as the cause of an injury to the national body', and they are thus associated with 'figures of hate' that gain affective value through the circulation of this image. Within discourses that produce asylum seekers as such figures, they become utilised to reinforce boundaries, because hate helps to align 'not only the "I" with the "we" [...] but the "you" with the "them"': 'hate functions to substantiate the threat of invasion and contamination'.[9]

Considering that the protagonists of both texts engage with discourses that construct and essentialise asylum seekers as figures of hate, and who are, while they are waiting for their asylum applications to be processed, socially isolated and geographically marginalised, Jacques Rancière's notion of dissensus is a constructive starting point to assess whether these dynamics can be resisted. Rancière suggests that, first and foremost, politics is 'an intervention in the visible and sayable', and thus, dissensus is at the core of politics.[10] Rancière uses his understanding of dissensus to oppose Giorgio Agamben's notion of bare life. Agamben differentiates between *zoē* and *bios*, or 'bare life' and 'politically qualified life', and he argues that, while refugees are detained in camps, they are stripped to their bare lives as they are held in a state of exception, or a double bind of inclusion and exclusion, that denies them political rights and agency. In Agamben's view, camps are apolitical spaces, and their inhabitants are subjected to sovereign state power, while they themselves are politically powerless.[11] In a direct answer to Agamben, Rancière refutes the notion that bare life and politicised life become separated; he rejects 'every difference that distinguishes between people who "live" in different spheres of existence' and dismisses 'categories of those who are or are not qualified for political life'. Bringing these two categories, or separated worlds, together, Rancière does not consider the gap between politicised and non-politicised life a disjunction, but rather an 'opening of an interval for political subjectivation', in which everyone has the 'capacity for staging scenes of dissensus'.[12] This, as Rancière argues further, endows everyone with political agency despite the fact that some, such as refugees and asylum seekers, might be considered as not having any political rights at all: 'Politics exists when the natural order of domination is interrupted by the institution of a part of those who have no part'.[13] Strongly advocating a link between politics and aesthetics, Rancière conceives of literature as involved in politics, and when literature can constitute 'a partition of the sensible', both political and aesthetic undertakings have the potential to disrupt extant forms of consensus to create new and innovative configurations, or practices, of expression.[14] Keeping in mind that those protagonists who are granted a voice in the two texts are asylum seekers, we can ask whether the texts' aesthetic choices can be viewed as scenes or acts of dissensus.

Narrative Voices and Ironic Distance

In Sianne Ngai's understanding, the tone of a literary text is a 'concept of *feeling* that encompasses attitude: a literary text's affective bearing, orientation, or "set toward" its audience and world'.[15] It is primarily the narrative voices of Karim, in *Ohrfeige*, and Miki, in *Enmandstelt*, which orient the texts towards their audiences with a particular affective quality. Miki and Karim are not only of similar age, share comparable itineraries and are treated in similar ways by the respective authorities in Denmark and Germany, but also have a similarly laconic tone, and a dry sense of humour, in common. These similar narrative voices set both texts towards their audiences with an attitude of irony, and, together with other formal features such as ironic realism, the affective value of this irony becomes significant when assessing the ways in which the texts invite the reader to engage with those politics marking the protagonists' arrivals as difficult. In Karim's case, his ironic narrative voice can be seen as part of what Moritz Schramm, in his analysis of Khider's work, contextualises as ironic realism. Schramm argues that, at first glance, Khider's works fulfil the need for a new proximity to the real world after the dominant tendencies in literature for intertextual self-reference that characterised the postmodern era in general. This need for literature's connections with a reality outside the literary realm is accommodated by *Ohrfeige*, and equally by *Enmandstelt*, in that both texts clearly position their characters in real locations and actual times: we know when Miki and Karim arrive in Denmark and Germany, the stations of their itineraries are indicated, and most places are named and can be found on a map, which, according to Schramm, triggers an 'Erkennungseffekt' [effect of recognition] in the reader. This ostensible objectivity, however, is cast into doubt when it becomes apparent that it is subjectively constructed, a fact that both texts point towards, and which renders the depicted reality contingent.[16] For instance, Sandholm, the place where Miki is transferred after his arrival, is indeed the largest reception centre for asylum seekers in Denmark, whereas Körsbärsholm, the place in Sweden where Miki intends to be reunited with his older brother Neno, is invented. The place name itself evokes images of cherry orchards and suggests idyllic connotations; as an imagined place, however, it belongs to a desired world that is out of reach for Miki. Miki's references to real and imagined places alike highlights the contingency and subjectively constructed nature of the depicted reality, and evokes an effect of recognition in the reader, while it simultaneously undermines it.

In *Ohrfeige*, it is the two framing devices in which the main narrative is embedded that distort the ostensible realism of Karim's account, and thwart an effect of recognition for the reader. At the beginning of the novel, Karim ties his case worker, Frau Schulz, to her office chair, and, in reference to the novel's title, slaps her in the face. Subsequently, he smokes a joint and gags her, so that he can finally tell his story without being interrupted. However, Karim decides to relate his story in his first language, Arabic, because, as his first sentences demonstrate, he speaks only broken German, whereas in Arabic, he can 'frei reden' [speak free] (10; 2). In a reversal of the othering he is exposed to, Karim states that Frau Schulz is from 'einer ganz anderen Welt' [a completely different world] (10; 2), and, thus, she would not understand him anyway, even if she spoke Arabic. As the whole narrative is rendered in perfect German in Karim's voice while we know that he actually speaks Arabic, Karim's decision is a writerly device, or a double-voiced discourse, that draws the reader's attention to the fictionality of Karim's story, and deconstructs an assumed sense of authenticity. Throughout the main narrative, the reader is constantly being reminded that Karim's story is constructed, as he addresses Frau Schulz directly, and reiterates her name numerous times. The second framing device, four brief interspersions into the main diegesis in italics, undermines a claim for authenticity further. In these interspersions, Karim is waiting for a people smuggler to take him to Finland after his refugee status has been revoked in Germany, and he is lying on the sofa, smoking one joint after the other. Only when Karim comes to in the end and wonders, '*Wo ist Frau Schulz? [...] Irgendwann werde ich sie erwischen und ohrfeigen*' [*Where's Frau Schulz? [...] when I find you, I'm going to give you an almighty slap in the face*] (220; 218, italics in original), the reader learns that Karim's encounter with Frau Schulz is a product of his cannabis-induced imagination. This complex linguistic play grants Karim the freedom to express himself freely, while, at the same time, it distances the reader from Karim's narrative by raising awareness of its fictionality.

In addition, the ironic tone of Karim's and of Miki's narrative voices creates distance not only between the protagonists and the events they depict, but also between those events and the reader. Schramm argues that in Khider's work, the ironic tone helps to build 'eine humoristisch-ironische Distanz zu den Dingen und zum beschriebenen Geschehen' [a humorous-ironic distance to the matter and the events described], and this observation could be applied to Mešković's *Enmandstelt* as well.[17] On arrival in Denmark, Miki is impressed that the Danish police treat him with kindness, and he muses, 'Hvis de behandler afskum, der lige er dukket op i deres land, så godt, gad vide hvordan de så behandler hinanden, disse danskere?' [If they treat scum that just turned up in their country so well, you wonder how they treat each other, these Danes] (30). When Miki refers to himself as 'scum', he shows himself as having full awareness of the public discourse on the undesirability of asylum seekers, and, by using the notion of asylum seekers as human waste ironically, Miki subversively reflects this very discourse back at the reader. Simultaneously, Miki utilises irony to call positive images of the Danish people into question. In this scene, ironic distancing works in different directions: it distances Miki from the perception of himself as 'scum'; it distances the reader from prejudiced opinions and invites them to reconsider their own perceptions of asylum seekers; when Miki scornfully suggests that the Danes are nice to the point of naivety, he distances the reader from generally positive notions of Danish-ness; and, being alienated from a familiar reference frame, Danish readers find their social and national self-understanding challenged. In *Ohrfeige*, a similar effect is achieved when Karim, on arrival in Germany, is subjected to a strip search, and comments, 'Zum ersten Mal in meinem Leben schob jemand seinen Finger in meinen Arsch' [For the first time in my life someone stuck his finger in my arse] (45; 37). The irony, or rather the unvarnished directness, with which this event is depicted distances Karim from the humiliation this transgression of physical boundaries entails. However, it also creates distance between this scene and the reader: because of the narrative tone, we laugh spontaneously instead of feeling for Karim, only to realise afterwards what we are actually laughing about, and that this scene, in fact, is anything but funny. When, as this discussion has illustrated, ironic realism applies to both texts, their formal features, together with the protagonists' ironic narrative voices, produce distance from the matter and the depicted events, which, in turn, enables 'eine kritische Auseinandersetzung mit der Wirklichkeit' [a critical engagement with reality].[18] Although these textual strategies pertain to fictional accounts of the harsh realities of asylum seekers, they may inspire critical reflections, and thus can be viewed as key features of the texts' political aesthetics.

Arrival in Liminality

As stated earlier, Karim, and also Miki, arrive for arbitrary reasons in countries other than they had planned. Karim thinks that he is on his way to his uncle Murad in Paris when the people smugglers abandon him in the middle of the night in Germany, and, mistakenly assuming that he is in France when the police arrest him, he says the words he rehearsed in English especially for this occasion: 'I am from Iraq. Seeking asylum. Asylum please' (43). Miki's contact, who is supposed to meet him in the railway station in Copenhagen to smuggle him into Sweden, does not appear, and when he is approached by a police officer, Miki follows the advice of the Croatian people smuggler Darko, who instructed him, 'Bare sig det ord' [Just say the word] (11), and says, 'jeg vil have asyl [...] De vil slå mig ihjel. Jeg har brug for hjælp!' [I want asylum [...] They will kill me. I need help!] (10). Since both protagonists are arrested by the police, their claims for asylum can be viewed as a double-voiced discourse in that they are 'a request and a demand', and simultaneously invoke 'notions of sanctuary and illegitimacy'. While Karim and Miki, with their 'insistence on the provision of refuge' express 'a counter-will' which disrupts the sovereign power of the states in which they are seeking refuge, they are, at the same time, forced to submit to the sovereign decisions made in Germany and Denmark respectively, despite not having wanted to arrive in these countries in the first place.[19] Both protagonists emphasise the arbitrariness of their situation and their dependency on illegal intermediaries, so that Miki sums up the reasons that thwart his plan to live with his brother in Sweden by stating that, 'Den navnløse menneskesmugler, den civilklædte politimand, Neno og nogle danske asylregler kom i vejen' [The nameless people smuggler, the policeman in civilian clothes, Neno and some Danish asylum regulations got in the way] (68). Karim, finding himself in almost identical circumstances, states that those who cash in on the vulnerable situation of asylum seekers such as 'die Vermittler, die Mafiosi, die Geldgeilen, die Schmuggler, die bestechlichen Polizisten und Beamten' [the middlemen, the mafiosi, the money-grubbers, the smugglers and the corrupt policemen and officials] are more necessary for survival 'als alle Mitarbeiter von AMNESTY INTERNATIONAL zusammen' [than [...] all the staff members of Amnesty International put together] (28; 20). These statements indicate that Karim's, and also Miki's, vulnerability is politically induced, because pan-European frameworks for the regulation of immigration, in combination with national immigration laws, force them into illegality, and, simultaneously, close national borders for them, so that they are denied the possibility to reach their destinations of choice.

After their arrests by the police, Miki is treated with sensitivity and care, whereas Karim, as we have seen, experiences a harshness that violates physical boundaries. Miki is given sandwiches and coffee and is informed about every step of his itinerary, whereas Karim is handcuffed and locked in a prison cell; when he asks for food, he is informed in English that, 'It's in the middle of the night. Ask tomorrow' (47). Neither Miki nor Karim have any control over their itineraries while they are in transit, but Miki enjoys nevertheless that he, instead of being 'fragtet af kriminelle typer' [transported by criminals] as on his journey to Denmark, is now being chauffeured by the police in a 'splinterny Mercedes' [brand new Mercedes], because, as he says, he is convinced that he is still able to make his way to Sweden: 'Jeg ville lægge Danmark bag mig som et ubetydeligt bump på vejen' [I would leave Denmark behind me like an insignificant bump in the road] (46). Conversely, Karim, again in handcuffs, is pushed into a car and, without any further information, driven to a building 'das wie ein Knast aussah' [that looked like a jail] (49; 42), and states that he is 'eingeschüchtert von der Härte und der Kälte' [intimidated by the harshness and the cold] (49; 41) that the policemen's ostentatious demonstration of power signals to him. On arrival, a fellow asylum seeker, and not the police themselves, crudely disillusions Karim's plans to reach France when he informs him that he is in a transit centre in Munich, but that he will be transported further: 'Dein Paris heißt jetzt Zirndorf' [Zirndorf is your Paris now] (51; 44). This cold welcome is further reflected upon when Karim, utilising the weather as a metaphor, and objecting to the cold, snowy Bavarian winter, asks, 'Was ist das für ein komisches Land, das so ein Scheißwetter hat?' [What kind of weird country is this where the weather's so shit?] (62; 55). Miki, also suffering from the cold, echoes Karim's sentiment when he complains about 'den del af vinteren, danskerne skamløst kalder forår' [this part of winter the Danes shamelessly call spring] (159). It is not surprising that a sense of displacement is keenly felt by both protagonists, considering that neither Miki nor Karim arrive in their potential host-countries by choice, while they are, nonetheless, compelled to reside there by virtue of national and transnational regulatory frameworks. Once Miki is entrusted to the care of his distant relative Zijo in a centre for asylum seekers in Lundslev, he realises that he will not be able to reach Sweden, and comments with, 'nu boede jeg altså i denne åndssvage by i dette forkerte land' [now I lived in this stupid town in this wrong country] (91). Similarly, Karim wonders about 'diese absurde Welt da draußen namens Bayern' [the absurd world outside known as Bavaria] (54; 47). Both protagonists express a sense of alienation because, in their view, it is not only wrong or absurd that they are in the countries in which they arbitrarily find themselves, but the countries themselves appear wrong to them. With regard to asylum seekers, Bromley argues that they challenge 'the dominant vocabularies' of nation-states that are produced and circulated to reinforce 'a culture of entitlement and identity'.[20] Karim's and Miki's statements question precisely such dominant discourses, and while they, through their perspectives from the margins of Danish and German societies, voice their own alienation, they simultaneously alienate Danish and German readers from a familiar and dominant imaginary.

Once Miki, and also Karim, are placed in centres for asylum seekers, it transpires that they are, in the way they are depicted, similarly organised in Denmark and

Germany. Miki is housed in a centre on the outskirts of the small town Lundslev on Fyn; in Miki's own words, the centre is located in 'Lundslevs industrikvarter [...] mellem kyllingefabrikken og renseanlægget' [Lundslev's industrial area [...] between the chicken factory and the cleaning company] (76), or, 'Mellem kødet og lorten' [Between the meat and the shit] (55). The centre where Karim is placed is situated in a similarly marginalised location on the outskirts of Bayreuth, and with an armed guard at the entrance who controls the residents' papers and shopping bags. Further parallels between the centres are that they are self-contained, and house administrative bodies relevant to seeking asylum on the premises, and that the residents are bound to the immediate surroundings of the place. While Miki does not state the extent to which his movement is restricted other than that he cannot live outside the centre, Karim is subject to what is called *Residenzpflicht* [mandatory residence], which means that he has to stay within a radius of thirty square kilometres around the centre. This restriction has the kind of effect on Karim where he feels detained against his will: 'Wir befinden uns in einem dreißig Quadratkilometer großen, eiskalten Gefängnis' [We are in an ice-cold, twelve-square-mile prison] (70; 61). When Engin F. Isin and Kim Rygiel discuss the living conditions of dispossessed people in various frontiers, zones and camps around the globe, they observe that exclusionary politics of asylum 'want to render asylum seekers inexistent' by placing them on the outskirts of cities and on the margins of the attention of citizens. Although in fictional form, the two texts reflect this observation and confirm its validity, as they depict protagonists who are geographically marginalised and forced to live 'under some form of conditional freedom and surveillance'.[21] In this sense, the two texts illustrate accurately the ways in which the protagonists' sense of liminality is politically effectuated, and that borders are indeed reproduced in those 'localities and spatialities of state and society' where states claim the right to detain and police asylum seekers.[22]

Social isolation and the denial of citizens' rights become part of Miki's and Karim's geographical marginalisation, as they are not allowed to work, and are not eligible for language courses.[23] Miki's and Karim's limited financial means, together with their lack of language proficiency and the self-containment of the centres, impedes their chances to become part of the social and cultural lives of the towns in which they live, while they actually desire contact with the locals. Karim and Miki articulate their isolation in similar ways; Karim says:

> Vor allem hätte ich mir Kontakt zu Bayreuthern gewünscht, aber die einzigen regelmäßigen Begegnungen mit Deutschen [...] waren die mit den Polizeibeamten oder mit dem Wachpersonal im Heim, also mit Menschen, die beruflich dazu gezwungen waren, uns nicht zu ignorieren.

> [I dearly wanted some contact with people from Bayreuth, but the only regular encounters we had with Germans [...] were with police officers or the hostel guards — that is, with people whose jobs dictated that they couldn't ignore us.] (120–21; 114)

Miki echoes these sentiments when he states that all the people he has met 'var enten politimænd, Røde Kors-medarbejdere eller læger. Med andre ord folk, der i kraft af deres arbejde — og ikke ligefrem lyst — var nødt til at tale med mig' [were either policemen, Red Cross workers, or doctors. In other words, people who, by virtue of their work — and not exactly because they wanted to — had to talk to me] (99). These statements illustrate that it is indeed 'strategies of silencing such as geographical and social isolation' that facilitate the protagonists' sense of liminality.[24] Those officials whom Miki and Karim describe as being compelled to talk to them help to maintain Miki's and Karim's social isolation, as they are operative in the execution of restrictive and exclusionary asylum policies. Moreover, when Karim states that some people were forced not to ignore him, he tacitly implies that other locals do ignore him by choice, and, emphasising this fact as a cause for his social isolation, he summarises, 'Wir standen mittendrin und doch waren wir meilenweit von all dem entfernt' (66–67) [It was all around us and yet we were so very far away from it all; 60]. Karim gives voice to the same politically induced liminality that the Kallay family, in *Der Wege der Wünsche*, feel: they find themselves in a new world, 'aber keine zum Anfassen' [but they couldn't touch it], and thus, they are forced to live 'im Niemandsland' [in a no man's land] (97). While the Kallay family, however, are travelling towards their destination, Miki and Karim have arrived somewhere, albeit not at their preferred destinations. In Miki's and Karim's cases, liminal zones extend into the national space after the protagonists have crossed national borders, and the geographical, social and political marginalisation that inscribes these zones continues to render Miki and Karim 'hardly perceptible, hardly audible and "voiceless"', while their status as refugees is pending.[25]

Miki and Karim describe their financial situations in detail, and they broach the issue of the ways in which their restricted finances accentuate their social isolation. Miki's relative Zijo informs him that, 'Paragraf 15 i den danske lov [...] giver os otte hundrede tyve kroner til mad og drikke hver anden uge, men den forbyder os at arbejde, gå i skole, lære dansk, bo uden for lejren, rejse til udlandet og så videre' [Article 15 of the Danish law [...] grants us 820 kroner for food and drink every other week, but it forbids us to work, go to school, learn Danish, live outside the camp, travel abroad and so on] (86).[26] In the beginning, Miki finds it difficult to accept money that he, in his opinion, does not deserve because he has not worked for it, but he becomes quickly accustomed to his *løn* [wages], as it is called in the centre. Miki begins to work as a paper delivery boy to improve his financial situation, but it poses a dilemma for him, because he 'vil betale skat' [wants to pay tax], but 'må ikke arbejde' [isn't allowed to work] (133). When the denial of the right to work clashes with Miki's limited finances, he can only earn money by doing so illegally. Karim describes a similar situation in a somewhat more drastic way when he states, 'Manche von uns verkauften ihre Ärsche und Schwänze, um sich ein paar Kröten dazuzuverdienen. Andere wurden zu Dieben oder Drogendealern. Der Rest von uns, wie ich, musste mit achtzig Mark monatlich auskommen' [Some of us sold their cocks and arses to earn a little dough on the side. Others became thieves or drug dealers. The rest of us, including me, had to survive on eighty marks per month] (151; 145). These depictions of Miki's and Karim's financial circumstances reveal that the Danish and German governments provide them with minimum shelter and enough money to eat, but they are otherwise excluded from citizens' rights, such as the right to work, or to learn. The solutions that Miki and Karim could employ to alter their destitution illustrate the 'especially fraught relations [...] with the law' while their applications for asylum are being processed, because the two protagonists inevitably break the law with their wish to work, and, if they want to improve their finances, they are forced into illegality.[27] Accordingly, both *Ohrfeige* and *Enmandstelt* portray accurately how 'exclusionary politics [...] of securitisation and criminalisation get entangled in a self-fulfilling cycle'; or how, in other words, exclusionary asylum discourses portray asylum seekers as a 'problem' or 'illegal', while it is, more often than not, restrictive policies which lead to illegality and prostitution.[20]

The sum of these intersecting aspects of geographical, social and political liminality produces affects which are not only personally felt and individually embodied, but which, in Tygstrup's words, 'persist as a material/immaterial halo or sphere' and hover 'indistinctly but nonetheless insistently above and within any field of human agency and interaction'.[29] For Miki's and Karim's predicaments, this means that these affects — boredom, tension and conflict — are felt within and above fields in which humans are stripped of their agency and are condemned to inaction. When Miki says, 'Disse måneder i Danmark var jo ikke mit liv. De var en pause midt i en film' [These months in Denmark were not my life. They were like a break in the middle of a film] (116), he confirms Agier's observation that the lives of asylum seekers are interrupted by 'a gap made up of distance and waiting'.[30] Miki describes further that he has no possibility to release emotional tension when his life is suspended in this way, and he states, 'Det værste er, at man ikke rigtig kan gøre noget. Man er tvunget til at holde sin vrede inde' [The worst is that you can't really do anything. You are forced to keep your anger inside] (95). Karim, too, substantiates the notion that habitation in the centre constitutes a gap in his life, and remarks that, additionally, this condition of waiting and inaction implies an ever-increasing state of intellectual under-challenge: 'Wir konnten nichts anderes tun, als zu warten, und wurden von Tag zu Tag dämlicher' [We could do nothing but wait, and every passing day dulled our wits a little more] (120; 114). These statements expose how Miki and Karim, after their journeys came to a halt against their intentions, are forcibly arrested in time and place, and held in a state of 'transient permanence' where they are 'infantilised, static and inert, subject to curfews and a behavioural regime of containment that strips them of agency, voice and adulthood'.[31] In this state, which reduces Miki's and Karim's lives to passivity, they appear indeed stripped to their bare lives, with, seemingly, no chance to resist the mechanisms bearing upon them.

The Demands of the Trauma Economy

In her conceptualisation of a trauma economy, Tomsky conceives of traumatic histories as narratives that circulate and gain marketable value according to the 'economic, cultural, discursive and political structures' that sharpen the attention of audiences to particular traumas, whereas others are neglected. I have suggested earlier that, in the context of seeking asylum, the term 'audiences' also includes officials such as case workers or judges, who decide whether or not an asylum seeker will be recognised as a refugee and is granted asylum. In this respect, Miki, in *Ennmandstelt*, and Karim, in *Ohrfeige*, have to utilise their histories to explain convincingly why they cannot continue living in their countries of birth. The consideration that these audiences are particularly prone to accept some histories as convincing, whereas they are indifferent towards others, places Miki and Karim in a predicament: in order to claim legal protection, they have to adapt their histories to the currents of the trauma economies in their respective countries of arrival. These currents are subject to changing national immigration politics and international events with their local ripple effects, and therefore, Miki's and Karim's histories are transformed into currencies which, as they hope, persist despite the volatility of 'the commodity market of traumatic memories'.[32]

One of the first hurdles that Miki and Karim encounter when their applications for asylum are being processed is that neither of them speaks the language of their potential host country. Therefore, they are interviewed by the authorities with the help of an interpreter, and, as Karim states, this dependency on a mediator adds a degree of contingency to his case. Karim does not understand the interpreter's Arabic too well, but he reassures the interviewer of the opposite because he is afraid that 'er [der Übersetzer] andernfalls kein gutes Wort bei dem Entscheider für mich einlegen würde' [he [the translator] wouldn't put in a good word for me with the decision maker] (111; 105). In Karim's view, the interpreter plays a significant role in the decision on his asylum application beyond the mere linguistic mediation of his account; hence, Karim's interpreter is assigned a part in the trauma economy, because he has the power to shape the attention of Karim's audience to his particular narrative. In addition, the mediation of an interpreter holds the potential that Miki's and Karim's accounts become contorted, and details are lost in translation. Every detail of their respective pasts, however, matters, because asylum seekers 'must recall details of personal experiences — often traumatic — and give a narrative account, judged sufficiently coherent and consistent, in the context of administrative and legal procedures in the receiving country'.[33] In this respect, Karim and Miki are facing the challenge of having to deliver a narrative that is coherent in terms of dates and facts, and, at the same time, convincing enough to explain why they should be granted asylum.

In *Ohrfeige*, this challenge is reflected upon when Karim is first advised by a fellow asylum seeker, 'Du musst die Daten und Namen auswendig lernen. Das gilt auch für Orts- und Zeitangaben' [You have to learn the dates and names by heart. Same for places and times] (74; 67), and then, in the same breath, that he has to lie about his reasons for seeking asylum and present this lie credibly: 'Geh die Lüge so lange im Kopf durch, bis du wirklich glaubst, sie sei wahr!' [Go through the lie in your head until you genuinely believe it's true!] (75; 68). Moreover, Karim wants to avoid being extradited to the first EU country which he arrived in or passed through, and to that effect, his friend practices his narrative with him for the interview:

'Du bist mit einem Lastwagen hergekommen. Und bist dabei in keinem anderen europäischen Land ausgestiegen. Nur so hast du nämlich das Recht auf Aufenthalt' [You came here by lorry. And you didn't set foot in any other European country on the way. That's the only way you'll have a right to asylum] (71; 64). While it remains concealed from the immigration authorities, the reader learns that Karim suffers from gynecomastia, an increase in the size of male breast tissue, which makes his chest look female. This, in Karim's anticipation, would lead to abuse and rape once he began compulsory military service in Iraq, and therefore he flees, but this story, and the concomitant fact that he would be executed for desertion on return to Iraq, is apparently not traumatic enough to secure him asylum. Since the reader is granted insight into the actual reasons for Karim's flight, the fact that he feels impelled to amend his biography can be read as a double-voiced discourse that highlights how volatile the market for traumatic memories is, and how arbitrary the reasons for giving asylum often are. Karim's friend highlights this arbitrariness when he tells him that in Germany, the parameters of the trauma economy for Iraqis seeking asylum are clearly delineated: 'Entweder hast du etwas gegen die Regierung getan und man sucht dich, oder du bist Christ, Kommunist, Mitglied einer schiitischen Partei, ein Homosexueller oder Teil einer Minderheit' [Either you've done something against the regime and they're hunting you, or you're a Christian, a communist, a member of a Shiite party, a homosexual or belong to a minority] (101; 95). None of these six criteria apply to Karim, and therefore, his friend advises him, 'Du musst dir eine komplett neue Lebensgeschichte einfallen lassen' [you have to come up with a completely new life story] (69; 62), despite Karim's observation that he had to experience 'so viele tragische Dinge [...] dass sie für mehrere Leben gereicht hätten' [enough tragic events to fill several lives]. But, as Karim realises with some disillusionment, 'vor dem deutschen Gesetz wurden sie schlagartig unwichtig, weil sie nicht ins Raster passten' [German law suddenly made those experiences appear trivial because [...] they didn't tick the right boxes] (75; 68). Correspondingly, Karim has to invent the narrative account which he presents to the authorities, or rather, he has to fictionalise his biography, although he is of the opinion that his life experiences have been traumatic enough as it is.

Miki, too, lies about his itinerary and his reasons for fleeing, although for different reasons: he has to protect the identity of his illegal intermediaries, and, by extension, his family. Before Miki embarked on his journey, the people smuggler Darko instructed him, 'Det er vigtigt, at du aldrig fortæller om mig, Boris eller nogen andre, der hjælper dig undervejs. Forstår du? Ellers vil både du og dine kære fortryde det' [It's important that you never tell anyone about me, Boris or anyone else who helped you along the way. Do you understand? Otherwise both you and your loved ones will regret it] (7). This threat to himself and his family causes Miki to tell the official in the interview in Sandholm that he travelled with a man unknown to him, and to say, when asked where he crossed the border into Denmark, 'Aner det ikke. Jeg sov det meste af vejen. Manden gav mig sovepiller' [No idea. I slept most of the time. The man gave me sleeping pills] (22). However, Miki has to make a convincing case for himself, because he had already been granted refuge in

Croatia, and therefore he tweaks his narrative to make his claim more urgent, and conceals the fact that his main reason for leaving was to be reunited with his brother in Sweden: 'Jeg nævnte selvfølgelig intet om, at jeg lige efter overfaldet stak af og ville til Sverige' [Obviously, I didn't mention that I ran away right after the attack and wanted to get to Sweden] (22). This attack took place in the refugee camp in Croatia, and, although Miki had been badly beaten, he embellishes the assault with 'et par andre pumpede patrioter, som havde kæmpet mod muslimer' [a couple of other iron-pumping patriots who had fought against Muslims] to emphasise his need for refuge. Hence, when prompted, Miki names as his reason to flee, 'For ikke at få tæsk igen!' [Not to get beaten again] (23), and claims that it was his father who, to protect Miki from further violence, 'satte mig ind i en bil, som blev kørt af en mand, jeg ikke kendte. Manden kørte mig til Danmark' [put me in a car that was driven by a man I didn't know. The man drove me to Denmark] (23). Only after this interview, Miki's brother reassures him with, 'Du skal nok få det [asyl]. Du er mindreårig. De sender ikke børn hjem til lande i krig' [You should get it [asylum]. You are a minor. They don't send children home to countries at war] (70). Although Miki and Karim are very close in age, the age difference is significant because Miki, unlike Karim, is treated as an unaccompanied minor by the authorities in Denmark, and therefore, his chances for being granted asylum are far greater than Karim's.

We learn surprisingly little about Miki's life before his time in the refugee camp in Croatia, and he alludes to his history only in passing when he, for instance, describes his home town Kasabica as 'et gennembrændt hul på kortet' [a burned hole on the map] (26). It is Miki's fellow countryman and asylum seeker Refko who supplies detail: 'De massevoldtagne kvinder hoppede ud af hotelvinduer, børn og gamle blev samlet i et hus og brændt ihjel' [The women who had been gang-raped jumped out of hotel windows, children and old people were gathered in a house and burned to death] (82). After Refko is offered therapeutic treatment in Denmark, he comments, 'Sådan er danskerne, du [...] Meget, meget sarte. Bare en ligbleg narkoman plyndrer en kiosk, får alle involverede straks psykologbehandling. Så sidder de på gulvet med lukkede øjne, holder hinanden i hånden og mediterer' [That's what the Danes are like [...] Very, very sensitive. It's enough that a deathly pale junkie robs a corner shop for everyone involved to get therapy. Then, they sit on the floor with their eyes closed, hold hands and meditate] (91). This reference to traumatic events through a secondary source distances Miki from similar events he might have witnessed, whereas Refko's ironic comment about the supposed disproportionality of the allocation of therapy distances Danish readers from their own self-understanding. By juxtaposing a robbery in Denmark with war atrocities, Refko implies that it is these atrocities that would actually deserve the attention of a therapist, which underscores their severity, but in Miki's asylum claim, they are not even mentioned.

We can see, then, that in Karim's and Miki's cases, the discursive and political structures of the German and Danish immigration authorities influence the ways in which the representations of the protagonists' biographies become altered and amended. In consequence, Karim's and Miki's pasts are turned into a currency, or a commodity, that has to be adapted to the demands of the trauma market if their claims for asylum are to be successful. Although Miki and Karim have fled from violence and war zones, and have, arguably, witnessed or experienced atrocities that would qualify them for refuge, the dynamics of the trauma market force them to lie about their pasts, which suggests that within some trauma economies, 'war trauma risks becoming a surfeit commodity and so decreases in value'.[34] While Miki and Karim have both arrived in countries other than they had originally intended, they see themselves nevertheless compelled to lie about their itineraries and their pasts when pan-European immigration regulations and the national demands of the trauma economy jeopardise their chances of being offered asylum in Denmark or Germany. This emphasises that it is precisely these dynamics of the trauma market that cause friction in Miki's and Karim's relationships with the law.

Refugee Status: A Chance for Self-Creation?

Notwithstanding their fraught relations with the law, Miki's and Karim's adaptation of their narrative accounts to the demands of the trauma market has the desired outcome, and at long last, both protagonists are granted refugee status. Despite their protagonists' similar experiences and equally laconic narrative voices, however, the two texts eventually follow diverging affective trajectories in conformity with the different developments in the protagonists' lives. We have seen that both Khider and Mešković employ formal strategies such as ironic realism, and the narrators' wry tone of voice, to orient the texts towards their audiences with an attitude of irony that, in the reader, creates an effect of recognition, and, simultaneously, of distance. While this irony can be considered the overarching 'affective bearing', or tone, of both texts, the respective affective changes in the narrative voices of the two protagonists undermine this irony ever so slightly.[35]

Shortly before Miki is granted asylum, the regulations that restrict him to a certain radius around the centre are loosened, without the text providing a reason for this change. Given his newly won freedom, Miki realises how trapped he feels in the liminality of the centre, and also in Lundslev itself: 'Jeg trængte til at komme væk fra denne lorteby' [I needed to get away from this shithole] (157). Miki uses this freedom to travel to the rock festival in Roskilde, and, once he finds himself among like-minded young people, his time in Lundslev 'forekom som en åndssvag drøm' [seemed like a daft dream] (183). Once again, Miki confirms that his time in the centre is characterised by its arrested temporality, which creates a gap between him and the social world; until now, his life has been put on hold, as he has done 'nothing but "pushing time"'.[36] In view of this liminality, the festival in Roskilde functions as a catalyst; once Miki is back in Lundslev, he has an epiphany and realises, 'Om fem uger var jeg atten år. Atten år! Og jeg havde intet' [In five weeks' time I would be eighteen. Eighteen! And I didn't have anything] (254). As a result of this epiphany, Miki begins to fight for his right to learn Danish and go to school. He knocks on doors, writes letters in broken English and slams his fist on the table in the office of the Danish Refugee Council, and, in an interview with the headmaster of a school he applied to, he stresses the urgency of his appeal: 'Det her handler ikke om skole' [This is not about school], adding in English: '*I just need life, you know. I don't have it*' (259, italics in original). Miki's latter comment highlights that he, while he lives in the centre, is indeed deprived of 'any chance for self-creation', because he is denied any political agency.[37] The loosening of spatial restrictions, however, grants Miki a fraction of political agency, which he seizes with both hands, and thus, it can be viewed as 'the opening of an interval for political subjectivation'.[38] Because, as Rancière states, 'There is politics when there is a part of those who have no part', Miki uses the interval that the loosened restrictions grant him as a foothold from where he, who previously did not have a part, expands his political agency in his development towards political subjectivation, and he becomes a part of the Danish body politic.[39]

Karim's case is more complex, but at first, Karim is relieved when he is finally granted refugee status and is placed — once again not by choice — in a shared flat for refugees in Niederhofen, a small town on the Danube. Echoing Miki's feeling of being trapped, Karim assumes that he has now escaped the liminality of the centre when he says, 'Es war als hätte man mich nach vielen Jahren aus dem Gefängnis entlassen' [It was as if I'd been released after many years in prison] (156; 151). Karim's life, however, remains restricted by exclusionary politics and policies that prescribe the ways in which he should become 'ein guter Bürger' [a good *Bürger*] (157; 152).[40] When Karim enquires at the job centre about his options to first learn German, and then find work, he is informed, 'Sie müssen aber erst ein Jahr lang arbeiten und Steuern zahlen. Danach können wir Ihnen einen Sprachkurs finanzieren' [but first you have to work and pay taxes for a year, and then we can fund a language course for you] (157; 151). This means that Karim has to prove himself as a good, tax-paying citizen before he is allowed to learn the language. In addition, this policy implies that Karim only qualifies for underpaid work where he is not required to speak German, such as the job at Burger King which the official offers him.

Karim's situation changes drastically with the 9/11 terror attacks and with the ensuing war on terror, which also has a local ripple effect on the small town Niederhofen in rural Bavaria; Karim's individual life is turned on its head, and he comments, 'das ist wohl Globalisierung' [That's what you call globalization] (165; 160). When xenophobia and Islamophobia tangibly increase in Niederhofen, Karim shaves off his beard, because, as he reasons, 'Seit dem 11. September wäre es töricht, so bärtig wie Osama bin Laden herumzulaufen' [It would be daft to go about wearing a bush like Osama bin Laden's after 9/11] (12; 4). Despite Karim's precautions, it is impossible for him to find work, because, as he states, 'der wichtigste Ausdruck für uns Araber in Deutschland' [the main term used to describe us Arabs in Germany] is now 'verdächtig' [suspicious] (164; 160). As a consequence, Karim is repeatedly interrogated by the police with pestering and absurd questions about his supposed affiliations with al-Qaida, or whether or not he ever carried out a bomb attack. Karim's situation is reminiscent of Khemiri's open letter to Beatrice Ask, in which Khemiri quotes her with, 'Det finns tidigare dömda som uppfattar att de alltid är ifråga satta' [There are some who have been previously convicted and feel that they are always being questioned]. In response to Ask's remark, Khemiri contemplates, 'Intressant ordval: "tidigare dömda". För det är precis det vi är. Alla vi som är skyldiga tills motsatsen har bevisats' [Interesting choice of words: 'previously convicted'. Because that's exactly what we are. All of us who are guilty until we prove otherwise] (130). In the same way, Karim is viewed as guilty until proven otherwise, and hence, he is subject to racialised and Islamophobic profiling, and to discriminatory interrogations, which, although in fictional form, directly compares with Khemiri's experiences in Sweden as he describes them in his letter to Ask. In the context of Karim's predicament in Germany after 9/11, Khemiri's ensuing questions of, 'När blir en personlig upplevelse en rasistisk struktur? När blir den diskriminering, förtryck, våld?' [When does a personal experience become a structure of racism? When does it become discrimination, oppression, violence?] (130) can only be understood as rhetorical. Considering that Karim describes how the German Foreign Office, after the official declaration of the end of the war in Iraq in May 2003, begins to revoke the refugee status of Iraqis it previously granted, Karim's personal experiences are embedded into structures of discrimination and racism which generalise everyone on the basis of appearance and origin in disregard of any personal circumstances.[41]

For Karim, and Miki alike, their recognition as political refugees constitutes a pivotal moment in their lives in their so-called host countries. However, as their subsequent treatment by the respective authorities in Denmark and Germany differs, the affective tone of their narrative voices begins to diverge, too: Miki's tone changes from irony to gratefulness with the fact that he is granted asylum and a place in a school, whereas Karim's voice becomes increasingly saturated with anger after the 9/11 terror attacks. Karim receives a letter informing him that his refugee status will be revoked, and when Karim, like so many other Iraqis, sees himself threatened with being deported back to Iraq, it highlights how dependent the trauma market for asylum seekers and refugees is on political national reactions to international events. On this volatile trauma market, the currency of Karim's fictionalised narrative account which helped him to gain refugee status has now lost all its value, so that Karim considers everything that he has achieved and fought for as 'ein gigantisches Nichts' [a gigantic pile of nothing]. When Karim further states, 'In Bagdad konnte ich nicht bleiben, in Deutschland darf ich nicht bleiben' [I couldn't stay in Baghdad, I'm not allowed to stay in Germany] (218; 215), he expresses how he finds himself in an impasse with no solution, and, reflecting on this impasse in an outburst of anger, he says:

> Unser Leben in Deutschland endet jetzt, genau hier, obwohl es nie wirklich angefangen hat. [...] Wir sind alle wie die geschmacklosen und billigen Produkte aus dem Ausland, die man bei Aldi und Lidl finden kann. Wir werden mit dem Lastwagen hierhergeschleppt wie Bananen oder Rinder, werden aufgestellt, sortiert, aufgeteilt und billig verkauft. Was übrig bleibt, kommt in den Müll.
>
> [Our lives in Germany end right here, right now — that's if they ever got really started. [...] We're like the cheap, tacky foreign products you find at Aldi or Lidl. We're hauled here on trucks like bananas or cattle, then arranged, graded, divided up and sold on the cheap. What's left is thrown into the bin.] (216; 213)

Karim suggests that he, although he has lived in Germany for more than three years, has never had the chance to leave the liminal zone, as it expands beyond the boundaries of centres for asylum seekers. Geographically and socially isolated, and without political agency, Karim feels that his whole life resembles a surplus commodity that can be sold cheaply, or that can be discarded when there is no market for it. Karim's words resonate with Bauman's observations about refugees, in which the latter states:

> All waste, including wasted humans, tends to be piled up indiscriminately on the same refuse tip [...] People without qualities have been deposited in a territory without denomination, while all roads leading back or forward to meaningful places and to the spots where socially legible meanings can be and are forged daily have been blocked for good.[42]

While Karim lived in Germany after he had been granted asylum, this path towards a place where he could eventually forge meaning and a social category for himself was not completely blocked, but it was made difficult by restrictive and exclusionary policies such as the decree that he has to work first, and learn German afterwards. Or, to employ Bauman's words to describe Karim's circumstances, his 'prospects of being recycled into [a] legitimate and acknowledged' member of human society were 'dim and infinitely remote'.[43] When Karim's refugee status is revoked, his path towards a place within German society has indeed been blocked for good.

Considering the developments in Karim's life, it is not surprising that his narrative voice partially loses its irony in favour of anger. In contrast, Miki's ironic narrative voice loses its irony somewhat when it becomes more hopeful with the prospect that he will be granted asylum. After Miki has secured himself a place in a Danish school, he reads for the first time in Danish in front of the class, and is 'forberedt på hån, spot og latterliggørelse' [prepared for scorn, mockery and ridicule] but instead, 'et overdøvende bifald eksploderede i lokalet' [a deafening applause exploded in the room] (264). In this classroom situation, Miki exposes himself in the sense that he makes himself vulnerable to others on an emotional level, as he expects his poorly spoken Danish to have a negative effect. When his performance, however, causes a positive affective reaction contrary to his expectations, these positive affects expand, and Miki's whole affective infrastructure changes, in accordance with Michael Richardson's observation that, 'Certain encounters can change bodies radically, can cause them to grow, enlighten, transform, strengthen them'.[44] Miki embodies these positive affects, since they transform him and change his narrative voice, and, when Miki is granted asylum, it puts an end to the liminality which has marked his life in Denmark to date, and he realises, 'Hvis jeg fik asyl, kunne jeg blive. Ikke bare i Danmark, men også på gymnasiet' [If I got asylum, I could stay. Not only in Denmark, but also in the secondary school] (306). For Miki, recognition as a political refugee means that he can start a new life in Denmark, because he is finally given the chance for self-realisation, and thus the opportunity to carve out a social category for himself in the microcosm of the Danish school. Hence, Miki's former ironic perspective on Danish society yields to one of positive surprise and gratitude reciprocal to the way in which he finds a social place, and he concludes: 'Det var tid til at sige "tak, mange tak"' [It was time to say 'thanks, thanks a lot'] (307).

The ending of *Enmandstelt* can be assessed in different ways. On the one hand, the text dissolves into a narrative of the happy immigrant, and, when Miki's previously ironic outlook on Danish society and Danish-ness gives way to one of appreciation and gratitude, Danish readers, instead of finding their self-understanding challenged, can feel good about themselves. In this respect, the text loses its critical distance, or attitude, which was maintained by Miki's ironic tone, and the text presents itself as supportive of the immigration policies that were previously criticised by means of this ironic narrative voice. On the other hand, it is precisely these immigration policies that finally grant Miki a minimum of political agency. Miki's political subjectivation allows him to fight for his right to attend language courses and go to school, and, when his political agency increases accordingly, Miki becomes recognised as part of Danish everyday society. From this perspective, the text can be regarded as supportive of Rancière's understanding of politics, in the sense that Miki actively interrupts 'the natural order of domination' and integrates himself into Danish societal life as 'a part of those who have no part'.[45] When Miki seizes 'the rights of those who have no rights', he becomes politicised and is granted the right to be heard.[46] In this light, the text's ending can also be read as underscoring the importance of political agency when it comes to self-realisation in the context of migration.

Conversely, Karim is denied any political agency within the main narrative of the text; only in the framing narrative can Karim exert political agency, albeit in his cannabis-induced imagination, in which he ties Frau Schulz to her chair and gags her, so that he is finally heard. Karim states that Frau Schulz is the person who has 'Macht über andere Menschen' [authority over other people] and who decides 'auf welche Weise ich existieren darf' [how I may or should live] (11; 3). When Karim's existence is thus dependent on asylum policies as they are put into effect by Frau Schulz, his general condition of precariousness is converted into precarity, considering that this precariousness is politically produced and reinforced. Karim's remark further illustrates that he is differentially exposed to this precarity, because once his refugee status is revoked, the social, economic and political conditions that would sustain Karim's life as a life are equally revoked, and he sees his whole existence jeopardised. When Karim, in his imagination, slaps Frau Schulz in the face, this slap is, in a metaphorical sense, directed at the German Foreign Office in general, and at the whole of the German administration, and Frau Schulz can be viewed as a synecdoche for this state apparatus. In this light, the text, from the very start, creates tension between a state of voicelessness engendered by various levels of liminality, and an imaginative form of resistance. In his fantasy, Karim seizes the political agency he is denied, and he violently opens an interval for his own political subjectivation and stages a scene of dissensus. From this point of view, the whole text can be seen as an act of resistance against being made voiceless, and as a subversion of exclusionary asylum policies, particularly when taking into account that the text's title makes this imaginary form of resistance the central theme of the text. In accordance with Slavoj Žižek's differentiation between subjective and objective violence, the violence of Karim's resistance should be assessed within the context that produces it. Žižek identifies subjective violence as the most visible form of violence, whereas he describes objective violence as 'invisible since it sustains the very zero-level standard against which we perceive something as subjectively violent'.[47] This objective violence is inherent in all those practices and policies which render Karim invisible and inaudible, and which hold him forcefully in a state of liminality; his visible outburst of subjective violence is merely the counterpart to these invisible forms of violence.

★   ★   ★   ★   ★

To summarise, for Miki and Karim, their processes of seeking asylum are marked by geographical, social and political liminality. While the protagonists' claims for asylum are processed and they are housed in centres for asylum seekers, the locality of these places and the exclusionary politics that govern them create a gap with the social world, and Miki and Karim find themselves forced into inaction while their lives are put on hold. This state is exceptional insofar as it is stretched in time and decreed by sovereign powers that place Miki and Karim 'outside the boundary of the common law';[48] they are detained in 'spaces of existential, social, political, and legal limbo' and are thus rendered invisible and voiceless. The centres for asylum seekers where Miki and Karim are accommodated 'govern precisely by attempting to prevent individuals from exercising political subjectivity', as Miki and Karim are reduced to passivity instead of action, and denied political agency.[49]

The period while Miki's and Karim's applications for asylum are being processed is further characterised by the protagonists' fraught relations with the law, as they cannot improve their destitute financial situation without breaking the law, and as they see themselves compelled to lie about their biographies to make their cases more convincing according to the demands of the trauma market. The time frames of Miki's and Karim's narratives are significant insofar as they demonstrate that authoritative decisions on refuge are dependent on global political developments. Within the fictional realms of the narratives, both texts reflect on actual immigration regulations at the time when the narratives are set: in Miki's case, it is immigration policies created especially for the increased influx of refugees from war-torn Yugoslavia, and in Karim's case, it is Saddam Hussein's dictatorship in Iraq, and later the 9/11 terror attacks and the ensuing war on terror with its local ripple effects. Karim's refugee status is revoked concomitantly with global developments, and therefore Khider's text illuminates how volatile the trauma economy is in the context of seeking asylum, and that the fictionalised narrative account that Karim presents to the authorities has, when it is viewed as a currency within this economy, 'no fixed value' despite his efforts to adapt it to the demands of this economy.[50] Karim emphasises this volatility further when he points out that decisions regarding his refugee status can be dependent on luck, or the goodwill of individuals who are responsible for his case: 'Je nachdem auf welchen Beamten man trifft, werden die Dinge erledigt oder eben nicht' [Whether things get done or not depends on which civil servant's name comes up] (142–43; 136).

With regard to political agency, it is only once the regulations are loosened that Miki is granted a fraction of a political existence. Miki seizes the little amount of political agency that he is granted and expands it when he fights for his right to attend a school of his choice, and, with resisting the authoritative structures that would limit him otherwise, Miki gains political subjectivity. While Miki overcomes exclusionary asylum politics within the literary realm of the text, the happy ending dilutes the text's overall ironic tone, which undermined these asylum politics. At the same time, Mešković's text highlights the importance of political agency with regard to self-realisation in the context of seeking asylum. In *Ohrfeige*, Karim is denied political agency while his case is being processed, and his rights as a citizen are limited by restrictive and exclusionary policies. Karim is not able to leave the liminal zone, since it expands into the German nation space beyond the confines of centres for asylum seekers, even after he is granted refugee status. When Karim's refugee status is revoked, all he is left with is his bare life, and he has the impression that he is treated like a surplus commodity that can be discarded when it has lost its value. While Karim, in the main diegesis, loses all political agency and has no possibility of resisting the exclusionary structures that dominate his life, the text itself offers forms of resistance on more than one level. On the one hand, stylistic devices such as ironic realism, and Karim's ironic narrative voice, distance the reader from the events Karim describes, and hold them up to the reader for critical reflection. On the other hand, Karim, in the framing narrative in which he speaks to Frau Schulz, does claim political agency for himself when he seizes the rights that are denied to him, and when he, albeit in his imagination, makes himself heard. In this sense, the text, instead of regarding it as an escape into fantasy, can be viewed as a form of resistance that is only possible in and through imagination: Karim refuses to be made one of 'the *unimaginables*', as he is reimagining himself.[51] When Bromley discusses how an affective disengagement from refugees is made possible, he argues that the refugee, as a figure, is dehumanised, essentialised and reduced 'to a set of invariable and negative characteristics and stereotypes', instead of being seen as 'a knowing subject, with autonomy and agency'. In order to avoid such exclusionary essentialism, Bromley suggests that we need 'the development of other lenses of perception, a greater aesthetic-political reflexivity and sensitivity [...] linguistic and stylistic resources which unsettle, defamiliarize, and disrupt expectations and preconceptions'.[52] *Ohrfeige* and *Enmandstelt* offer precisely such other lenses of perception that Bromley calls for, since the texts, with their narrative strategies, contrast existing discourses, defamiliarise the reader from potentially stereotyped preconceptions, and may foster a greater aesthetic-political reflexivity and sensitivity.

Notes to Chapter 2

1. Farrier, p. 6.
2. Although both texts focus on the subjective experiences of their protagonists, they implicitly engage in fictional form with actual European and national immigration regulations at the time in which the novels are set. Denmark and Germany are, like all EU member states, committed

to protecting refugees according to the 1950 Geneva Convention (see John McCormick, *European Union Politics* (Basingstoke: Palgrave Macmillan, 2011), p. 397), but in Karim's case, and as it is the year 2000, the Dublin Convention applies. This framework (replaced by the Dublin II Regulation in 2003, and the Dublin III Regulation in 2013) establishes the EU country responsible for the evaluation of an asylum application, which is usually the first country where an asylum seeker enters the EU, which means that an asylum seeker can only apply for asylum in any one EU country, and might be sent back to the first EU country they arrived in or passed through. This framework is not applicable to Miki, because he arrives in Denmark in 1994, and the Dublin Convention first came into force in 1997 (see 'Dublin Convention', in *A Dictionary of Law*, ed. by Jonathan Law (Oxford: Oxford University Press, 2018)). According to Diane Sainsbury, in *Welfare States and Immigrant Rights: The Politics of Inclusion and Exclusion* (Oxford: Oxford University Press, 2012), p. 230, Miki is instead liable to national immigration regulations such as the 1983 *Udlændingeloven* [Aliens Law], and a law that was ratified in 1992 for the protection of refugees from former Yugoslavia to grant them temporary residence permits (see 'Lov om midlertidig opholdstilladelse til visse personer fra det tidligere Jugoslavien m.v.', *Onlaw*, 933 (28 November 1992) <https://onlaw.dk/lov/lov-nr-933-af-28–11–1992> [accessed 24 August 2019]).

3. Terri Tomsky, 'From Sarajevo to 9/11: Travelling Memory and the Trauma Economy', *Parallax*, 17 (2011), 49–60 (pp. 49, 53).

4. Agier, *Borderlands*, p. 36.

5. Bauman, *Liquid Times*, p. 45, italics in original.

6. UN General Assembly, 'Universal Declaration of Human Rights', United Nations, 217 (III) A, art. 14 (1948) <http://www.un.org/en/universal-declaration-human-rights> [accessed 13 March 2017]; Vicki Squire, *The Exclusionary Politics of Asylum* (Basingstoke: Palgrave Macmillan, 2009), p. 13.

7. Farrier, p. 6.

8. Roger Bromley, 'Displacement, Asylum and Narratives of Nation: Giving Voice to Refugees in the Film "La Forteress"', in *The Culture of Migration*, ed. by Sten Pultz Moslund and others (London: I. B. Tauris, 2015), pp. 41–58 (p. 42).

9. Ahmed, *Cultural Politics*, pp. 47, 53.

10. Jacques Rancière, 'Ten Theses on Politics', in *Dissensus: On Politics and Aesthetics*, ed. and trans. by Steven Corcoran (London: Continuum, 2010), pp. 35–52 (p. 37).

11. Giorgio Agamben, *Homo Sacer: Sovereign Power and Bare Life*, trans. by Daniel Heller-Roazen (Stanford: Stanford University Press, 1995), p. 7.

12. Jacques Rancière, 'Who is the Subject of the Rights of Man?', in *Dissensus: On Politics and Aesthetics*, ed. and trans. by Steven Corcoran (London: Continuum, 2010), pp. 70–83 (p. 77).

13. Jacques Rancière, *Disagreement: Politics and Philosophy*, trans. by Julie Rose (Minneapolis: University of Minnesota Press, 1999), p. 11.

14. Jacques Rancière, 'The Politics of Literature', in *Dissensus: On Politics and Aesthetics*, ed. and trans. by Steven Corcoran (London: Continuum, 2010), pp. 160–76 (p. 166).

15. Sianne Ngai, *Ugly Feelings* (Cambridge, MA: Harvard University Press, 2007), p. 43, italics in original.

16. Moritz Schramm, 'Ironischer Realismus: Selbstdifferenz und Wirklichkeitsnähe bei Abbas Khider', in *Neue Realismen in der Gegenwartsliteratur*, ed. by Søren R. Fauth and Rolf Parr (Munich: Fink, 2016), pp. 71–84 (p. 72).

17. 'Ironischer Realismus', p. 72.

18. Ibid.

19. Farrier, pp. 6, 7.

20. Bromley, 'Displacement', p. 43.

21. Engin F. Isin and Kim Rygiel, 'Abject Spaces: Frontiers, Zones, Camps', in *The Logics of Biopower and the War on Terror: Living, Dying, Surviving*, ed. by Elizabeth Dauphinee and Christina Masters (Basingstoke: Palgrave Macmillan, 2007), pp. 181–203 (pp. 195, 193).

22. Rajaram and Grundy-Warr, p. x.

23. While Karim is liable to national German asylum regulations, in Miki's case, the so-called

Jugoslaverloven applies. This law was considered controversial because it reinforced precisely the kind of liminality Miki is experiencing. The law introduced *midlertidig opholdstilladelse* [temporary residence permit] as a term and practice with the aim to deport refugees once the war in Yugoslavia was over. This left refugees in a situation of waiting and frustration, as they were treated differently from other asylum seekers: they were denied the right to work or learn Danish, and kept in isolation instead of being integrated into Danish society (see Camilla Pedersen, 'Venteland — bosniske flygtninge i Danmark', in *Folkedrab*, <http://www.folkedrab. dk/artikler/venteland-bosniske-flygtninge-i-danmark> [accessed 20 April 2017]).

24. Isin and Rygiel, p. 189.
25. Agier, *Borderlands*, p. 36.
26. Zijo refers to, and slightly misquotes, the 1992 *Lov om midlertidig opholdstilladelse* [Temporary Residence Permit Act].
27. Farrier, p. 6.
28. Squire, p. 16.
29. Tygstrup, 'Affective Spaces', p. 201.
30. Michel Agier, *On the Margins of the World: The Refugee Experience Today*, trans. by David Fernbach (Cambridge: Polity Press, 2008), p. 29.
31. Isin and Rygiel, p. 193; Bromley, 'Displacement', p. 47.
32. Tomsky, pp. 54–55.
33. Jane Herlihy and others, 'Just Tell Us What Happened to You: Autobiographical Memory and Seeking Asylum', *Applied Cognitive Psychology*, 26 (2012), 661–76 (p. 661).
34. Tomsky, p. 49.
35. Ngai, p. 43.
36. Agier, *Borderlands* p. 36.
37. Farrier, p. 6.
38. Rancière, 'Who is the Subject', p. 77.
39. Rancière, *Disagreement*, p. 11.
40. *Bürger* translates as 'citizen'; the German word is used in the translation to retain the play on words between Burger King and *Bürger* when Karim becomes confused because he thinks the official is asking him to become a burger.
41. According to Markus Sperl, in 'Fortress Europe and the Iraqi "Intruders": Iraqi Asylum-Seekers and the EU, 2003–2007', *New Issues in Refugee Research*, research paper 144, UNHCR (2007), pp. 1–19 (p. 9), the German government considered the threat of persecution no longer present after the fall of the Ba'ath Party in Iraq in 2003: 'the German Federal Ministry of the Interior [took] the unique step of systematically revoking the refugee status of thousands of Iraqis who were granted protection before 2003', and '18,000 Iraqi refugees who entered the country before the 2003 invasion thus had their refugee status revoked, placing them in a situation of uncertainty and precariousness'.
42. *Liquid Times*, pp. 41–42.
43. Ibid., p. 42.
44. Richardson, p. 35.
45. Rancière, *Disagreement*, p. 11.
46. Rancière, 'Who is the Subject', p. 74.
47. Slavoj Žižek, *Violence* (London: Profile, 2008), p. 1.
48. Agier, *Borderlands* p. 36.
49. Isin and Rygiel, pp. 188–89.
50. Tomsky, p. 49.
51. Bauman, *Liquid Times*, p. 45, italics in original.
52. Bromley, 'Displacement', pp. 19, 20.

CHAPTER 3

❖

Travel:
Unequal Encounters in
Vigdis Hjorth's *Snakk til meg* and
Kirsten Thorup's *Tilfældets gud*

The two texts selected for the present chapter constitute a shift in perspective as they portray two white, female Scandinavian protagonists who, on their holidays, encounter those they perceive as 'other', or different from themselves and the cultural background they come from. Kirsten Thorup's *Tilfældets gud* (2011) follows Ana, a 43-year-old Danish career woman in the finance sector, who has dedicated her whole life to Rower, the multinational investment company she works for, and who travels to Gambia to counter work-related stress. On the beach belonging to her luxurious hotel, Ana encounters Mariama, a fifteen-year-old local girl selling fruits and nuts, with whom she develops a platonic relationship. In Vigdis Hjorth's *Snakk til meg* (2011), the Norwegian protagonist Ingeborg, an almost fifty-year-old librarian, travels to Cuba for a holiday, where she encounters Enrique, six years younger than her and a local musician, with whom she begins a sexual relationship. When both Ana, in *Tilfældets gud*, and Ingeborg, in *Snakk til meg*, decide to make it possible for Mariama, and Enrique respectively, to come to Europe, it soon becomes obvious that the notion of transnational mobility applies to the different characters to disparate degrees, and once Ana has placed Mariama in the care of friends in London, and Enrique lives with Ingeborg in Norway, these two transnational relationships are put to the test.

Although the encounters between Ana and Mariama, and Ingeborg and Enrique, come about by chance, the ensuing contact is sought out and willed, and guided by the Scandinavian protagonists' desire to come closer to the 'other'. As the respective focus of the two texts themselves is on their Scandinavian female protagonists, the texts invite a reading that centres on the ways in which their transnational encounters challenge Ana's and Ingeborg's self-understanding as Scandinavian women, and thus, I will take into account, from a gender perspective, how Ana's, and also Ingeborg's, perceptions of themselves change in and through these encounters. However, as my focus is on those characters who are perceived or constructed as 'other', reading the texts against this line of enquiry will highlight how Mariama and Enrique are affected in these encounters. I draw on the notion of affective economies and Sara Ahmed's concept of stranger fetishism to explore how the encounters between the texts' protagonists are embodied; and in what ways Ana's and Ingeborg's desire fetishises Mariama and Enrique; and how, when this fetishisation commodifies the 'other', the idea of Mariama's and Enrique's consumable difference unravels once the protagonists are in London and Norway respectively. The concept of affective economies also enables me to point out the power relations underpinning these encounters, and helps to highlight the ways in which financial disparity, as well as the protagonists' dissimilar opportunities to partake in transnational mobility, makes them unequal. Regarding inequalities, I shall probe whether or not the texts portray the power relations dominating the depicted encounters as problematic, and to what extent the narrative voices, as well as the texts themselves, critically engage with the disparate allocation of global mobility and the political dimensions underlying the protagonists' actions and reflections.

While I will discuss the concepts of stranger fetishism and affective economies in due course, it is relevant to outline the texts' structures and narrative voices, and how these voices are deployed to characterise the protagonists Ana and Ingeborg, as these overarching aspects shape the critical understanding of the texts themselves, and of the ways in which the depicted encounters and their inherent inequalities are potentially problematised. In *Snakk til meg*, Ingeborg is the first-person narrator, and in eight parts of different length spanning a time period from December 2005 to February 2009, she recounts her relationship with Enrique and reflects on it. It transpires only some fifty pages into the text that Ingeborg's account is addressed to her adult son Torgrim, from whom she is estranged, and that the title, reiterated throughout the text, is a plea to Torgrim to contact her. Although Torgrim never actually reads Ingeborg's narrative, it is written with an agenda, a fact that should raise our suspicion with regard to the trustworthiness of her account, because it poses the question, to what degree she instrumentalises her relationship with Enrique to elicit a response in Torgrim. In addition, Ingeborg's narrative is written retrospectively, and in relation to the story she is telling Ingeborg's narrating self reflects and comments on her former self from the position of a higher narratorial authority. Considering her agenda, this fact should substantiate our suspicion, as Ingeborg's reflections, instead of helping her to understand herself better, might equally have the purpose to explain herself to her son, and manipulate him, and by extension the reader, in particular ways.

Without giving dates or the exact time span, *Tilfældets gud* covers the period of several years, and is divided into three parts, beginning with 'Mørket derude' [The Darkness Out There] which describes Ana's encounter with Mariama and their ensuing contact. The second part, 'Konsekvensen af Mariama' [The Consequences of Mariama], revolves around Ana's wish to become the girl's sponsor in Gambia, and, when Mariama insists on wanting to come to Europe with her, Ana comes to the decision that she wants to realise Mariama's dream. It is easier for Ana to find a place to stay for Mariama in London than in Copenhagen, and therefore, she moves to London herself, in the hope to find work with Rower's local branch. The last part, 'Imagination', details how Ana and Mariama's relationship unravels when Ana finds her expectations disappointed, and when Mariama does not comply with the image Ana has created of her. In the first two parts, Ana is the sole focaliser of the third-person narrator, whereas in the last part of the novel, the narrator's focus shifts subtly, so that it oscillates between Mariama's and Ana's consciousnesses. While Ana's voice permeates that of the narrator in dialogue and free indirect discourse, the narrator, with a certain ironic distance, comments repeatedly on Ana's self-assured opinions and her value system, and, in this way, undermines them and holds them up to the reader for ridicule.

This brief delineation of the texts' narrative voices insinuates that *Tilfældets gud* is, from the outset, critical of its protagonist Ana and the politics that underlie her character. In contrast, in *Snakk til meg*, Ingeborg's narrative voice is intended to manipulate her son, and thus holds the possibility for simultaneously influencing the reader in the same way. Therefore, it is the reader's task to resist this manipulation, and to disentangle the potentially problematic political undercurrent from Ingeborg's narrative voice, to explore the ways in which the text itself might be critical, even if Ingeborg fails to understand the political implications of her relationship with Enrique.

Stranger Fetishism in the Liminal Tourist Zone

The sociologist John Urry suggests that tourism produces 'distinct kinds of liminal zones' which are, for the tourist, characterised by a suspension from everyday obligations, and therefore grant 'licence for permissive and playful "non-serious" behaviour'.[1] The liminal zones discussed in chapters 1 and 2 are infinitely suspended in time, and force those detained there into inaction, whereas liminality, in the context of tourism, is limited in time, and can be experienced as an experimental freedom balanced between the binary opposites of the familiar and the faraway, the everyday and the extraordinary. Tourism within this liminal zone, however, is by no means neutral, as Graham Huggan points out when he discusses the relationship between tourism and exoticism. Huggan argues that, by making the culturally exotic other accessible, 'tourism continues to feed off social, political and economic differences', and, while it disguises these very differences through exoticist aesthetics, the relation between tourists and those they encounter is commodified from the outset.[2] In a similar vein but from the angle of affect, Annegret Heitmann views tourism as Mary Louise Pratt's famous 'contact zone' in which 'people from the rich industrialized nations and "the Global South"' meet, and in which tourists are confronted 'with alterity characterized by poverty'.[3] This binary between rich and poor, Heitmann suggests, can potentially contaminate the positive feelings that a holiday in an exotic location is generally expected to evoke: 'Given these experiences of fundamental inequality, it stands to reason that happiness on vacations in poor countries or former colonies is compromised by feelings of powerlessness or guilt-ridden responsibility'.[4] While it could be useful to investigate whether guilt, or other affects for that matter, emerges in the encounters depicted in the two texts, I consider it more important regarding the power relations inherent in the dichotomies of rich and poor, and black and white, to examine what effect this guilt has not only on those experiencing it, but also on those characterised by their poverty or alterity. In terms of these power relations, Avtar Brah observes that, 'What matters most is how and why, in a given context, a specific binary [...] takes shape, acquires a seeming coherence and stability, and configures with other constructions [...] In other words, *how these signifiers slide into one another in the articulation of power*'.[5] Brah's assertion is pertinent to those binaries depicted in the two texts, insofar as she pinpoints how boundaries and unequal power relations are strengthened when certain signifiers become conflated.

In a first reference to the novel's title, *Tilfældets gud* begins with the sentence, 'Ved skæbnens ironi var det blevet Vestafrika og ikke Seychellerne' [By some irony of fate it turned out to be West Africa and not the Seychelles] (11; 9), and Ingeborg, in *Snakk til meg*, describes the choice of her destination with, 'En bruker leverte inn en reisebok om Cuba og fortalte at han hadde hatt det bra, at øya var trygg [...] så tilfeldig var det' [A library user handed back a travel guide about Cuba and said that he had had a good time, and that the island was safe [...] it was that random] (7). Choosing exotic destinations in poor and formerly colonised countries arbitrarily, both Ana and Ingeborg take their transnational mobility for granted. Ingeborg emphasises, however, that security is important to her, a fact that also applies to Ana and is reflected in hotel choices and leisure time activities: Ingeborg drinks coffee 'på Hotel Inglaterra' [at the Hotel Inglaterra] (12) and dines 'i hotellets italienske restaurant' [in the hotel's Italian restaurant] (16–17), and Ana's hotel is '[e]ngelskejet og stilfuldt' [under English ownership and tastefully designed] (11; 9). Ingeborg keeps to areas designated for tourists where 'hele området var bevoktet' [the whole area was guarded] (13), and describes, 'Hendte det jeg plutselig [...] befant meg i en gate uten turister, hvite mennesker, hastet jeg i det jeg håpet var riktig retning mot mine likemenn' [When I suddenly [...] found myself in a street without tourists, white people, I hurried in what I hoped was the right direction towards my equals] (13), whereas Ana relaxes on the beach of her hotel, 'hvor soldater i camouflageuniformer og pistoler i bæltet patruljerede' [where soldiers patrolled in camouflage uniform with pistols in their belts] (11; 9), and states that she needs to get used to 'at hendes beskyttere på stranden var sorte og ikke hvide' [that her guardians on the beach were black and not white] (11–12; 10).

These scenes illustrate that a sense of security is achieved through both familiarity and bourgeois relations; the European references function as a safeguard against foreign and unfamiliar surroundings, and when Ingeborg, and Ana alike, stake out the most basic determinants of sameness and otherness by using skin colour, or race, as 'a trope of ultimate, irreducible difference', they admit that this racialised difference disconcerts them.[6] Through Ana's and Ingeborg's fear, the binary of black and white acquires stability and 'brings into play relations of social and political antagonism that *mark some others as stranger than other others*'.[7] When the affect of fear circulates in this way and adheres to some places and people, it becomes the protagonists' means of evaluating their surroundings: fear makes them turn towards their fellow Western tourists because they are 'other', but not frightening, and away from potentially threatening other others, the locals in Gambia and Cuba. When the liminal zone of the tourist space is one chosen at random, affectively charged with fear and restricted to areas that are almost guarded like a prison, Ana and Ingeborg are kept away from the social reality in Gambia and Cuba respectively; it is of no concern to them. Instead, they can indulge their fascination with exoticised otherness despite their fear, and from a comfortable distance: 'Hun måtte indsnuse det mørke kontinent i vareudbuddets koncentrerede form og erhverve sig noget trendy afrikansk design til ingen penge omregnet i euro' [She had to inhale the dark continent in the concentrated form of the displayed wares and acquire some trendy African design for practically nothing when converted to euros] (19; 16). In the hotel's shop, Ana can consume the whole of Africa safely and cheaply, and when, for her, the desirable exoticised difference is contained in the products she purchases, this scene illuminates the 'immediate relationship between commodity fetishism and stranger fetishism'.[8] In addition, as Heitmann rightly points out, 'The complete segregation reduplicates the colonial divide between "us" and "them"'.[9]

Out of necessity, however, there is an intersection between tourists and locals which renders the boundaries of the liminal tourist zone porous, because tourists are dependent on services provided by locals, and, in turn, the livelihoods of locals are dependent on the tourist industry. This intersection makes it possible that the encounters between Ingeborg and Enrique, and Ana and Mariama, come about: through Enrique, together with his band, being officially employed by the hotel to play every evening in the garden of the hotel, and through Mariama selling snacks illegally on the beach, always in fear of being chased away by the guards. When Ingeborg describes how she sits in the hotel garden with a glass of wine, listening to the band, she appreciates what Urry calls 'the right to gaze at hosts', but when this gaze is reversed, and it is not 'the "exotic natives" who are being gazed upon' but Ingeborg herself, it comes entirely unexpected for her: 'Denne dagen skjedde noe uventet' [This day, something unexpected happened] (16). Four times on the same page, Ingeborg reiterates that, 'Denne høye mannen så på meg' [This tall man looked at me] (17), which expresses her surprise that it is not Enrique who is 'the *object* of the tourist gaze', but that he, inversely, makes her the object of his gaze and has transgressed her bodily space with a look.[10]

Ingeborg's depiction of the ensuing courtship lets us believe that it is Enrique who utilises 'the seduction of difference', and that he instrumentalises his corporality, the racialised differentiation of his black skin against Ingeborg's white to seduce her, whereas she is supposedly passive and defenceless in the face of his embodied masculinity.[11] When Enrique, whom Ingeborg perceives as 'overveldende stor og svart' [overwhelmingly big and black] (19), comes to her table, she comments, 'jeg lot det skje' [I let it happen] (30), and, emphasising her powerlessness by way of iteration, she states: 'jeg klarte ikke reise meg, stanse det, bremse' [I couldn't get up, stop it, slow down] (40). Enrique and Ingeborg incorporate the very myth Cornel West addresses when he states that 'the dominant sexual myths of black women and men portray whites as being "out of control" — seduced, tempted, overcome, overpowered by black bodies': Enrique is portrayed as the agent of seduction, whereas Ingeborg is seduced by Enrique's black body.[12] Enrique approaches Ingeborg, and she admits, 'Jeg kjente uro da jeg forsto han var på vei til meg' [I felt uneasy when I understood that he was coming towards me] (18), which, in bell hooks's words, indicates that for Ingeborg, the encounter with otherness is 'clearly marked as more exciting, more intense, and more threatening. The lure is the combination of pleasure and danger'.[13] From the outset, Enrique's embodied difference is particularly attractive to Ingeborg, because it promises to be more stimulating than anything she has known so far, while, at the same time, it unsettles and scares her. This fear can be seen as 'a basic ingredient of white racism', since it is usually rooted in the perception that black sexuality is 'a form of power over which whites have little control'.[14] In addition, yet another aspect of 'racist sexist thinking about the black body' is, that it 'has always projected onto the black body a hypersexuality'.[15] By admitting to her simultaneous attraction to, and fear of, Enrique's sexualised body, Ingeborg reveals the racism underlying her desire for Enrique.

Ana's encounter with Mariama does not begin with a look, but with Mariama's voice first entering Ana's bodily space, which happens '[u]den noget forvarsel' [[w]ithout any warning] (14; 12), which expresses a surprise similar to Ingeborg's. Mariama asks Ana in English, 'Want something?' (14), and Mariama really seems to offer something that Ana, without being fully aware of it, wants, which is suggested by her strong reaction. Mariama's voice 'ramte hendes øre og fortsatte ind gennem øregangen. En overjordisk skønhed, en sølvklokkes fine klang opfyldte hende. [...] En dirrende barnestemme trængte ind under huden og rørte hende' [struck her ear and continued in along the auditory canal. She was filled with an unearthly beauty, the fine tinkling of a silver bell. [...] A quivering child's voice forced its way beneath her skin and moved her] (14–15; 12–13). The intertextual reference to Hans Christian Andersen's fairy tale 'Klokken' [The Bell] underlines Ana's Danish-ness against Mariama's otherness with Andersen being firmly rooted in the Danish national canon, while it simultaneously suggests that this encounter has a sublime quality for Ana. The encounter is physical as it penetrates Ana's ear and gets under her skin; yet it is also not from this world, at least not the world with which Ana is familiar. Ana's value system is based on materialism and rationality, and she only trusts 'hvad der kunne måles og vejes, høres og ses med det blotte øje eller i et mikroskop' [what could be measured and weighed, heard and seen with the naked eye or under a microscope] (15; 12). This ostensibly rational control, impartially depicted by the narrator, is undermined when the narrator describes Ana's reaction to physical contact in general, and in doing so discloses one of Ana's weaknesses to the reader: 'Berøring med en fremmeds hud fyldte hende med ubehag og en kvalmende svimmelhed' [The touch of a stranger's skin filled her with antipathy and nauseous dizziness] (19; 17). On the basis of this knowledge, it is not surprising that Ana's hand freezes when Mariama takes a hold of it while they go for a walk. Ana's frozen hand is contrasted with 'Mariamas lille varme, levende hånd' [Mariama's warm little living hand] (19; 17), and the narrator comments, 'Hun kunne ikke huske hun havde oplevet noget lignende' [She could not remember having experienced anything like it] (19; 17). Through the binary opposites of warm and cold, differentiation is negotiated on the level of the skin, but Ana does not withdraw her hand. This skin contact, instead of merely creating separation through difference, illustrates how Mariama becomes an object of desire for Ana because she possesses something Ana lacks, and also manages to breach the boundaries of Ana's rationality by touching her physically and emotionally.

To recapitulate, Ahmed's concept of stranger fetishism implies that white Westerners tend to produce the stranger as a figure, or a fetish, by recognising the other as strange or different, thus ontologising the stranger because their being is determined from the outside by their status as strangers. The other becomes fixed in a juxtaposition of proximity and distance, and through practices and techniques of differentiation, an image of the stranger is constructed as being different, and thus related to, and simultaneously separated from, particular others.[16] When Ana reflects that in Mariama, she had found 'sin sjæl [...] den manglende brik hun havde ledt efter i sin individuelle udvikling hen imod at blive "et helt menneske" [...] Mariama var alt det hun ikke var, hendes platoniske halvdel' [her soul [...] the missing piece she had been searching for in her individual development towards becoming 'a whole person' [...] Mariama was everything she was not, her platonic other half] (50; 45), she makes Mariama a fetish. In Ana's imagination, Mariama is related to, even part of, her, but she has to be different to be able to complement Ana's being and make her whole.

This notion is further substantiated by the symbolism implicit in the two women's names, Ana, short for Mariana, and Mariama. In his article on *Tilfældets gud*, Jørgen Veisland states, 'The letters "m" and "n" are phonetically so close that they may signify sameness and difference at the same time', and further that, ' "ana" turns into "ama", *l'âme*, spirit, mind'.[17] In this light, the narrator's assurance that in Ana's view, 'al snak om det åndelige og immaterielle [var] den rene overtro' [all talk of spiritual and immaterial manifestations was pure superstition] (15; 12), ridicules Ana's rational approach to life, and exposes it as false, considering her spiritual desire for Mariama. This desire, however, fixes Mariama in her difference, and the girl becomes fetishised in much the same way as Ingeborg's desire, although physical and not spiritual, fetishises Enrique. When Ingeborg and Enrique eventually spend the night together, Ingeborg foregrounds once again that she surrenders to a force that renders her powerless when she recounts, 'Strøk ham ikke, viljeløs, lam, det var han som gjorde det' [Didn't caress him, no will of my own, paralysed, it was he who did it] (41). Nonetheless, Ingeborg cannot help but being seduced by Enrique's body: 'Overarmshuden strukket så stramt over musklene at det liksom ikke var noe mellom. Svart mer maskulint enn hvitt, brunt, gult, svart det mest maskuline, voldsomste. Jeg likte fargen, svartheten hans' [The skin on his upper arms stretched so tightly over the muscles as if there was nothing in-between. Black, more masculine than white, brown, yellow, black, the most masculine, most violent. I liked his colour, his blackness] (71). To satisfy Ingeborg's desire, Enrique has to be different, and to this end, Ingeborg fixes him in a form of stereotyped masculinity that reduces Enrique to his sexualised, racialised and supposedly hyper-virile body. In the liminal tourist zone, Ingeborg allows herself a deviation from the everyday, and because 'the exploration into the world of difference, into the body of the Other' promises, although seemingly dangerous, a greater pleasure than what Ingeborg knows, Enrique has to remain in his fetish form.[18] Ana's and Ingeborg's fascination with, and desire for, difference fetishises Mariama and Enrique in equal measure; and, as the following discussion will demonstrate, the financial disparity between the two Scandinavian women and their desired 'others' makes it possible for all characters to enter into affective economies, which, for Ana and Ingeborg, holds the promise that they can secure the fetishised images of Mariama and Enrique permanently.

Affective Economies: The Stranger as Commodity

We have seen earlier that the liminal tourist zone is characterised by social, political and economic differences, and that the relations between tourists and locals in this zone are, precisely because of these differences, commodified from the outset. The encounters between Ana and Mariama, and Ingeborg and Enrique, are no exception: they are marked by economic disparities between the two Scandinavian women, who are affluent, and Enrique and Mariama, who are, particularly in comparison with Ingeborg and Ana, poor. As a result of these disparities, and as it is one way of satisfying their desire, Ingeborg and Ana pay to keep Enrique and Mariama by their side, a fact that establishes a direct link between stranger fetishism and consumer culture. To assess the ways in which the economic imbalances between the protagonists in *Snakk til meg* and *Tilfældets gud* shape and dictate their affective relationships, I complement Ahmed's concept of affective economies with a more literal understanding of the term as an exchange of money for affective goods in the way Megan Daigle propounds it. Ahmed argues that emotions can be seen as an economy in that they are always in motion and generated in relation, and that therefore, 'affect does not reside positively in the sign or commodity, but is produced as an effect of its circulation'.[19] It is the circulation of affect between individuals, and between the individual and a social body, that establishes differences and creates boundaries. Consequently, the more particular affects circulate, the more they stick to particular objects or signs and increase their affective value. Hence, as Ahmed argues, 'the accumulation of affective value shapes the surfaces of bodies and worlds'.[20]

   We have already seen how the circulation of desire shapes racialised bodily surfaces in the relations of proximity and distance that characterise stranger fetishism; when money enters these relations, it reinforces affective dynamics, as Daigle demonstrates in her study on the intersections of love, sexuality and politics in contemporary Cuba, *From Cuba With Love*. To contextualise her approach, Daigle describes how the collapse of the Soviet Union in the early 1990s and the United States embargo on Cuba brought about a time of material shortages and poverty that is still a reality for many Cubans today. During this period, the Cuban government opened the country up for mass tourism in an attempt to alter this destitute situation, which helped to pave the way for what Daigle calls 'a tourist-oriented sexual-affective economy' which deals not only in material goods, but also in 'affect, love, and solidarity'. This means that many Cubans pursued romantic or sexual liaisons with tourists 'as viable means of accessing hard currency, consumer goods, travel, and emigration'.[21] Ingeborg's sexual desire for Enrique in Hjorth's novel, together with the reiteration of the phrase *jeg betalte* [I paid] multiple times throughout her narrative, makes an analysis of her relationship with Enrique through the angle of a sexual-affective economy self-evident. In Thorup's novel, Ana's relationship with Mariama is platonic, yet similarly dictated by the exchange of money for non-material goods, and thus, their relationship can be equally assessed within the parameters of a tourist-oriented affective economy. When, according to Daigle's observations, affective value can be bought with money, the question is not only how money within affective economies promotes stranger fetishism, but also which particular affects emerge, or gain momentum in their circulation, when money becomes involved.

Before Ingeborg, in *Snakk til meg*, travels to Cuba, she describes her situation as, 'Jeg hadde penger. Foreldrene mine var døde, huset solgt, sønnen flyttet til Stockholm for å studere, jeg hadde ikke noe forhold' [I had money. My parents were dead, the house sold, my son moved to Stockholm to study, I had no relationship] (7). In short, Ingeborg is a free, independent and affluent woman, used to being alone. In the past, Ingeborg travelled widely with her son or colleagues, mainly to formerly communist or developing countries, because, as she explains to Enrique, 'når jeg reiste i land som hadde et annet fokus enn det materielle, skjedde det noe' [when I travelled in countries with a different focus than the material, something happened] (24). When Ingeborg learns that Enrique has never left Cuba, she realises that not everyone can 'bevege seg fra verdenshjørne til verdenshjørne' [move from one corner of the world to the other] (24), and that the transnational mobility she takes for granted is denied to others. Confronted with her Western privilege, Ingeborg has to admit to herself that her travels, instead of being motivated by her 'politisk korrekte holdning til norsk forbrukskultur' [politically correct attitude towards Norwegian consumer culture], are rather inspired by '[e]n eksklusivitet jeg ikke følte ellers' [[a]n exclusivity I didn't feel otherwise] (25). When Ingeborg's value system is reflected back at her through Enrique's perspective, her criticism of what she deems Norwegian materialism and of global injustices is exposed as hypocritical, and Ingeborg feels guilty for her privileged position, and ashamed.

Shame, however, emerges not only in their conversations, but dominates also Ingeborg's physical contact with Enrique, so that she, after their first night together, reflects, 'hadde kommet under ham mot min vilje, skam og gru' [had come under him against my will, shame and horror] (42). In this context, the feeling of shame enables Ingeborg to maintain the role of the passive victim of a seduction that is only successful because of her supposed innocence. Ingeborg tries to convince her son, and simultaneously the reader, of her naivety when she says that she was 'uerfaren' [inexperienced] and had never had 'nærkontakt med andre enn hvite mennesker' [close contact with anyone other than white people] (32). While this allows her to hold on to the particular narrative of, 'En middelaldrende bibliotekar reiser til Cuba, lar seg sjarmere av en syngende latino og faller' [A middle-aged librarian travels to Cuba, lets herself be charmed by a singing Latino and falls] (103–04), Ingeborg herself undermines her ostensible innocence. Watching a young, muscular local man in the street, she admits, 'før jeg arresterte meg selv, hadde jeg sett ham for meg naken over meg i bevegelse' [before I could stop myself, I had seen him moving naked over me], and she discloses that she feels 'en lyst jeg ikke hadde kjent på lenge, aldri, ikke engang da jeg var forelsket' [a desire I hadn't felt in a long time, never, not even when I was in love] (29). Because this sexual desire is new to Ingeborg, it becomes closely linked to her exoticisation and sexualisation of men of colour in general, and Enrique in particular, and she involuntarily verifies bell hooks's assertion that:

> Whites seek the black body to confirm that it is the exotic supersexed flesh of their fantasies. Within this economy of desire, which is anything but equal, the "hypermasculine black male sexuality" is [...] tamed by a process of commodification that denies its agency and makes it serve the desires of others, especially white sexual lust.[22]

Ingeborg, however, presents herself as unaware of the inequalities that she reinforces with her desire, and instead, she perceives her journey to Cuba and her encounter with Enrique as challenging her self-understanding as a Scandinavian woman, and as a result, she feels shame and guilt.

This shame, however, does not vitiate Ingeborg's desire, to which Enrique responds when he suggestively tells her 'at cubanerne var mer enn normalt opptatt av seksualitet' [that Cubans were concerned with sexuality more than was normal], and, in the same breath, that sex 'på Cuba var en av svært få fornøyelser som var gratis' [in Cuba was one of the few pleasures that was for free] (35). Enrique plays on a national stereotype, or Cuba's 'libidinous reputation', according to which Cubans are 'both desirable and sexually energetic', while he, simultaneously, tries to allay any potential suspicions that he exchanges his body for financial compensation.[23] Enrique's spiel is meant to seduce Ingeborg, and it works; at the same time, it is misleading, considering that Ingeborg pays for everything else apart from sex, such as drinks and concert tickets when they meet, and presents for Enrique's friends and family. In their study on sex tourism in the Caribbean, Julia O'Connell Davidson and Jacqueline Sanchez Taylor propose that, 'The informal nature of the sexual transactions' gives Western women the permission 'to believe that the meals, cash, and gifts they provide for their sexual partners do not represent a form of payment for services rendered but rather an expression of their munificence'.[24] This suggests that Enrique engages consciously in a sexual-affective economy that allows Ingeborg to believe that she, instead of paying for sexual services, is charitable. While the notion that Enrique is the sole agent in this economy would serve Ingeborg's construction of herself as the naïve and helpless victim of his seduction, Ingeborg is well aware that Enrique's motives are anything but romantic. She asks herself, 'Hva så han i meg, et pass? Europa?' [What did he see in me, a passport? Europe?]

(71), and suspects that 'han har forsøkt før' [he has tried this before] (87): namely, seducing white, affluent European women to obtain a legal passage to Europe. When Ingeborg enters into a relationship with Enrique despite these suspicions, her participation in the sexual-affective economy is on a par with Enrique's and just as conscious — the exploitation is mutual. While Ingeborg does not see it like this herself and tries to disguise her agency with victimhood and munificence, the reader is able to see through this disguise. This complicates the reader's affective engagement with Ingeborg, because it gives the impression that she, as an unreliable narrator, manipulates us for the purpose of upholding a particular image of herself; while instead, she is actively involved in 'the production of the stranger as a commodity fetish' through her desire for a stereotyped and exoticised notion of masculinity that she can pay for.[25]

In *Tilfældets gud*, Ana and Mariama's relationship is, from the beginning, established as a business connection where money is exchanged for affective goods such as time and company. When Ana engages Mariama in conversation, the girl points out that she is actually working on the beach selling snacks, indicating that her time is valuable. Ana reacts with, 'Jeg køber hele bakken, hvor meget skal du have?' [I'll buy the whole trayful, how much do you want?] (17; 15). Quickly grasping how affective economy works, Mariama suggests, 'Jeg venter på dig hver dag og gir dig en god pris for at gå en tur på stranden' [I shall wait for you every day and give you a good price for a walk on the beach] (24; 21), and she summarises their business-like relationship with, 'Jeg holder dig med selskab, og du betaler for det' [I keep you company and you pay for it] (53; 48). The text is replete with rhetorical patterns such as these, which indicates that both characters are fully aware of the fact that they manoeuvre within an affective economy, and, when the narrator comments on this fact with, 'De forstod hinanden' [They understood each other] (26; 23), it suggests that Ana and Mariama, despite their economic disparity, operate at eye level and feel comfortable with this arrangement. Out of her desire for Mariama, Ana reassures her, 'Jeg vil give dig alt, hvad der kan købes for penge' [I'll give you everything money can buy] (46; 41), which is, ultimately, a school education in Europe and a legal way out of her precarious situation. By asserting that, 'Deres forhold var blevet forvandlet til en følsom forretningsforbindelse med Ana som investor' [Their relationship had been transformed into a sensitive business connection with Ana as the investor] (47; 42), the narrator identifies the power imbalance between Mariama and Ana and makes the connection between stranger fetishism and consumer culture. Ana, in a similar way to Ingeborg, is actively involved in producing the 'other' as a commodity fetish.

The notion of Mariama as a commodity fetish is substantiated when Ana enters into negotiations with Aunt Rosie, who functions as Mariama's guardian, to decide whether she should become the girl's sponsor in Gambia or take her to Europe. While Aunt Rosie is Ana's immediate contact, Big Man, the patriarch of the extended family, oversees Aunt Rosie in similar ways to Rower's business executives monitoring Ana's work performance. When Ana arrives at Aunt Rosie's shack, the reader learns that 'Ana havde ikke noget imod en forhandlingsrunde med Rosie. Hendes "no nonsense"-attitude var en udfordring som Ana følte sig på bølgelængde med' [Ana had no objection to a round of negotiations with Rosie. Her 'no-nonsense' attitude was a challenge which made Ana feel she was on the same wavelength] (68–69; 62). Veisland rightly argues that this direct comparison between Ana's world of corporate global finance and African family organisation reveals the close entanglement of Western corporate practices and postcolonial structures, which, by way of unequal power relations, 'have invaded African family and work relations causing them to deteriorate'.[26] While it certainly holds true that the text, with this juxtaposition, highlights that precarity is politically generated and causes only 'certain populations [to] suffer from failing social and economic networks of support', these oppressive structures can be resisted.[27] Aunt Rosie's principles for doing business are based on trust, and when Ana repeatedly demands guarantees that her money is reaching Mariama's school, Aunt Rosie, feisty and 'med hænderne i siden' [with her hands on her hips] (70; 63), tells Ana to leave. Literally opposing the encroachment of capitalist corporate practices, embodied by Ana, Aunt Rosie distances herself from these practices and insists on her own methods. Moreover, Aunt Rosie deflects Ana's patronising attitude when she says, 'Hvem tror du, du er? Kommer her på en lille bekvem sightseeing [...] Hvorfor tar du ikke billeder? [...] Er mit hus ikke elendigt nok til dig?' [Who do you think you are? Coming here for a bit of fancy sightseeing [...] Why do you not take photos? [...] Is my house not miserable enough for you?] (71; 64). By pointing out the implicit voyeurism in Ana's demeanour, Aunt Rosie refuses to be victimised by Ana's alleged benevolence, and Ana's superiority, barely held together anyway, becomes unhinged: she starts to cry, agrees to Aunt Rosie's conditions, and pays. Despite Aunt Rosie's resistance to corporate practices, she is presented as a seasoned player in affective economies when she proposes that Ana can either support Mariama financially, or the girl has to 'gifte sig med en eller anden gammel mand og blive hans tredje kone' [marry some old man and become his third wife] (71; 64). Manipulating Ana's compassion and desire for Mariama, Aunt Rosie raises Mariama's affective value, while she, simultaneously, gives Ana the opportunity to disguise their joint venture of turning Mariama into a commodity fetish with her financial generosity.

Both texts depict affective economies which are different in nature, yet similar in structure. Moreover, the dynamics of these affective economies intensify once the Scandinavian protagonists decide to bring Enrique and Mariama with them to Europe, because restrictive immigration procedures add affective value to the desired difference of Enrique and Mariama, or, to put it bluntly, they put the price up. The second part of *Tilfældets gud* describes two parallel developments: how Ana's working life in Copenhagen disintegrates because of 'hendes ustabile psykiske tilstand' [her unstable mental state] (140; 126), and how she, in numerous phone conversations with Aunt Rosie and Big Man, negotiates the price for Mariama's legal passage to Europe. Big Man, who procures Mariama's paperwork, such as a passport, visa and birth certificate, demands €15,000 for the passport alone, and Ana, prepared to pay whatever it takes, 'følte sig pludselig taknemmelig over, at penge ikke var noget problem for hende, at hun kunne tillade sig at dele ud af dem' [suddenly felt grateful that money was not a problem for her, that she was free to share it] (122; 110). Nevertheless, Ana's life unravels, and we learn that she, despite Rower's intensive coaching programme, 'befandt sig nu i frit fald' [was in free fall] (145; 131); and, once she has moved to London to await Mariama's arrival, she turns with an increasing degree to alcohol, self-medication and gambling. At the same time, Ana's expectations strengthen her affective bond with Mariama towards obsession, so that she, once again emphasising the notion of sameness in difference, nurtures a fantasy in which Mariama 'foldede sig ud og blev en smuk, intelligent ung kvinde formet i hendes billede. De skulle blive som søstre der lignede hinanden og dog var så vidt forskellige' [would [...] blossom into an attractive, intelligent young woman formed in her image. They would become like sisters who resembled each other and yet were utterly different] (165; 149). In her analysis of *Tilfældets gud*, Elisabeth Oxfeldt suggests that Ana 'is caught between ugly and confused drives of altruism and narcissism': 'she wants to "do good" as a sponsor in a businesslike manner' and, at the same time, 'she thinks of Mariama as a child, a daughter, a sister, and a friend'.[28] Oxfeldt's assertion underscores how problematic it is that Ana conflates affective interests and financial matters: Ana utilises her financial superiority within the affective economy to construct herself simultaneously as Mariama's benefactress and close companion, while she is seemingly unconcerned, or unaware of the fact, that these dynamics turn Mariama into a commodity fetish.

At first, Ana's desire for Mariama seems surprising, considering that she appears independent and confident, is highly affluent, successful as a career woman, drives a Porsche, lives in a big central flat in Copenhagen, and leads a transnational lifestyle that takes her to every corner of the world. This façade, however, is destabilised when we learn that Ana came into the world as a donor child and that she 'skammede sig over sin laboratorietilblivelse' [was ashamed of her test-tube origins], because she considers herself 'et kunstprodukt' [an artificial product] (107; 96). When, as a teenager, Ana learns about her origins, she feels betrayed by her parents, cuts ties with her family and later replaces them with the corporate structures of international finance: 'Rower er min familie, hvor jeg får kærlighed og varme' [Rower is my family, where I get love and warmth] (118; 107). Nonetheless, as Janet Garton points out in the afterword to her translation of the novel, Ana's 'material success has not compensated her for the fact that she feels incomplete and unloved, a half-person who was created with donated sperm'.[29] This explains Ana's wish for completeness, and why she intends to utilise Mariama, as the object of desire, to complement her being. It also demonstrates why Mariama needs to stay fixed in a particular image, and, additionally, has to develop according to the capitalist laws that govern Ana's life: success and progress. To serve Ana's purpose, Mariama has to remain Ana's opposite, but also receive an expensive college education so that Ana's 'store planer med Mariama som en succeshistorie' [great plans for Mariama as a success story] (303; 275) can become realised. In this light, Ana's benevolence is self-preoccupied rather than arising out of an affective responsibility that would have Mariama's well-being as its central concern. Moreover, the narrator states that Ana 'ville ikke leve resten af sit liv med selvbebrejdelser og dårlig samvittighed over, at hun ikke havde gjort alt' [would not spend the rest of her life reproaching herself and feeling guilty that she had not done everything] (164; 149). This substantiates Oxfeldt's observation that Ana suffers from 'White-savior syndrome', because her wish to help Mariama stems from a form of guilt that makes Ana more concerned for herself than for Mariama, and hence, her benevolence is 'aimed more at maintaining an image of her, the Westerner, as "good" than at combatting racial structures of oppression'.[30] At least until Mariama's arrival in London, Ana's financial advantage over Mariama grants her a power within the affective economy that allows her to use her guilt and desire to construct a particular image not only of Mariama, but also of herself.

When Ingeborg and Enrique, in *Snakk til meg*, visit Enrique's family, Ingeborg, instead of staying 'i morens ettroms for en billig penge [...] insisterte på hotellet' [in his mother's bedsit for cheap money [...] insisted on the hotel] because, as she states, 'jeg var sjefen' [I was the boss] (134). When it comes to physical contact, Ingeborg prefers to regard herself as helpless in the face of Enrique's sexual prowess, whereas her spending capacity allows her to assert her superiority over Enrique in the same way that white Western women 'employ fantasies of Otherness' to affirm 'their own privilege as Westerners'.[31] This privilege is predominantly related to Ingeborg's affluence, and therefore, her financial means grant her power within the sexual-affective economy; and, when restrictive regulations put obstacles in the way of Enrique visiting her in Norway, this power is increased in the same way as Ana's is. When Ingeborg helps Enrique to apply for a visitor visa, they are informed that processing the application can take up to six months; the queues for every one of the offices that has to be visited in Havana are long, as is the list of required documentation; every single document, and also its translation, costs money, and Ingeborg pays. On her return to Norway, Ingeborg goes through a similar bureaucratic procedure with an additional interview by the police, who investigate her motivation for Enrique's visit. This is necessary, the policeman elucidates, because, 'Norge kan ikke være trampoline for cubanere som vil ut av Cuba. Lander i Norge og forsvinner til Spania [...] Det er et stort problem, vi har et felles europeisk regelverk og et stort ansvar' [Norway can't be a trampoline for Cubans who want to leave Cuba. They land in Norway and disappear to Spain [...] It's a big problem, we have a common European regulatory framework and a major responsibility] (114–15). When the policeman deems Enrique a threat to the whole of Europe, it demonstrates that transnational mobility is a construct based on disparity, and, from the European angle, on exclusionary politics that operate through affect. Discussing the affectivity of threat, Brian Massumi argues, 'Threat does have an actual mode of existence: fear, as foreshadowing. Threat has an impending reality in the present. This actual reality is affective'.[32] In this sense, threat is directed towards the future with actual implications for the present. Threat is an as yet non-actualised potential that nonetheless justifies measures in the present, such as the police interview. In addition, threat sticks to people affectively: they become the threat. From this angle, Enrique is viewed as a threat because he might, potentially and in the future, violate European immigration regulations, which leads to the rejection of his visitor visa. When Ingeborg is confronted with this setback, she asks herself whether it would be better to give up, but she perseveres, travels back to Cuba and marries

Enrique in Havana as the only legal option of bringing him to Norway by way of family reunification. This wedding is only possible because, as Ingeborg states, 'En norsk statsborger kan gifte seg med hvem hun vil, hvor hun vil, når hun vil' [A Norwegian citizen can marry whom she wants, where she wants, when she wants] (192), which exposes double standards, and reasserts Ingeborg's privilege, as well as her power, in the sexual-affective economy.

The bureaucratic process to bring Enrique to Norway offends Ingeborg, but not because the Norwegian authorities construct a particular image of Enrique, but because they distrust her: 'Det krenket meg, jeg hadde alltid vært lojal' [It hurt me, I had always been loyal] (108). This distrust unsettles Ingeborg's national self-understanding, and as a result, she becomes defiant and states, 'Det handlet ikke om Enrique lenger, kanskje gjorde det aldri det, det var myndighetene mot meg' [It wasn't about Enrique any more, maybe it never was, it was the authorities against me] (109). What is more, Ingeborg weighs up her options and reflects, 'Leve som "før". Det føltes umulig. Gi fra meg denne spenningen, denne betydningen, å være noens håp' [To live like 'before'. It felt impossible. Give up on this excitement, this meaning, to be someone's hope] (124). Ingeborg's statements reveal that her reasons to marry Enrique were neither altruistic nor romantic — they were not even related to Enrique as a person. Just like Ana, in *Tilfældets gud*, Ingeborg suffers from 'White-savior syndrome' and utilises her ostensible benevolence to maintain the image of herself as the Scandinavian woman doing 'good'. This helps Ingeborg to combat the guilt over her privileged position, because she can tell herself that she uses her financial advantage to help Enrique, while she really does not want to live without the excitement Enrique brought into her life; a life which Ingeborg describes as, 'den fargeløse, udramatiske ikke-tilværelsen i den søvnige strenge småbyen' [the colourless, undramatic non-existence in the sleepy, stiff little town] (128). Just as bell hooks argues that, 'Within commodity culture, ethnicity becomes spice, seasoning that can liven up the dull dish that is mainstream white culture', Enrique has become for Ingeborg the 'new delight, more intense, more satisfying than normal ways of doing and feeling'.[33] While Ingeborg expects Enrique to stimulate her life in Norway, he also serves as a catalyst for her in terms of self-realisation. When Ingeborg, with reference to her repeated travels to Cuba, states, 'Jeg kunne Charles de Gaulle, verdensvant på Gardermoen' [I knew my way around Charles de Gaulle, urbane in Gardermoen airport] (200), she confirms a degree of sophistication she did not possess before she met Enrique. The transnational orientation of her relationship with Enrique results for Ingeborg in 'at alt var forandret, at jeg også tilhørte den store verden' [that everything was changed, that I also belonged to the big world] (120), and she concludes, 'Jeg er ikke den jeg var' [I'm not who I used to be] (201). For all the reader knows, Enrique stays 'fixed in the "beyond" of the commodity form', whereas the sexual-affective economy works in an emancipatory sense for Ingeborg.[34]

Both texts depict affective economies in which money is exchanged for affective goods to satisfy Ingeborg's, and also Ana's, desire for exoticised difference. The financial advantage of the two Scandinavian women allows them to keep Enrique and Mariama in their immediate proximity, while they, simultaneously, fix them in their commodity form. Ingeborg, and Ana as well, palliate this fact with the notion of benefaction, and hence, the fantasy of strangerness becomes affectively charged: Ingeborg and Ana do not have to feel guilty for their Western privileges, and instead, they can feel good about themselves because they are munificent and use their affluence to help disadvantaged 'others'. Within these affective economies, however, Enrique and Mariama are not without agency. Deliberately and consciously, they engage in affective economies by responding to Ingeborg's and Ana's desires, pursuing their own objectives, namely, a legal passage to Europe. Consequently, the next section turns to the questions of whether Ana and Ingeborg can perpetuate the fixing of Mariama and Enrique in fetish form once the two texts' unequal pairs are in London and Norway respectively, and when the context changes from liminal tourist zones to Ingeborg's and Ana's own cultural surroundings.

Transformations, or Bringing the Stranger Home

When stranger fetishism and consumer culture intersect, the other's difference is, more often than not, exoticised as if ready for consumption, and accordingly, as Ahmed argues, 'The fascination with difference [...] allows the appropriation of difference into the permeable "constitution" of the consumer self'. This suggests that the 'other' is denied any form of agency, and that fetishised otherness serves the sole purpose of satisfying the consuming subject's desire for this otherness, so that the consuming self may be enriched or transformed. We have already seen that affective economies enable Ana and Ingeborg to fix Mariama and Enrique in a combination of fetish and commodity form, and when the two Scandinavian women decide to bring Mariama and Enrique to Europe, these decisions indicate that Ana and Ingeborg expect Mariama and Enrique to remain permanently fixed in this form, while they themselves may change through their close association with the desired 'other'. Utilising an analogy with food, Ahmed highlights the exploitative nature of the intersection of consumer culture with stranger fetishism when she says that 'black people are spicy and different. The white consuming subject is invited to eat the other, to take it in, digest it, and shit out the waste'.[35] In view of this graphic image, we can ask whether or not the relationships between Ana and Mariama, and Ingeborg and Enrique, once the characters are in Europe, are as exploitative as Ahmed suggests. To put it another way, the question is whether or not the appropriation of Mariama's and Enrique's difference into the permeable constitutions of Ana's and Ingeborg's selves is actually possible. Considering that Enrique and Mariama are not without agency within the affective economies, we must ask whether they have the possibility to resist their being fixed in particular images, or whether the texts themselves employ narrative strategies that undermine Ingeborg's and Ana's intended appropriation of Enrique and Mariama.

In Hjorth's novel, Ingeborg's desire for Enrique originates primarily from her fascination with a particular form of masculinity, and to that effect, the transformations taking place once the couple are in Norway are best examined from a gender perspective. The fact that Ingeborg, in Cornel West's words, has bought into '[t]he dominant myth of black male sexual prowess'[36] begs the question of how Ingeborg's perception of Enrique's masculinity changes when he is removed from his familiar surroundings, and how, in turn, her shift in perception changes their relationship, and the two characters individually. Enrique, in one of their first conversations, summarises what he knows about Norway: 'Rikt, sa han, olje, sa han, kaldt, likestilling' [Rich, he said, oil, he said, cold, equality] (18–19). Enrique explains that, in contrast to Norwegian gender equality, in Cuba 'er det mannfolka som bestemmer' [it's the men who call the shots]; but, accepting her money under the table so that he can pay the restaurant bill, he adds, 'om det ikke er sånn, må det se sånn ut' [if it isn't like this, it has to look like it] (143). Enrique demonstrates that he is well aware of the constructed nature of Cuban patriarchal masculinity, and because he is dependent on Ingeborg in his desire to leave Cuba, he, with keeping up appearances, finds a playful solution for the supposed threat that his poverty poses to his masculinity. Once the couple are in Norway, however, this becomes increasingly difficult, as Ingeborg describes: 'Jeg insisterte på å kjøre, kunne veiene, skiltene, han likte det ikke. At jeg fylte bensinen, betalte bensinen' [I insisted on driving, knew the routes, signs, he didn't like it. That I filled up the car, paid for the petrol] (250). In this scene, it is not only Enrique's poverty that threatens a patriarchal notion of masculinity, but also Ingeborg's overt dominance, and the fact that Enrique is unfamiliar with the surroundings. Ingeborg's sexualised and exoticised image of Enrique does not withstand Norwegian immigration procedures and the obligatory police interview in connection with Enrique's application for a residence permit. When Ingeborg picks him up after the interview, she views him as 'en slagen mann. Ingen vittigheter, ingen forføring, ikke noe overskudd, velkommen hit' [a defeated man. No wittiness, no seducing, no abundance, welcome to Norway] (248). Ingeborg holds Norway in general, and the Norwegian immigration authorities in particular, responsible for Enrique's supposed crisis of masculinity, but it is she who demands Enrique to embody a particular conception of sexualised, racialised masculinity. As Ingeborg sees it, their Norwegian domesticity, combined with Enrique's unfamiliarity with the Norwegian language, robs Enrique of his confidence, which, for Ingeborg, is an essential part of his masculinity. Trying to teach Enrique Norwegian, she comments, 'all suverenitet [...] forduftet, ikke jeger med bytte [...] ikke mann lenger, forvitret for øynene mine' [all aplomb [...] vanished into thin air, not a hunter with a prey [...] not a man any more, withered before my eyes] (252). For Ingeborg, Enrique's masculinity only functions in its natural habitat, and when the circumstances change, she finds her idea of Enrique disappointed, as the image of his masculinity unravels before her eyes.

When the masculinity that Ingeborg fixed unto Enrique becomes unfixed, Enrique is emasculated in Ingeborg's eyes, and as a consequence, he ceases to be an object of desire for her. What is more, Ingeborg achieves her own two objectives: firstly, she manages to bring Enrique legally to Norway; and secondly, her son Torgrim finally calls her. In Ingeborg's fight against the Norwegian immigration authorities, Enrique becomes depersonalised, and when Ingeborg states that she has 'vunnet over politi og utenriksdepartement' [won over the police and the Foreign Office] (225) against all the odds, he has fulfilled his purpose in this struggle. Torgrim has heard about Ingeborg's relationship with Enrique through the grapevine, and he only calls to scream at her and cut off all ties. Ingeborg explains that her discord with Torgrim 'hektet på en svart mann fra Cuba' [hinged on a black man from Cuba], and instead of questioning Torgrim's racist motives, Ingeborg feels 'en slags glede eller tilfredshet: Jeg betyr noe' [a kind of joy or satisfaction: I mean something] (260). We have seen earlier that Ingeborg uses Enrique to fill her life with meaning, since she thinks of herself as his benefactress, his hope; now, Enrique indirectly assists her in eliciting an emotional response from her son, and again, it is the augmentation of her ego that matters most to her. She regards Torgrim's break with her 'nesten som en renselse' [almost like a cleansing] (260) and realises that this cathartic process frees her from any expectations her motherhood might entail, such as, 'Bildene, rollene, alle krav jeg har bakset for å oppfylle' [The images, the roles, all the demands that I struggled to fulfil]. Hence, as she comments, Torgrim 'har befridd meg og jeg kan være meg selv' [has freed me and I can be myself]. While Torgrim's reaction to her relationship with Enrique has an emancipatory effect, Ingeborg also acknowledges that this would not have been possible without Enrique, because through her relationship with him, she was granted 'et nytt syn' [a new vision] (266) of herself, and in this sense, Enrique can be seen as a catalyst in Ingeborg's self-actualisation as a woman.

Once she is set free, Ingeborg and her narrative have no need for Enrique any longer, and he is abolished. In a clever narrative manoeuvre that serves her purpose, Enrique simply disappears, 'sikkert til Spania' [probably to Spain] (261), as she reckons. Ingeborg presents herself in line with the exclusionary immigration policies that constructed Enrique as a threat when she assumes that the misgivings of the police are justified. While Ingeborg previously was successful in her fight against the Norwegian immigration authorities, it is, in the end, her loyalty for the Norwegian state that gains the upper hand. In hindsight, Ingeborg reflects on their relationship after Enrique has left, and says:

> Kanskje jeg elsket ham en gang på en mate, den sterke mørke kroppen hans over min i sitt alvor. Pliktfølelsen, det han tok på seg, at han gjorde det. Det var vel verdt det sett fra min side, håper det også vil være det for ham og familien, som han gjorde det for.

> [Maybe I loved him once in a way, his strong dark body over mine in his seriousness. His sense of duty, what he took on, that he did this. It was well worth it for me, I hope it was also worth it for him and his family, who he did it for.] (261)

Ingeborg reduces Enrique once again to his stereotyped, exoticised and sexualised body, which she appreciates as long as he can uphold this image. While Ingeborg admits that she does not know anything about Enrique's feelings, she assumes simultaneously that he acted out of a sense of duty for his family. Hence, she appropriates Enrique's thoughts and his motivation to enter into a relationship with her, while she, throughout her entire narrative, never explicitly mentions, but only guesses at, his motives. In addition, Ingeborg's interpretation that it was an exercise of duty for Enrique to have sex with her, and her conclusion that it was worth it, confirms the sexual-affective economy as a quid pro quo where she got what she paid for. At the same time, Ingeborg can sustain the image of herself as a benefactress not only for Enrique, but, by extension, for his whole family. To the reader, Ingeborg appears unconcerned regarding the way that she fetishises Enrique's body and appropriates his thoughts and feelings, and she fails to understand that her attitude towards Enrique might be problematic. It is, however, obvious that Ingeborg uses her relationship with Enrique to wrench an emotional response from her son, and that she employs manipulative narrative strategies to achieve this objective, which makes her an unreliable narrator, and complicates our affective engagement with her. The text itself may guide the reader to assessing Ingeborg's attitude towards Enrique critically, and to discovering how problematic the politics of appropriation underlying Ingeborg's attitude actually are. This entails disentangling the text's possible critique from Ingeborg's own uncritical stance and her dominant narrative voice, and we have to work hard to this end. In contrast, the narrative structure in *Tilfældets gud* makes critical engagement with Ana's problematic politics easier, and therefore much more likely.

Earlier, I have argued that Ana holds on to a particular image of Mariama that fixes the girl simultaneously in sameness and difference, and that Ana expects to regain a sense of wholeness through her close, yet distant, relationship with Mariama. However, this incorporation of Mariama into Ana's self does not quite go to plan, because the girl's development diverges from Ana's conception, and Ana finds her expectations disappointed. Besides, Ana hopes to find employment with the local branch of Rower in London, but she is not rehired, and when she is faced with diminishing financial resources and Mariama's costly college education, she turns to alcohol and medication, and resorts to the only value she believes in, chance, and begins to gamble online. Ana is unable to cope with Mariama's deviation from her imagined form, and she is therefore 'utilfreds med sig selv og sin manglende evne til at håndtere forholdet til den mere selvstændige og uafhængige Mariama' [dissatisfied with herself and her lack of ability to handle her relationship with the more independent and autonomous Mariama] (192; 174). Mariama's developing independence threatens the parameters of the affective economy, because it jeopardises the role of the white saviour that Ana has constructed for herself, and her means of feeling good about herself for helping Mariama. When, as a result of Mariama's self-determination, the happiness Ana expected fails to appear, Ana's anxiety increases, and she experiences 'paranoide angstanfald' [paranoid panic attacks] (251; 228), while she presumes that Mariama double-crosses her: 'Hun var buret inde i angsten og bildte sig ind, at Mariama helt fra begyndelsen havde haft en skjult dagsorden, der skulle lokke hende i en fælde' [She was walled up in her fear, and imagined that Mariama had had a hidden agenda right from the start, in order to lure her into a trap] (251; 228). After learning that Mariama sent photographs of Ana to her family in Gambia, Ana suspects 'at nogen vil bruge dem til at lave voodoo på mig' [that someone will use them to put voodoo on me] (256; 233). Ana's formerly rational attitude crumbles, and she extends her irrational assumptions to all people of colour and perceives their ubiquity in London as a threat. Her paranoia turns into outright racism when the narrator states that she sees 'sorte alle vegne' [black people everywhere], which, for Ana, means that she is 'omgivet av dæmoner' [surrounded by demons] (255; 232). Ana thinks that Mariama is one of these demons because Mariama, in Ana's view, 'Gemmer sig bag en maske' [Conceals herself behind a mask] (256; 232) only to spy on and deceive her. Rower's counsellor, whom Ana sees for stress coaching, demonstrates insight when he suggests that Ana demonises Mariama to explain the fact that she is losing control over her life; and yet, Ana cannot help but feel a 'mystisk nærhed' [mystical closeness] to Mariama, and states that her feelings for the girl are not 'sværmerier eller indbildning, men en realitet der krævede handling' [a fantasy or delusion, but a reality which demanded action] (267; 243). Considering Ana's delicate emotional and mental condition, this call for action poses a threat to Mariama and her newly won independence, because Ana cannot allow Mariama to deviate from the image she has created of her.

While Ana tries to deny Mariama detachment from this image, the narrative structure reflects and respects Mariama's development into an independent individual: in the third part of the text, Mariama is focalised to a greater extent, and the narrator oscillates between Ana's and Mariama's psyches, so that Mariama's personality becomes visible for the reader autonomously from Ana. Ever so subtly, Thorup's aesthetic choice undermines the unequal power relations that bind Ana and Mariama together, while it simultaneously highlights how problematic Ana's intended appropriation of Mariama is. While Mariama is attending college, she takes on a part-time job in addition to her studies to support her family in Gambia, but eventually, and despite the Diazepam she takes, Mariama surrenders to the pressure, drops out of school and disappears, which intensifies Ana's anxiety immensely.

The narrator's alternation between Ana's and Mariama's perspectives grants the reader separate insights into the ways in which Mariama makes her own decisions regarding her life, and into Ana's life unravelling. These two parallel processes are interlinked; eventually, they converge, and in a last dramatic encounter, the two women meet at eye level. Ana, dishevelled and in borrowed clothes after a long and exhausting search, finds Mariama by chance in the queue of a soup kitchen. In the following dialogue, the narrator's mediation is suspended, which highlights the equality between Ana and Mariama in this scene. Ana accuses Mariama and says, 'Du tager imod kost og logi, lommepenge, tøjpenge, for slet ikke at tale om, at det koster en formue at gå på college. Du har spillet med falske kort' [You have been given board and lodging, pocket money, clothes money, not to mention the fact that it costs a fortune to go to college. You did it all under false pretences] (305; 278). Ana exposes her beneficent attitude as false when she indicates that she, in exchange for her money, expects Mariama to develop within the frame that she has set for her. When Ana sees her expectations disappointed, she feels betrayed, and when Mariama tries to reassure her with, 'Alt hvad jeg er i dag, er jeg takket være dig' [Everything I am today, I am thanks to you], Ana counters with, 'Du er ingenting.

Projektet er tabt på gulvet' [You are nothing. The project has failed completely] (306; 278). When Mariama refuses to allow her exoticised otherness to be integrated into Ana's world, she loses all relevance for Ana, and Ana forfeits her hope of being made into a whole being. Ana cannot allow this to happen, and in a sudden surge of anger and panic, she slaps Mariama in the face, who then falls and hits the kerb, and the reader is left with the sounds of an approaching ambulance.

To prepare the ground for this scene, and to emphasise the momentary equality between the two women, the narrator states that, while Mariama 'havde ikke mistet sit tjekkede college-look' [had not lost her smart college look] (298; 271), Ana's 'elegance, hendes suveræne livsstil [...] var forsvundet' [elegance, the well-groomed stylishness [...] had disappeared], so that Mariama finds herself vis-à-vis 'et afklædt menneske, hverken rig eller fattig, men bare et menneske som hun selv' [a naked human being, neither rich nor poor, just a human being like herself (307; 279). For an instant, they are balanced in an equilibrium where binary opposites are suspended, and between these two equal human bodies opens a dynamic space in which their encounter could become truly transformational for both of them. This potential, however, is destroyed by Ana, and, as Veisland rightly argues, within this chance encounter 'chance is twisted and loses its sense of unique opportunity'.[37] But as Ana feels so closely connected to Mariama, she cannot hurt Mariama without hurting herself: she 'havde dræbt sin sjæl' [had killed her soul] (311; 283). Or, to reverse this statement, when Mariama dispossesses Ana of the possibility to recover her soul, Ana's intended countermove is to dispossess Mariama of her life altogether. The text's ending remains ambiguous because we never learn if Mariama survives. Chance, as the only value Ana believes in, becomes her last resort, and she plays roulette in the nearest casino, convinced that if she wins, 'ville hun også vinde Mariama tilbage' [she would also win back Mariama] (313; 285). Or, as Oxfeldt accurately observes, with her arrogance and desperation, Ana 'wants to reassert an order of chance and inequality in which she comes out the winner, not just of cash, but also of Mariama';[38] and yet, it transpires that, 'Tilfældighedernes og statistikkens love var ubønhørlige' [The laws of chance and statistics were inexorable] (314; 286). In Ana's racist paranoia, the colour black has acquired a threatening symbolic meaning, and therefore she places her bets on red, and wins four times consecutively. She then places the highest stake possible on red again, but the ball falls back on black. In this moment of poetic justice, chance, or the god of chance, retains the upper hand, and Ana is punished for interfering with chance by turning it into violence.

★   ★   ★   ★   ★

Liminal tourist zones, with their inherent suspension from the everyday, set the scene for Ana's and Ingeborg's encounters with Mariama and Enrique in Gambia and Cuba respectively, and allow the Scandinavian women to fix Mariama and Enrique in fetish form through their desire for the other's exoticised difference. This desire, paired with the financial disparity between Ana and Mariama, and Ingeborg and Enrique, enables the characters to enter into affective economies which are different in nature, yet similar in structure, because affective value can be purchased with money in both cases. Within these affective economies, Mariama's and Enrique's exoticised difference is transformed into a commodity, and when the Scandinavian women decide to take Mariama and Enrique with them to Europe, exclusionary immigration policies increase the price for their desired difference, which reinforces the unequal power balance in the two relationships. When Mariama and Enrique deviate from their fixed images, however, Ana's and Ingeborg's intentions to appropriate their desired otherness fail. Nevertheless, Ingeborg's encounter with Enrique is cathartic for her and has an emancipating effect, so that she comes to terms with herself and concludes, 'jeg [er] en middelaldrende bibliotekar, ikke mer, ikke mindre' [I [am] a middle-aged librarian, no more, no less] (267). The text, however, makes it clear that this emancipation is only made possible by Ingeborg's exploitation of Enrique, who becomes further marginalised as he disappears from Ingeborg's narrative, and his fate remains unknown. Similarly, the reader never learns of the consequences that Ana's attack has on Mariama. While Mariama, at least to this point, has emancipated herself, Ana's life disintegrates, and Ana's violent attempt to interrupt this development and reinstate hierarchy cannot stall this process.

In terms of the happiness that is, supposedly, concomitant with Scandinavian privilege, both *Tilfældets gud* and *Snakk til meg* can be viewed as questioning 'the happiness of the Nordic woman by confronting her with less privileged global [others]'. At first, the Scandinavian women's financial advantage allows them to see themselves as benefactresses, which alleviates their feelings of guilt over their privileged positions and enables them to feel good about themselves. Yet, these positive feelings cannot be sustained, and in this sense, the two texts can be seen as 'an affective counter-discourse to the scientific happiness discourse of research institutions and reports that focus on evaluative happiness'.[39] For Ana and Ingeborg, their prosperity, and the lifestyle that this affluence facilitates, is not enough to make them happy, and their situational happiness is tied to the consumption of difference. When, in Ana's case, this happiness fails to appear, her emotions turn into hate, jealousy and fear, and as Ingeborg's situational happiness is dependent on her exploitation and ensuing disposal of Enrique, it appears tainted to the reader.

The endings of the two texts can be seen in the light of Deleuze and Guattari's famous lines of flight, a term they use to describe 'a path of mutation precipitated through the actualisation of connections among bodies'.[40] Within these connections lies the potential to release and increase the capacities of bodies to affect and to be affected, to act and to respond. When these responses are based on the fine adjustment of attentiveness to situated others and their differences, this act of attentive listening can lead to affective responsibility, and to the emergence of something new in the embodied encounter. However, as Deleuze and Guattari argue, a line of flight implies the danger that, 'instead of connecting with other lines and each time augmenting its valence', it can turn to '*destruction, abolition pure and simple, the passion of abolition*'.[41] When Mariama's and Enrique's fetishised difference becomes unfixed, they lose their affective value for Ana and Ingeborg, and the lines of flight that connect them forfeit their creative potential; the line that connects Enrique and Ingeborg turns into a line of abolition, and the line that binds Mariama to Ana turns into a line of violent destruction. When the reader is thus confronted with the ambiguous, yet violent, outcomes of these processes of fetishisation and commodification, both texts throw into sharp relief how affective economies can create unequal power structures, and how problematic the underlying politics of appropriation are. In order to arrive at this insight in *Snakk til meg*, the reader has to resist Ingeborg's manipulation to be able to separate her uncritical stance from the position the text itself might assume. While this complicates the reader's affective engagement with either Enrique or Ingeborg, the instances of Ingeborg's unreliability as a narrator can be viewed as caveats in the text which draw the reader's attention to the fact that her motives are questionable, and thus invite a critical reading of Ingeborg's narrative. Thorup's novel also complicates the reader's affective engagement, but in different ways than Hjorth's text: from the outset, the narrator's ironic distance from Ana exposes her attitudes and opinions as problematic. In addition, the narrator increasingly focalises Mariama as the text progresses, and Thorup's aesthetic choice undermines Ana's intended appropriation of Mariama, and makes the politics underlying Ana's character visible to the reader. In this sense, *Tilfældets gud* invites the reader's critical engagement with Ana's character and the concomitant politics in a much more open way than Ingeborg's character and her narrative do in *Snakk til meg*.

Notes to Chapter 3

1. John Urry, *The Tourist Gaze* (London: Sage, 1990), pp. 10, 11.
2. Graham Huggan, *The Postcolonial Exotic* (London: Routledge, 2001), pp. 177, 178.
3. Mary Louise Pratt, *Imperial Eyes: Travel Writing and Transculturation* (London: Routledge, 2008), p. 7; Annegret Heitmann, 'Female Tourists Going Global: — Danish Travel Narratives between Happiness and Guilt', *Scandinavian Studies*, 89 (2017), 512–29 (p. 514).
4. Heitmann, p. 514.
5. Brah, p. 185, italics in original.
6. Henry Louis Gates Jr, 'Introduction', in *'Race,' Writing and Difference*, ed. by Gates, Jr (Chicago: University of Chicago Press, 1986), pp. 1–20 (p. 5).
7. Ahmed, *Strange Encounters*, p. 25, italics in original.
8. Ibid., p. 114.
9. Heitmann, p. 517.
10. Urry, pp. 10, 15, 9, italics in original.
11. bell hooks, *Black Looks: Race and Representation* (Boston, MA: South End Press, 1992), p. 23.
12. Cornel West, *Race Matters* (New York: Vintage Books, 1994), p. 125.
13. hooks, *Black Looks*, p. 26.
14. West, p. 125.
15. bell hooks, *We Real Cool: Black Men and Masculinity* (London: Routledge, 2004), p. 67.
16. Ahmed, *Strange Encounters*, pp. 3–5.
17. Jørgen Veisland, 'A Mysterious Closeness: Africa and Europe in Kirsten Thorup's "The God of Chance"', *Forum for World Literature Studies*, 5 (2013), 276–88 (pp. 276, 280).
18. hooks, *Black Looks*, p. 24.
19. Ahmed, *Cultural Politics*, p. 45.
20. Sara Ahmed, 'Affective Economies', *Social Text*, 22 (2004), 117–39 (p. 121).
21. Megan Daigle, *From Cuba with Love* (Oakland: University of California Press, 2015), p. 4.

22. hooks, *We Real Cool*, p. 79.

23. Daigle, p. 7.

24. Julia O'Connell Davidson and Jacqueline Sanchez Taylor, 'Fantasy Islands: Exploring the Demand for Sex Tourism', in *Men's Lives*, ed. by Michael S. Kimmel and Michael A. Messner, 6th edn (London: Allyn & Bacon, 2004) pp. 454–66 (p. 461).

25. Ahmed, *Strange Encounters*, p. 116.

26. Veisland, p. 277.

27. Butler, p. 25.

28. Elisabeth Oxfeldt, '"I Come from Crap Country and You Come from Luxury Country": Ugly Encounters in Scandinavian Au-Pair Novels', *Scandinavian Studies*, 89 (2017), 468–86 (pp. 477–78).

29. Janet Garton, 'Afrerword', in *The God of Chance*, by Kirsten Thorup (London: Norvik Press, 2013) pp. 289–94 (p. 289).

30. Oxfeldt, 'I Come from Crap Country', p. 479.

31. O'Connell Davidson and Sanchez Taylor, p. 462.

32. Massumi, 'Future Birth', p. 54.

33. hooks, *Black Looks*, p. 21

34. Ahmed, *Strange Encounters*, p. 118.

35. Ibid., pp. 118, 117.

36. West, p. 127.

37. Veisland, p. 287.

38. Oxfeldt, 'I Come from Crap Country', p. 479.

39. Ibid., pp. 484, 470.

40. Tamsin Lorraine, 'Lines of Flight', in *The Deleuze Dictionary*, ed. by Adrian Parr (Edinburgh: Edinburgh University Press, 2010), pp. 147–48 (p. 147).

41. Deleuze and Guattari, p. 268, italics in original.

CHAPTER 4

❖

Indifference, or
The Limits of Affective Responsibility in
Aasne Linnestå's *Opphold*, Negar Naseh's
De fördrivna and Lone Aburas's *Politisk Roman*

Central to the present chapter are three texts which revolve around three Scandinavian protagonists who encounter asylum seekers and refugees, and who position themselves affectively in one way or another to those 'others': the Danish novel *Politisk roman* (2013) by Lone Aburas; the Norwegian novel *Opphold* (2014) by Aasne Linnestå; and the Swedish novel *De fördrivna* (2016) by Negar Naseh. At first glance, the focus on these novels appears reminiscent of the previous chapter, but in chapter 3, the contact between the Scandinavian protagonists and those they perceive as 'other' is sought out and willed, and Ingeborg's and Ana's motivations to enter into those relationships is driven by a desire for experiencing difference. Now, however, the Scandinavian protagonists find themselves in relations of 'unwilled proximity' with others and respond to this 'obtrusive alterity' affectively in more varied and less unequivocal ways.[1] It is precisely these affective responses I am interested in, and whether or not relations of unwilled proximity with 'others' incite a sense of affective responsibility in the protagonists towards those whom, to paraphrase Judith Butler, they do not know; towards those who test their sense of belonging, and who defy the norms of likeness available to them.

Assuming that a sense of responsibility can be instigated affectively, the affects in question, one would think, are to be found somewhere on the scale of sympathy, pity, compassion or empathy. These four terms, however, are by no means interchangeable, as Aleida Assmann and Ines Detmers clarify when they distinguish empathy from its close cognates, sympathy, pity and compassion. Assmann and Detmers define sympathy as 'an emotion that creates an often mutual attraction and affinity that binds two people together through a sense of similarity in their characters, experience, or values', while they describe pity and compassion as 'unidirectional feelings that flow from a person in a subject position who is in a neutral state towards a person in an object position who is in a bad state'.[2] The latter definition already points towards a hierarchy, or inequality, between the one feeling pity or compassion and the recipient, and towards the conception that pity and compassion are usually focused on pain, suffering or distress. Lauren Berlant confirms this when she states, 'In operation, compassion is a term denoting privilege: the sufferer is *over there*'.[3] When Sara Ahmed argues that, 'To be moved by the suffering of some others [...] is also to be elevated into a place that remains untouched by other others', she underscores the notion that this inequality becomes even more pronounced with regard to someone who is radically different from oneself.[4] In a similar vein, and akin to Butler's suggestion that a sense of responsibility is shaped by 'norms of likeness', Berlant argues that a compassionate response to distress, or the felt obligation to alleviate suffering, is socially and politically mediated: 'it is crucial to appreciate the multitude of conventions around the relations of feeling to practice where compassion is concerned'.[5] In contrast, empathy, in Assmann and Detmers's view, is not reduced solely to the alleviation of suffering, but is 'more generally the hallmark of social intelligence'.[6] Assmann and Detmers set empathy apart from pity, sympathy and compassion by arguing that, in its most desirable form, empathy is 'no longer a volatile affective disposition' when it is 'stabilized in insights, attitudes, and concrete actions'.[7] Then, empathy can turn into affective responsibility and pro-social action, but this ethical level of empathy may contradict the same conventions and norms which, in Butler's and Berlant's views, mediate compassion: 'the acts of empathic observation and concern may not be prescribed by the norms and conventions of one's society'. This statement does not imply that these norms and conventions are necessarily an obstacle for empathy, but that they might be, particularly with regard to empathy towards someone radically different from oneself. When affective responses to difference are mediated by conventions, difference creates distance and, potentially, 'precludes the possibility of spontaneous emotional ties, and blocks empathy', while an unmediated empathic response holds the possibility that this distance may be eradicated.[8]

It certainly holds true that compassionate or empathic responses to others can be mediated or impeded by social and cultural norms or conventions; in addition, those arguably ethical feelings are often accompanied, or contaminated, by what Sianne Ngai calls 'ugly feelings'. This term circumscribes 'minor and generally unprestigious feelings' such as envy, indifference, anxiety or irritation; feelings that are 'explicitly *amoral* and *noncathartic*, offering no satisfaction of virtue, however oblique, nor any therapeutic or purifying release'.[9] When it comes to scenes of distress or vulnerability which would generally call for a compassionate response in the spectator, Berlant argues that it is possible that, instead, these scenes 'produce a desire to withhold compassionate attachment', and 'all the spectator wants to do is to turn away quickly and harshly'.[10] The witnessing of vulnerability and suffering, rather than generating affects that lead to affective responsibility and supportive action, can bring out negative affects that curb action. Moreover, as Ngai contends, 'these moments of conspicuous inactivity remain affectively charged' with a general sense of 'affective disorientation', which Ngai further describes as 'a meta-feeling in which one feels confused about *what* one is feeling'.[11] While affects such as compassion or empathy could potentially lead to political or social action, these so-called minor affects suspend agency, as they create affective ambiguity and inertia.

This brief discussion of ethical feelings and their possible contamination by 'ugly feelings' provides the critical framework to highlight how the texts' protagonists respond affectively to 'others'. Empathy, and indifference or other related negative responses, can be directly linked with what Elisabeth Oxfeldt calls 'skandinaviske skyldfølelser', or 'Scandinavian Guilt'.[12] Oxfeldt expounds that, broadly speaking, Scandinavians perceive themselves as highly privileged, and, while they 'nyter godt av sine privilegier' [enjoy their privileges], they are, simultaneously, aware that these privileges are predicated on 'strukturell, politisk og økonomisk undertrykkelse av Andre' [structural, political and economic repression of Others], which, in turn, produces a feeling of unease, or 'dårlig samvittighet og skyldfølelser overfor en global, lidende Annen' [a guilty conscience and feelings of guilt towards a global, suffering Other]. Considering that the Nordic countries consistently top the ranking lists as the happiest countries in the world and are usually construed as the hallmark for 'lykke, velstand, tillit og likhet' [happiness, prosperity, trust and equality], this feeling of guilt 'kan bli ekstra stor og komme ekstra tydelig til uttrykk' [can become especially strong and can be expressed particularly clearly] in Scandinavia. Cautioning against generalisations, however, Oxfeldt points out that it is important to keep in mind that the Scandinavian we-group which potentially feels this sense of guilt is a construction, because the Scandinavian societies are less homogeneous than this construction suggests; in addition, neither are all Scandinavians privileged, nor do all privileged Scandinavians display signs of guilt.[13]

Oxfeldt sets Scandinavian Guilt apart from other forms of national guilt when she states that, while Scandinavian Guilt is 'en del av vestlig skyld' [a part of Western guilt], it is different from other European forms of guilt such as, for instance, German guilt, because the Scandinavian countries do not define themselves via a sense of shame related to history, 'slik Tyskland har måttet gjøre det etter annen verdenskrig' [in the same way Germany had to after the Second World War]. Oxfeldt also differentiates between Scandinavian Guilt and an American collective feeling of guilt when she argues that American guilt is usually related to historical injustices on the national level, whereas Scandinavian Guilt correlates with more recent global developments.[14] Yet, Shelby Steele's reflections on a particularly American form of guilt are nevertheless incisive regarding individual reactions to guilt. In the previous chapter, we have seen that the Scandinavian protagonists Ingeborg and Ana mitigate feelings of guilt about their privileges by viewing themselves as benefactresses, since they, through their financial advantages, make it possible that the desired 'others' can emigrate to Europe. Guilt, instead of inspiring altruism, becomes self-serving, because it spurs affective dynamics which aid Ingeborg and Ana in their pursuit of feeling good about themselves. Directing his reflections on guilt towards the relationship between white Americans and African Americans, Steele cautions against precisely such self-serving implementations of guilt. The awareness of guilt, as Steele argues, always contains 'the fear of what the guilty knowledge says about us', and therefore, as Steele goes on to say, guilt 'generates as much self-preoccupation as concern for others. The nature of this preoccupation is always the redemption of innocence, the reestablishment of good feeling about oneself'.[15] When the fear for one's own self is not dispelled, action resulting from feelings of guilt will always be self-centred, because the primary aim of such action is to ensure that one can feel good about oneself.

Bearing in mind that 'emotions *do things*', this chapter explores what Scandinavian Guilt, or any other affect for that matter, does: do the texts' protagonists suppress or negate their feelings of guilt, or do these feelings inspire affective responsibility, and, ultimately, pro-social action and solidarity with underprivileged 'others'? The three texts portray individual protagonists and their personal affective reactions; and yet, personally experienced emotions are closely related to collectives, because these emotions align individuals with, or alienate them from, a social body.[16] This suggests that personal emotions are not only mediated by collectives, but that they, in turn, shape social, cultural and political space as well. Moreover, emotions can be viewed 'as a mediation between the aesthetic and the political in a nontrivial way'.[17] Ahmed's and Ngai's perspectives grant insight into the social, cultural and political structures into which the protagonists' affective responses are embedded; reading the texts' depictions of affective responsibility through these perspectives will allow me to highlight the mechanisms that mediate the protagonists' affective responses. In conjunction with affective responsibility and the reader, Assmann and Detmers point out that empathy produced in the fictional realm of a text 'differs from empathy activated in personal interaction', and that it is, obviously, not on the same level with lived experiences. When the texts, however, depict various ways in which empathy, or any other affects, are produced or blocked in fictional characters, this portrayal 'can work as a propaedeutic for the understanding of others and strengthen conscious reflections on the state of the other'.[18] In this light, the present chapter illuminates how Linnestå, Naseh and Aburas, through certain deliberate aesthetic choices, offer the reader a conscious reflection on the state of asylum seekers and refugees.

In the Norwegian novel *Opphold* by Aasne Linnestå, the reader follows Mikkel, the first-person narrator and father of the three children Synne, Marianne and Eivind, who, returning with the children from a summer holiday, finds their house in Oslo empty and his wife Sylvia gone. Mikkel reports his wife missing, and in the following six months, he tries to hold their lives together, while the police search for Sylvia, until they find her frozen to death on the top of a mountain. Mikkel's narrative is paralleled and interwoven with the story of the Javadi family, who fled from Iran to Norway to seek asylum, and who, at the same time that Sylvia is found dead, have their applications for asylum rejected and are deported back to Iran. Seeing the vulnerability of all five members of the Javadi family, Mikkel finds himself in a dilemma: how can he help these strangers, when he has barely enough strength to look after his own family? Negar Naseh's *De fördrivna* is an intimate portrait of the psychological dynamics in the relationship of Miriam and Filip, a Swedish married couple who have moved to Sicily with their baby daughter Olivia, and bought a house there, so that they can work in peace and quiet, compared to the noisier Stockholm, and in a warmer climate. The relationship between Miriam and Filip is characterised by tension, which intensifies when Filip's best friend

Ashkan arrives with his wife Erika, because the four characters do not get along as well as they thought they would. In a combination of omniscient narration, character focalisation and free indirect discourse, the reader becomes familiar with these tensions partly through the perspectives of the respective partners when the narrator's focalisation oscillates between Miriam and Filip, and partly through the ways in which the narrator overtly comments on the protagonists' personality traits, or the developments between all four protagonists. Ashkan, a journalist and visiting Italy to research the fate of refugees on the island of Lampedusa, confronts Miriam and Filip regarding their supposed lack of interest in his research project. When Ashkan challenges Miriam and Filip, both are individually compelled to position themselves in relation to undocumented migrants, and to ask themselves whether there is anything they should do in support of the refugees' cause, or not. Lone Aburas's *Politisk roman* is the portrait of a Danish couple and their dysfunctional patchwork family, encompassing Robert and his two daughters Sally, who is eleven years old, and Martha, who is seventeen, and Rebecca and her sixteen-year-old son Oskar. One day, Robert is struck by the thought that it is hypocritical of him merely to wear a badge 'med teksten *Jeg skjuler en flygtning*' [with the text *I'm hiding a refugee*] (5, italics in original), and, deciding that urgent action is required, he moves the undocumented migrant Amir into their flat in Copenhagen to hide him from the authorities, and prevent his deportation. Narrated from the perspective of Robert's partner Rebecca, the text's dynamics, and the affective responses of Rebecca and the whole family, revolve and develop around Amir's presence in the flat, and around the question of whether Robert's political action is misguided, or not. *Politisk roman* is a highly satirical text, and by means of irony, hyperbole, and, most of all, Rebecca's caustic narrative voice, the attitudes of the respective family members are held up to the reader for ridicule.

These brief synopses indicate that all three texts engage with the ethical question of what the protagonists' responsibility towards those they do not know might be, as they portray Scandinavian protagonists in relations of 'unwilled proximity' with asylum seekers and refugees, or with those they perceive as radically other, and whose alterity is felt as obtrusive. This 'obtrusive alterity', as Butler argues, 'can be, and often is, what animates responsiveness', and this responsiveness 'may include a wide range of affects'.[19] The depictions of the protagonists' personalities indicate that they, although for diverging reasons and in different ways, are affectively predisposed towards the 'others' they encounter. Therefore, I shall outline these affective predispositions, and then investigate the protagonists' wide range of affects towards the 'others' they come up against. On the assumption that it is the protagonists' closer contact with, and deeper knowledge of, these 'others', which may change their affective predispositions and feelings throughout the course of the three texts, we can ask whether this closer contact inspires a greater sense of responsibility in the protagonists, or whether it renders them more indifferent.

Relations of Unwilled Proximity and Affective Predispositions

Miriam, in *De fördrivna*, is an anaesthetist, and by virtue of her profession, she has a keen interest in sleeping disorders and the alleviation of pain; but with regard to her baby daughter Olivia, Miriam's interest in monitoring her sleep verges on the obsessive. Throughout the entire text, the words *Olivia sover* [Olivia is sleeping] are reiterated multiple times, and indeed, her child does sleep: at any time during the day; or on the shoulder of one of her parents; at times when it is seemingly too noisy; and even during excursions to the beach. Yet, Miriam cannot abandon her fear of sudden cot death, and therefore, she insists that Olivia sleeps on her back at night. Moreover, Miriam's profession grants her access to a range of strong analgesics and sedatives, and she self-medicates generously because it 'kännas avslappande' [feels relaxing]; in addition, Miriam 'har provat att ge barnet några droppar Theralen ett par gånger' [has tried to give her child some Theralen drops a couple of times] (105) to make her fall asleep more easily. Miriam and Filip quarrel because Filip is irritated by Miriam's preoccupation with Olivia's sleeping patterns, and he criticises his wife for her smoking and drinking habits: 'Hennes sätt att röka och nuförtiden också att dricka är överdriven' [Her smoking, as well as her drinking these days, is excessive] (85). Miriam's proclivity for the use of any kind of narcotic can be viewed as a metaphor for her wish to affectively exclude the world: Miriam does not want to feel troubled in her pastoral idyllic Sicilian surroundings, which Filip paints as an idealised image when he suggests, 'Här är hon omgiven av vårblommor. Av pinjeträd och olivlundar. Det finns ingenting hon ångrar med flytten' [Here she is surrounded by spring flowers. By stone pine trees and olive groves. There is nothing she regrets about the move] (17).[20] Filip's criticism of his wife, despite his self-assurances, is rendered through the narrator's focalisation of Filip by way of free indirect discourse, and highlights the tense psychological dynamics in Miriam and Filip's partnership. The arrival of Ashkan and Erika causes further tension, and this happens for more than one reason. The two women do not get on with each other, and the narrator discloses that, 'varken hon [Erika] eller Miriam försöker bli vänner längre' [neither she [Erika] nor Miriam are trying to become friends any more] (38). While Filip thinks of Ashkan as his best friend, the narrator's focalisation of Filip reveals that he thinks that Ashkan has traits 'som irriterar' [which annoy] him, that is, 'att vännen kan tolka allt han säger på ett negativt sätt' [that his friend can interpret everything he says in a negative way] (53). Ashkan, in turn, is provoked by Miriam's ignorance whenever he tries to discuss his project with her: 'Miriams aningslöshet när han frågade henne om det som pågår i Medelhavet irriterade honom' [Miriam's ignorance when he asked her about what was going on in the Mediterranean annoyed him] (59). While the protagonists, among themselves, pretend to uphold the appearance of harmony, the intricate play of focalisation, narrator commentary, free indirect discourse and brief interior monologues reveals the protagonists' actual opinions of each other. In addition, these narrative strategies display how, in the complex relations between these four characters, disparaging feelings such as irritation and anger emerge. From the outset, these negative feelings charge the situation affectively, and undermine the ostensible harmony by exposing it as false.

The text's structural composition emphasises this tension further, as it juxtaposes two obverse ways of migrating: Miriam and Filip's privileged, unhindered relocation from Stockholm to Sicily, and the fate of asylum seekers and undocumented migrants on Lampedusa. Ashkan's role in the text is that of a catalyst insofar as he highlights these tensions and provokes affective responses in Miriam and Filip regarding underprivileged 'others', and he compels them to position themselves with regard to feelings of guilt, shame or responsibility. In a conversation after dinner, Ashkan 'pratade om att det hade dött fyra tusen personer i Medelhavet förra året' [talked about how four thousand people had died in the Mediterranean last year] (67), and then goes on to mentioning that they 'tidigare under dagen badat i samma hav' [had swum in the same sea earlier in the day] (68). In this scene, irony is used to emphasise the incongruity between refugees swimming for their lives, and the four friends swimming for leisure. When Miriam considers herself confronted with a comparison between the fatal destiny of undocumented migrants and her own privileged position, she concedes 'att samtalet gjorde henne nedstämd' [that the conversation made her depressed] (68). Nevertheless, Miriam's vague feeling of unease is diminished by her self-absorption; a fact that Ashkan points towards when he provocatively asks Miriam about her knowledge 'om det som pågår där ute' [of what's going on out there] (50), and also when he says to himself, 'Antagligen var Miriam alltför fokuserad på dottern för att förstå frågan' [Miriam was probably far too focused on her daughter to understand the question] (59–60). While Ashkan's comment can be interpreted as cynical and disparaging about Miriam, his assumption is confirmed when the narrator focalises on Miriam and her reflections upon 'den stora flyktingströmmen' [the big stream of refugees]: 'Det har inte känts tillräckligt angeläget och dessutom har hon inte haft tid. [...] Hon är fortfarande osäker på vilken ö han menar' [It hasn't felt urgent enough and apart from that, she didn't have the time. [...] She's still not sure which island he means] (55–56). Miriam is presented as naïve and ignorant when she admits that the fate of refugees does not concern her, and when she cannot identify the island as Lampedusa; but she justifies her ignorance with the fact that she is too preoccupied to be able to engage affectively with anything other than her daughter. While this justification helps Miriam to assuage her guilty conscience, it also allows her to remain indifferent.

To assess Filip's affective response to Ashkan's provocation, Oxfeldt's critique of Pascal Bruckner's theory of reactions to guilt is particularly insightful. In his polemical publication *The Tyranny of Guilt*, Bruckner takes the generalising view that Europeans prefer 'guilt to responsibility' because 'the former is easier to bear'; Europeans, in Bruckner's opinion, are paralysed by guilt feelings about the past, which allows them to remain indifferent, and prevents responsible action in the present: 'moral and metaphysical culpability is used to elude any real political responsibility'. As a solution, Bruckner suggests that Europeans should aspire to the American model, and, instead of letting themselves be enslaved by guilt, defend traditional European values and embrace former victories, because, as Bruckner argues, 'it is better to praise the triumphs than the mourning', and, 'To the duty to remember we need to oppose the duty to our glories'.[21] Oxfeldt rightly points out that Bruckner's answer to guilt is problematic insofar as it represents an increasingly widespread attitude where, 'Man føler ikke skyld, men stolthet' [You do not feel guilt, but pride]: in a refusal of guilt, people assume responsibility 'i form av aggressivitet og selvhevdelse' [in the form of aggression and self-assertion] and insist that they 'har gjort seg fortjent til de privilegiene man har' [have earned the privileges they have].[22] Filip is a perfect example for this attitude. In his own view, he deserves his privileges, because he 'har arbetat hart för att husköpet ens skulle vara genomförbart' [has worked hard just to make the purchase of the house feasible] (54), and thus, as he states unambiguously, he refuses any feelings of guilt or shame; he 'orkar inte skämmas för att de har det bra här' [is unable to bring himself to feel ashamed that they are having a good time here] (53). Replacing a potential sense of guilt with pride does not lead to greater affective responsibility and ensuing pro-social action for Filip; pride allows him to stay indifferent towards those who suffer at the periphery of his immediate attention, and, in Filip's case, Bruckner's debatable theory does not hold true.

In much the same way as Miriam and Filip are self-absorbed, so is Mikkel, in *Opphold*, predominantly concerned about those emotionally closest to him: his absent wife, and his children. Obviously, Mikkel is in a situation of crisis after the disappearance of his wife Sylvia, and hence, he looks after his children's well-being, while he worries and reminisces about Sylvia. In the interest of his family, Mikkel outwardly disregards his own anxieties, or rather, tries not to show them to his children, which is evident when he states that, 'hver gang rastløsheten og fortvilelsen meldte seg, måtte jeg ta meg sammen' [every time the restlessness and despair set in, I had to pull myself together] (17). Mikkel acknowledges that it requires a considerable amount of effort to hold everything together, while he simultaneously points towards the vulnerability that Sylvia's absence produces in his family: 'Trekker meg opp, og videre, inn til ungene, det sårbare flertallet' [Pull myself up, and along, in to the kids, the vulnerable majority] (66). We ostensibly perceive a man who is physically and emotionally exhausted, but also a man who tries with effort to control those feelings which emerge in the void that his wife's disappearance has left in his life: fear, sorrow and anxiety. That Mikkel has to draw on his reserves of strength to do so suggests that the feelings he is trying to contain are overwhelmingly strong, so that Mikkel has hardly any empathic capacities left for anything beyond his immediate concerns, while the responsibility for his family, resting solely on his shoulders, bears down on him: 'Det er jeg som holder oss oppe, og sammen' [It's me who keeps us going and together] (73).

Considering the emotional strain caused by Mikkel's own worries, it is hardly surprising that he reacts with indifference towards the Javadi family when he becomes aware of their worries. Tellingly, it is the children who, without having learned prejudices (yet), strike up a connection over the border that separates them — the garden fence. Mitra, the youngest member of the Javadi family and of similar age as Mikkel's son Eivind, jolts Mikkel from his self-absorption, and, re-engaging with his surroundings, he reflects on the house on the other side of the fence: 'så lenge jeg kan huske har dette nabohuset vært bebodd av utlendinger som aldri blir værende over tid' [as long as I can remember, there have been foreigners living in the house next door, who have never stayed long]. Although Mikkel admits that he never became acquainted with any of the residents, he assumes that, 'Sannsynligvis har en del av dem vært asylsøkere' [Probably, some of them have been asylum seekers]. Without disclosing how, he identifies some of the former residents as Somalians and guesses, 'nå har de sannsynligvis fordufta igjen, de også' [now they, too, have probably bunked off] (25). Mikkel's reflections reveal the ignorance which has dominated his attitude towards the inhabitants of this house to date, and he presents himself as oblivious of asylum procedures when he assumes, with a derogatory word choice such as *fordufta* [bunked off] that the Somalians left of their own accord — it does not occur to him that they were most likely deported. Moreover, when Mikkel says that 'nå står det der [...] til villastrøkets store bekymring' [now it stands there [...] and bothers all the posh people in their nice houses] (25), the house, in a metonymic slide, comes to stand for its inhabitants, and Mikkel emphasises the hostile attitude of the whole neighbourhood towards asylum seekers. This attitude demonstrates how 'exclusionary norms' are constituted by 'fields of recognizability': in comparison with the (presumably white native) Norwegian residents of this affluent suburban area, the asylum seekers are underprivileged, and, judging by Mikkel's description, of colour.[23] When norms of social standing and racialised prejudices come to bear upon these asylum seekers, they are met with coldness, because they defy the norms of likeness available to the residents, and the mere existence of this house and its purpose undermine the social self-understanding of the whole neighbourhood.

When Mikkel says, 'det er det samme for meg hvem som bor der. Jeg har nok med jobben og flokken min' [it doesn't make any difference to me who lives there. I've got enough to do with my job and my flock] (26), he involuntarily assures the reader of his self-centredness and the concomitant indifference for those he perceives as strangers, while he simultaneously justifies his affective disinterest. Although Mikkel was indifferent towards the house's residents before the crisis in his family, he now emphasises that, in the present situation, his affective-empathic capacities are truly exhausted by those closest to him. Before Sylvia's disappearance, she and Mikkel, instead of engaging with the people beyond the garden fence, gave the house a nick name: 'Gjennomtrekket' (25).[24] By employing yet another metonymy, Sylvia and Mikkel use this term to bestow a particular quality upon the house, while the term actually describes the transitory and liminal status of its temporary residents. Simultaneously, the term denotes that asylum seekers can be kept at a distance, as they, despite their transitoriness, become arrested in this term, and fixed in their otherness. Stigmatised by a derogatory cipher, the asylum seekers become depersonalised and dehumanised, which, in turn, prevents Mikkel from engaging with them. Indifference emerges from the combination of two factors: Mikkel's own vulnerability instigated by a crisis in his family, and the fact that the asylum seekers' radical difference impedes the forming of emotional bonds and blocks Mikkel's empathy. However, as Butler asserts, 'Something exceeds the frame that troubles our sense of reality; in other words, something occurs that does not conform to our established understanding of things'.[25] Mitra does not conform to Mikkel's understanding that he does not have to show any affective responsibility towards his neighbours, because her appearance singles her out from the anonymous and universalised group of asylum seekers, and undercuts Mikkel's easy solution. Mitra's presence, and by extension that of the whole Javadi family, is corporeal and individualised instead of anonymous; this kind of presence demands recognition and prevents Mikkel from keeping the Javadi family out of his field of recognisability by means of marginalisation.

Both Mikkel in *Ophold* and Miriam in *De fördrivna* reason with themselves that their empathic capacities are under strain to justify why they remain indifferent, and therefore passive, towards underprivileged 'others'. In a similar vein, Rebecca, in *Politisk roman*, states that her affective capacities are exhausted by her personal life, and that she cannot engage affectively with anything that exceeds the scope of her family. Hence, when she compares her own emotional strain with her partner Robert's desire to hide an undocumented migrant in their flat, his idea appears preposterous to her: 'Jeg har nok at gøre med at holde sammen på mig selv. Jeg orker ikke flere personlige katastrofer' [I've got enough to do with keeping myself together. I can't take any more personal disasters] (6). Rebecca's remark acknowledges a vulnerability which, as it turns out, revolves around her relationship with her son Oskar, who, she notes, 'har [...] udvist en næsten hadefuld afsky over for mig' [has [...] shown an almost hateful disgust for me] (12), because he, in Rebecca's opinion, blames her for his father Theo having left them. Rebecca's vulnerability and affective preoccupation are reminiscent of the ways in which Mikkel's situation of crisis affectively overwhelms him. Unlike Mikkel, however, Rebecca does not feel the need to justify her indifference; and, while Miriam's indifference is accompanied by a feeling of unease, Rebecca's is not. Accordingly, Rebecca presents herself on the first page of the text as hard, cold and outright hostile to the suffering or distress of others when she opens her narrative with, 'En hjemløs har besluttet sig for at dø ved indgangen til Lidl' [A homeless person has decided to die in the entrance to Lidl] (5). Perceiving those who are vulnerable solely responsible for their own fate allows Rebecca to remain emotionally detached, and she can distance herself from any potential feelings of empathy for people who are ostensibly weaker, or less privileged, than herself. When Rebecca goes on to remark that the homeless person lacks 'evnen til at se sig selv udefra, ellers var han vel ikke endt sådan' [the ability to see himself from the outside, otherwise he would not have ended like this] (5), she presumes that a homeless person's appearance, and even their place of death, is a matter of freedom of decision, and therefore of agency, whereas, in fact, the opposite is more likely the case. In this sense, the text itself, from the very beginning, problematises indifference through irony, which emerges in the discrepancy between Rebecca's extreme views, and the harsh reality of homeless people.

Rebecca's callousness also extends into her personal life, which becomes evident when she states, 'Hver dag er en øvelse i at holde ud. Hverken Robert eller jeg orker endnu en gang at skulle finde nye partnere' [Every day is an exercise in endurance. Neither Robert nor I have the strength to find new partners again] (5). While Rebecca's tone suggests a degree of disillusionment, she also indicates that her relationship with Robert is a partnership of convenience by stating that it is too strenuous for her to find someone more suitable. Rebecca's emotional detachment is further underscored when she begins an affair with the neighbour, and when she, after the neighbour expresses romantic feelings for her, tells him that Robert is terminally ill, and comments, 'Heldigvis sætter min lille nødløgn gang i hans libido' [Luckily, my little white lie starts up his libido] (132). Rebecca lies to the man she has an affair with as a means to an end, and to her partner to maintain the status quo, and the reader perceives an ostensibly cold-hearted woman who uses people close to her to serve her purposes. When Rebecca states, 'Jeg dur ikke til at formulere mig om følelser' [I don't know how to express emotions] (6), she seemingly confirms her emotional detachment, and yet her attitude is somewhat hypocritical, considering that she repeatedly articulates those feelings Ngai calls 'explicitly amoral', and which offer 'no satisfaction of virtue'.[26] Rebecca expresses herself not through positive emotions, but through feelings of irritation and indifference, and presents herself to the reader as callous, insensitive and amoral; in short, she is not in the slightest inclined to engage affectively with the plights of others.

It is certainly correct that Rebecca's callousness has, as Oxfeldt points out, the function to 'forsvare noget, der er ved at bryde sammen' [defend something that is about to collapse], and that it can be seen as a mechanism to offset her concern for her son, and to counter her fear of losing him.[27] Nevertheless, I would argue that Rebecca's ostentatiously voiced indifference is, more often than not, an expression of her right-wing politics, and of her exclusionary and racist views on migrants. Hence, it is not surprising that she opposes Robert's plan to hide an undocumented migrant in their flat; and indeed, her immediate reaction is to say that she 'ikke bryder [sig] om at have fremmede boende' [doesn't like having foreigners living in her home] (9). Rebecca's xenophobia turns into outright racism when she finally meets Amir, and remarks that he 'har en ansigtskulør, der unægtelig er endnu værre' [has a complexion that is undeniably even worse] (15) than that of the intermediary who brought Amir into their flat. Rebecca's resentment is further emphasised when she states that she 'ikke gider have myndighederne på nakken, fordi han [Robert] skal dulme sin samvittighed' [doesn't feel like having the authorities on her back, because he [Robert] wants to soothe his guilty conscience] (9). Rebecca admits that she is relatively unperturbed by feelings of guilt when she says, 'Af og til får jeg dårlig samvittighed over ikke at have dårlig samvittighed, men det er en flygtig følelse' [Sometimes I feel guilty for not having a guilty conscience, but it is a fleeting feeling] (5). Therefore, she cannot understand Robert's urge to act out of a sense of guilt, and, from her viewpoint, Robert's desire to help Amir is self-centred, and Amir is turned into what Ahmed calls a 'happiness means': 'If objects provide a means for making us happy, then in directing ourselves toward this or that object, we are aiming somewhere else: toward a happiness that is presumed to follow'.[28] When Rebecca blames Robert for wanting to soothe his feelings of guilt, she points out that Robert's help, instead of being directed towards Amir, is actually aimed at his own needs and a near future in which he hopes to feel happy because his guilt is ameliorated, whereas Amir becomes objectified in the process. Robert's daughter Martha confirms this when she considers her father's empathy as excessive, and the resulting political activism as misguided: 'Jeg mener, hvorfor skal du altid overdrive din sympati for de svage, hvorfor kan du ikke bare lave noget frivilligt lortearbejde ligesom alle andre' [I mean, why do you always have to exaggerate your sympathy for the weak, why can't you do some shitty volunteer job like everyone else] (17). In Martha's view, at least the family's status quo would remain unchallenged if only Robert would content himself with insignificant action to feel good about himself. Martha exposes Robert's supposedly empathic attitude as sanctimonious, and, when she accuses the majority of Danes of the same hypocrisy, she ridicules a genuine sense of Scandinavian Guilt by suggesting that activism stemming from guilt is, most frequently, done 'selfishly for the appearance of concern', instead of selflessly, and out of concern for others.[29]

Robert's purportedly liberal mindset is further ridiculed when Rebecca derides him for his 'politisk korrekte linsesuppe' [politically correct lentil soup] (56) and his opinion that Lidl is 'et politisk ukorrekt lavprissupermarked' [a politically incorrect discount supermarket] (45). While Rebecca's critique of Robert underscores her own indifference and political incorrectness, the text contrasts two opposing political attitudes. These attitudes are primarily rendered through Rebecca's mordant tone, and by employing a narrative voice which articulates itself through disproportionate and hyperbolic statements, Aburas satirises both Rebecca's conservative attitude and Robert's liberal one. Rebecca and Robert, however, have one point of agreement: they are both of the opinion that there is something wrong with the Danish welfare state. But as their political stances diverge, the Danish state is criticised from a conservative and, simultaneously, a liberal point of view. Rebecca teaches geography at an adult education centre, and, condescendingly assuming that the majority of her course participants are 'arbejdsløse, tvunget herhen af deres sagsbehandlere' [unemployed, forced here by their case workers], which, in her view, explains their 'generelle uvilje til at presse sig selv' [general unwillingness to push themselves], she says, 'Var det ikke for velfærdsstaten, der med sin forfejlede kærlighed holder hånden under os alle, var de for længst gået til' [If it wasn't for the welfare state, which, with its misguided love, protects us all, they would have been long gone] (13). Rebecca's assertion coheres with her previous remark regarding the homeless person, in which she contends that everyone is solely responsible for their own fate, notwithstanding any vulnerabilities or weaknesses. With respect to her course participants, she suggests that the Danish welfare state is responsible for facilitating and prolonging their ostensibly unmotivated passivity, and that they, without state support, could not be as unambitious as she perceives them to be.

From Rebecca's point of view, the Danish welfare state is protective of people whom she considers disinclined to work, whereas Robert deems the Danish welfare state too exclusionary with regard to immigration politics and in need of political transformation. Thus, he considers his idea to help Amir not only as altruistic, but also, and more importantly, as a revolutionary political act. When Robert states, 'Jeg vil forme vores land på den rigtige måde' [I want to shape our country in the right way] (14), he indicates that he perceives his action as politically subversive, and that it will expedite some sort of political renewal, but he does not clarify what exactly he would like to change. Rebecca points towards the naivety in Robert's self-image as a political activist when she states, 'Robert lever gerne i troen på, at man kan være en overprivilegeret nar, samtidig med at man påvirker samfundet i en såkaldt undergravende retning' [Robert wants to live in the belief that you can be an overprivileged fool, while at the same time influencing society in a so-called subversive way] (57). Robert's political idealism appears to be absurd and laughable in its aimless and unreasonable self-importance, and when it is further ridiculed by Rebecca, satire is produced through Rebecca's hyperbolic caustic voice, and also through the contrast between Rebecca's callousness and Robert's hypocrisy. This form of satire, as a literary device, distances the reader from both Rebecca's conservative attitude and Robert's supposedly liberal stance, and, while the text's characters and their actions are ridiculed, very little is said about Amir himself, as the refugee in the family's midst remains mute, and is overlooked and marginalised by Robert and Rebecca in their self-centred concerns. By visualising the incongruity between this self-centredness and Amir's invisibility, satire in Aburas's text draws attention to contextual frameworks, and the reader is asked to consider whether there is a type of political or pro-social action better suited to the needs of refugees than the characters' misguided responses.

All three texts portray protagonists who are too preoccupied with their own lives to have the empathic capacities to engage with anything beyond their immediate concerns. They are confronted with 'others' who are in various degrees of spatial distance from themselves: for Filip and Miriam in *De fördrivna*, the migrants are an anonymous mass mentioned only by Ashkan, and not even on the same island; for Mikkel in *Opphold*, the Javadi family are over the border of the garden fence; and in *Politisk roman*, the undocumented migrant Amir enters the personal space of Rebecca and Robert's family by living in their home. Despite these various spatial relations, the protagonists' affective responses are not dissimilar: apart from Robert in *Politisk roman*, the protagonists in all three texts utilise their personal preoccupations either to appease their guilty consciences, or to justify to themselves that they remain indifferent towards the needs and suffering of those they encounter. When they are too engrossed in their own lives and families to be able to engage affectively with 'others', we can ask whether or not the protagonists' affective responses change once the contact with those 'others' becomes intensified.

Indifference: Interrupted or Reaffirmed?

In *De fördrivna*, Ashkan accuses Miriam of being 'ett lysande exempel på vit melankoli' [a shining example of white melancholy] (68), and, explaining the term to her, he adds, 'Vit melankoli är när vita personer får höra talas om de orättvisor som sker i världen till följd av våra olika hudfärger och reagerar med att känna sig ledsna och nedstämda över att en mer okomplicerad tid är förbi' [White melancholy is when white people hear about the injustices which happen in the world because of our different skin colours and react with feeling sad and depressed that a simpler time has passed] (68). Although Ashkan uses the term 'white melancholy' as a definition for an emotional state of white people in general, it can be directly related to the concept of Scandinavian Guilt, as it is similar to the way in which Scandinavian Guilt exhibits a feeling of unease 'overfor en global, lidende Annen' [towards a global, suffering Other].[30] Ashkan's definition, however, indicates that this feeling of unease is by no means altruistic, but rather self-centred because it implies the bemoaning of a less complicated time. In a particularly Swedish context, Tobias Hübinette and Catrin Lundström argue that this less complicated time refers to a double bind of seemingly incompatible perceptions of an old Sweden as a homogeneous, white society, and of a progressive Sweden as a country of anti-racism, gender equality and feminism. The advocates of both camps see their images of Sweden threatened by 'the recent influx and contemporary presence of non-white and non-Western migrants', which has led to a situation in which conservatives mourn the loss of a white, homogeneous Sweden, whereas progressive people regret that Sweden has lost its leading position and image of being the most liberal country in the world, because the cultural differences of some migrants supposedly contaminate this image. Therefore, conservative and progressive Swedes are equally 'yearning to return to the safe days of white homogeneity when it was easier to be either a racist or an anti-racist', because those perceived as 'other' were not within Swedish national borders.[31] Now, in times of cultural flux, accelerated globalisation and immigration, otherness is visible *in situ*, which makes it all the more difficult to remain indifferent. This leads to mourning for the loss of a time in which it was easier to find justification for not engaging with racialised others, and to absolve oneself from responsibility simply because those 'others' were of no immediate concern.

When Ashkan accuses Miriam of suffering from white melancholy, she does not even live in Sweden, and yet, she bemoans that it is impossible for her to disengage from the distress of refugees on Lampedusa when she states that Ashkan's account 'är jobbigt att höra' [is painful to hear], and that she 'blir så fruktansvärt illa berörd' [is so badly affected] (68). Nevertheless, Ashkan's deliberate provocations rouse Miriam from her drug-infused indifference, and she feels not only uneasy or depressed, but also guilty in relation to those suffering 'others', despite the fact that she is affectively preoccupied with her daughter. This guilt inspires Miriam to read an arbitrary selection of articles about undocumented migrants and a book Ashkan leaves for her.[32] At the same time, Miriam is overcome with 'en planlöshet [...] [e]n handfallenhet' [an aimlessness [...] [a] helplessness] (126), which indicates that she finds herself in a situation of 'conspicuous inactivity' which remains 'affectively charged' as it produces 'the inherently ambiguous affect of affective disorientation': Miriam is in 'a state of feeling vaguely "unsettled" or "confused"', and thus she does not know how to put her sense of guilt into practice.[33] While Miriam gains greater knowledge about refugees on an abstract level, it becomes apparent that her approach lacks practical implementations when her theoretical knowledge clashes with reality. On the way to the beach, Miriam stops her car to buy sandwiches at a shop located among greenhouses and recalls an article: 'Hon har läst om hur de afrikanska migranternas arbetsförhållanden är slavlika, att de sover och äter i växthusen' [She has read that the working conditions for African migrants are slave-like, that they sleep and eat in the greenhouse]; and, 'När Miriam vänder sig om [...] står där en ung afrikansk man. [...] De ser på varandra; han uttryckslöst, hon förvirrat' [When Miriam turns around [...] there is a young African man standing there. [...] They look at each other; he blankly, she confused] (139). When the man turns his back and walks away from her, Miriam shouts after him in English, 'Sir, I'm sorry!' (140). This scene substantiates Miriam's feeling of guilt, but it also illustrates how diffuse this sense of guilt is, as we never learn what Miriam is actually sorry for. This encounter certainly instigates some sort of vague ethical imperative in Miriam, the feeling that she should do something, but as she does not know what, her compassion becomes interfused with confusion and helplessness, and she is held in a state of affective ambiguity. Discussing compassion in a humanitarian context, Devika Sharma argues that 'compassion is, in its very structure, an asymmetrical feeling that is typically directed downwards in social and geopolitical hierarchies'. If we assume that Miriam feels sorry for the fate she ascribes to the African man, her compassion highlights and reinforces these geopolitical hierarchies, as she feels compassion from a subject position, which places the recipient of her compassion in an object position. Miriam's compassion 'does not serve as a counterweight to suffering and injustice', but instead, it sheds light on the contemporary global contrasts between privileged and non-privileged migration: Miriam assumes that the African man has to work under slave-like conditions because he lacks the legal documentation for immigration, such as a visa, a passport and a work permit, whereas she migrated to Sicily unhindered, with the appropriate documentation, and the financial means to buy a house and build a life there.[34]

Despite the fact that Filip, unlike Miriam, does not display feelings of guilt or compassion, let alone the need for pro-social action, he accompanies Ashkan to the island of Lampedusa. While Ashkan conducts research for his article, Filip sits on the terrace of a restaurant, with Campari and cigarettes, and wonders,

> Inga turister. Och vad skulle de göra på den här avlägset belägna ön med dåligt rykte? [...] Han kan inte tänka sig hur de illa rustade båtarna med flyktingar kan ta sig iland här. Båtarna måste krossas mot klipporna. [...] Första klunken och första blosset är den perfekta kombinationen.
>
> [No tourists. And what would they do anyway on this remote island with a bad reputation? [...] He can't imagine how the poorly equipped boats full of refugees are supposed to land here. The boats will surely be wrecked on the rocks [...] The first swig and the first drag are the perfect combination.] (86)

It crosses Filip's mind briefly that many of the refugees who try to reach Lampedusa in their inadequate boats die, but instead of being affected by this in any way, he views this fact as a disadvantage for Lampedusa as a tourist destination. This scene juxtaposes Filip's reality with that of the refugees insofar as he acknowledges the

death of a large number of refugees, while he sets his own immediate priorities —
the perfect combination of drinking and smoking.

Filip maintains his indifference to the violent events outside his safe environment
by turning a blind eye, a gesture which Slavoj Žižek calls 'fetishist disavowal' and
explains with: 'I know it, but I refuse to fully assume the consequences of this
knowledge, so that I can continue acting as if I don't know it'.[35] Filip can remain
unaffected by virtue of this fetishist disavowal and enjoy the trip to Lampedusa
as a short bourgeois break from parental duties; he is content to be '[e]nsam och
berusad och snart mätt' [[a]lone and inebriated and soon full] (100). Dying people
in his vicinity cannot spoil Filip's leisurely afternoon, which underscores both
Filip's indifference, and the refugees' marginalisation. This discrepancy becomes
even more pronounced when Filip 'tar fram en skissbok ur innerfickan och tecknar
snabbt av tallriken med det som återstår av fisken och i bakgrunden vinglaset och
den tomma vinflaskan' [takes out a sketch book from his inner pocket and quickly
draws the plate with the remains of the fish, the wine glass and the empty wine
bottle in the background] (100), while Ashkan takes pictures of the graveyard and
'båtkyrkogården' [the boat graveyard] (92). Here, the text invites the reader to
reimagine Filip's drawings of his late lunch and Ashkan's photographs of graveyards,
and when these visual images take form in the mind of the reader, the contrast
between them illustrates the aforementioned geopolitical inequality, and highlights
once more the disparity between privileged and unprivileged migration.

In yet another juxtaposition of stark contrasts, Ashkan finds the graveyard where
refugees are buried: 'Bakom en vägg med kryptor och gravar där färggranna
plastblommor och sirliga namn- och datuminskriptioner pryder stenarna ligger
de anonyma flyktingarnas gravar. Enkla träkors eller betonggjutna stenar med ett
nummer, och i ett fåtal fall en årtalsmarkering' [Behind a wall with crypts and
graves where colourful plastic flowers and dainty inscriptions of names and dates
adorn the headstones lie the graves of the anonymous refugees. Simple wooden
crosses or stones cast in concrete with a number, and — in a few cases — a year]
(93). Decorated and personalised graves are contrasted with those of the refugees,
which are spatially marginalised and remain anonymous. The arrangement of these
personalised and anonymous graves substantiates Butler's argument that 'there is
no life and no death without a relation to some frame'. When, as Butler asserts,
'grievability is a presupposition for the life that matters', these graves bear witness
to the fact that lives have been lost under conditions in which they were treated as
if they did not matter. Since the refugees who have died remain anonymous, they
cannot be mourned individually in this graveyard, and the lives themselves become
devalued, as if they have not been lived at all, which means that the 'ontological
status' of these refugees 'is compromised and suspended'. Even in death, the
refugees have fallen out of their former frames and networks, while they are socially
and politically unrecognised by new frames. These refugees became 'differentially
exposed to injury, violence, and death', as their lives did not receive what they
needed to be sustained as lives.[36]

Making her case for the concept of a relational ontology, Butler argues that
a sense of precariousness is ontological to all human beings, because we are

'fundamentally dependent on, and conditioned by, a sustained and sustainable world'.[37] On the premise of this dependency, Butler develops an ethical imperative, or rather, an ethical responsiveness towards others from which responsibility and pro-social action may follow. When environments and institutions fail to sustain human life, Butler considers it necessary to 'focus not just on the value of this or that life, or on the question of survivability in the abstract, but on the sustaining social conditions of life'.[38] Implicitly engaging with the lack of such sustaining conditions, Federica Mazzara challenges the discursive association of refugees on Lampedusa with the notion of 'crisis', and questions 'the socio-political construction of [refugees] as illegal and irregular'. When, as Mazzara argues, the influx of refugees on Lampedusa is publicly treated as 'a narrative of "emergency"', this kind of discourse constructs refugees as a threat by viewing them as 'an invasion of desperate and potentially dangerous masses that are destabilizing the order of well-delimited and protected national spaces', and it hinders the formation of alliances which could lead to life-sustaining measures.[39] When the graveyard of refugees is seen as a metaphor, it illustrates the drastic consequences for human lives when affective responses, instead of leading to pro-social action, consolidate exclusionary discourses and practices. Hence, *De fördrivna* engages in fictional form with the socio-political construction of refugees as illegal by illuminating their politically induced precarity.

★   ★   ★   ★   ★

Filip's disconnection from the fate of refugees is made easy insofar as they are in his vicinity, though as yet, for him at least, an anonymous mass. For Mikkel in *Opphold*, an affective disengagement from the Javadi family is harder, because they are spatially closer, and, initiated by the little girl Mitra, humanised and personalised. When Mitra's mother Afsoon rings Mikkel's doorbell to introduce herself, his reaction suggests that he considers his insularity invaded: he 'går noen skritt tilbake' [takes a few steps backwards] and realises that he is 'sikkert en anelse reservert' [clearly being a little offish] (39). Nevertheless, Mikkel asks her politely if he can help, and although Afsoon replies that she just wanted to say hello, he can see 'at det er noe hun trenger' [that there is something she needs] (39) — something he is not able or willing to give, judging by his reservation. Once again, it happens to be one of the children who manages to reach beyond Mikkel's indifference when he spontaneously invites Mitra's older brother Amir 'over til vår side av gjerdet' [over to our side of the fence] (56). Once Amir crosses the border of the garden fence, he helps Mikkel to bury a dead swan, and Mikkel, taken by surprise, states: 'jeg merker plutselig en varme for gutten' [I suddenly feel a warmth for the boy] (56–57). In this instance, when Amir is recognised by Mikkel as an individual human being, affect is the force that opens up a dynamic 'space of transformational encounter', in which Mikkel's initial indifference and formerly rigid boundaries become porous.[40] In a Deleuzian-nomadic approach to the political, Rosi Braidotti argues that the political can be viewed as a 'counter-actualisation of alternative states of affairs', and, as Braidotti goes on to say, 'Based on the principle that we do not know what a body can do, the becoming-political ultimately aims at transformations in the very structures of subjectivity'.[41] In this respect, the brief affectively charged moment between Mikkel and Amir holds a political, or micro-political, potential, for when Mikkel's indifference becomes displaced, the structures of his own subjectivity may change in the same way that his boundaries of sameness and otherness may be realigned, which, for Mikkel, affords the opportunity for new alliances with hitherto unrecognised strangers.

Mikkel's ensuing struggle, however, illustrates how difficult it is to maintain these counter-actualisations, as he is caught in conflicting affective responses towards the Javadi family: he has the desire to stay indifferent because his affective capacities are already strained, and yet, he cannot help but feel compassion, and the ethical imperative that he should do something. The term compassion is deliberately chosen because Mikkel's compassion encapsulates a hierarchy similar to that of Miriam's when she apologises to the African man. In both cases, compassion denotes 'privilege; the sufferer is *over there*'. For Mikkel, the Javadi family are 'over there' when they are over the garden fence, in an 'object position', and Mikkel's compassion flows unidirectionally from his 'subject position'. Although he is by no means in a neutral state himself, the Javadi family are, arguably, worse off, and thus, the term 'compassion' comprises the hierarchy which characterises the relationship between Mikkel and the Javadi family. Moreover, as Mikkel's priority lies with his own family, the distress of the Javadi family produces 'a desire to withhold compassionate attachment'.[42] The only reason why Mikkel does not turn his back is that Mitra's initial border crossing serves Mikkel's self-interest and care for his family: 'Sånn sett var det et sjakktrekk å få Mitra over gjerdet og inn i vår hage, og det er vel en slags lykke jeg kjenner akkurat nå ved tanken på at disse to har en sånn kontakt' [Actually, it was a clever move to get Mitra over the fence and into our garden, and right now, I feel a kind of joy at the thought that these two have such a good connection] (67). Mikkel experiences joy because his son's friendship with Mitra distracts the boy from the absence of his mother. Through the gradual approximation of his own and the Javadi family, Mikkel comes to realise that the Javadi family are less different from himself than he originally assumed asylum seekers to be, especially considering that he, at least to date, has simultaneously captured and distanced them in the term *gjennomtrekket*. When the three children of the Javadi family are gathered in his kitchen, Mikkel is surprised that they 'snakker så godt som perfekt norsk' [speak virtually perfect Norwegian] (83), and that they have decidedly Norwegian preferences when it comes to traditional Norwegian food such as waffles: 'med brunost' [with brown cheese] (Mitra), 'med jordbærsyltetøy' [with strawberry jam] (Amir), and 'rømme' [cream] (Lila) (83). This mundane scene illustrates how approximation is a two-way process in which Mikkel's norms of recognisability become displaced. Mikkel still operates within a framework of sameness and difference when he maps the children of the Javadi family against his own cultural norms; nonetheless, as those he regards as other are not that 'other' after all, Mikkel's framework may change, because it is now open to the potential inclusion of those who were previously excluded because of their otherness.

The repositioning of the Javadi family within frames of sameness and difference, however, does not prevent Mikkel's intention of distancing himself from the Javadi family's vulnerability and distress. When he realises that '[d]et er noe Afsoon trenger å prate om' [there is something Afsoon needs to talk about] but appreciates that Afsoon 'ikke er av dem som presser seg på' [is not the sort to push herself on you] (68), he feels bad 'for the sufferers, but only so that they will go away quickly'.[43] Yet, some information transgresses Mikkel's deliberately retained indifference, and he learns, 'Det aller viktigste for dem er å få oppholdstillatelse i Norge [...] Hun nevnte [...] at de har anket, og at dette er en vanskelig tid for dem' [What's most important for them is to get a residence permit in Norway [...] She mentioned [...] that they have appealed and that it is a difficult time for them] (68–69). Mikkel himself is going through a difficult time, and therefore, he proclaims: 'Jeg orker ikke å bekymre meg for familien Javadi også' [I'm not able to worry about the Javadi family, too] (69). Although Mikkel repeatedly tries to convince himself, and simultaneously the reader, that his affective capacities are exhausted, he reveals that his indifference is infiltrated by compassion, and a sense of guilt, when he says, 'I det hele tatt er det mye jeg burde ha foretatt meg for denne familien, men det holder med hjem og jobb' [All in all, I should have done much more for this family, but I've got enough on my plate with home and work] (96). Mikkel's affective state resembles that of Miriam in De fördrivna, as he also finds himself in a situation of 'affective disorientation', which leads to affective ambiguity: he feels compassion, but as he sees himself unable to help, guilt emerges, and, at the same time, the wish to withdraw his compassion.[44] If Mikkel's inner ethical imperative would only allow him, he would prefer 'to turn away quickly and harshly'.[45]

To silence this ethical imperative, Mikkel defers responsibility: 'Jeg må bare kunne stole på at [...] de rette myndigheter [...] tar sin del av ansvaret' [I just have to trust that [...] the right authorities [...] take on their share of responsibility] (96); but the authorities Mikkel relies on for being the responsible party in his stead disappoint his expectations. Mikkel asks Afsoon about their situation and immediately 'angrer [...] spørsmålet' [regrets [...] the question]; Afsoon tells him that, 'Vi har fått avslag. Vi er ikke syke nok, ikke opposisjonelle nok, ikke tilstrekkelig forfulgte. [...] Vi klarte ikke å si det tydelig nok, Mikkel, hvor redde vi er' [We've been rejected. We're not sick enough, not oppositional enough, not persecuted enough [...] We didn't manage to say it clearly enough, Mikkel, how scared we are] (115). Mikkel's question and his concomitant regret illustrate that he is torn between compassion, and the desire to withhold this compassion. He is already affectively implicated in the lives of the Javadi family, but he tries nevertheless to attenuate the impact of witnessing their distress by justifying his ostensible indifference yet again with his own preoccupation: 'Noe i meg har ikke plass. Ikke til dette, for jeg [...] eier ingen ekstra rom, og alt Afsoon forteller meg gjennomsyres av en virkelighet jeg ikke kan ta inn, ikke nå, jeg har også et liv' [Something in me doesn't have enough space. Not for this, because I [...] don't have any extra space, and everything Afsoon tells me is coloured by a reality I can't take in, not now, I've also got a life] (116). Looking at his own life and that of the Javadi family side by side, Mikkel argues that he first has to take care of his family before he can look after others, and he withdraws his affective engagement, creating a schism in his responsibility, or what Butler calls 'a differential at the level of affective and moral responsiveness'. When, as Butler suggests, 'responsibility requires responsiveness', this differential arises because we can only respond 'to what is before us with the resources that are available to us'.[46] Mikkel's resources are exhausted, and thus, his humanity becomes divided between those for whom he feels urgent concern, and those whose lives do not touch him; or so he tries to convince himself.

Eventually, Mikkel's conflicting affective responses converge into compassion once he realises that the fate of the Javadi family has a direct impact on his own family: 'Så slår det ned [...] Dette rammer også oss. Mitra. Utsendelsen. Eivind' [Then it hits me [...] This also affects us. Mitra. The deportation. Eivind] (120). The Javadi family are threatened with deportation because exclusionary immigration politics consider their lives not precarious enough to be sustained by the Norwegian state, which, contradictorily, only reinforces their precarity. Witnessing this precarity helps Mikkel to overcome his indifference, and, although triggered by a self-serving concern for his children, his compassion becomes unblocked. He feels 'the obligation to recognize and alleviate suffering',[47] and compassion becomes translated into affective responsibility and the ethical imperative to do something: 'Noe jeg må gjøre. For dem. For familien Javadi. For oss. Gjøre. Gjøre. Utføre. Handle' [I have to do something. For them. For the Javadi family. For us. Get my act together. Do something. Do something. Do it. Act] (123). When, as Berlant argues, compassion implies 'a social relation [...] with the emphasis on the spectator's experience of feeling compassion and its subsequent relation to material practice', Mikkel's emotions move him towards the Javadi family and inspire him to alleviate their distress: the potential loss of the Javadi children and the concomitant consequences for the well-being of his own children spur his affective agency.[48] However, the question remains how Mikkel is supposed to translate his emotions into practice: is there something he can effectively do to support the Javadi family, and prevent their deportation?

★   ★   ★   ★   ★

In *Politisk roman*, the spatial distance between the Scandinavian protagonists and the 'other' is even further reduced than in *De fördrivna* and *Opphold* when Robert moves Amir into the same flat where he lives with his family. Therefore, the individual family members are compelled to position themselves affectively in one way or another to this proximity, and, as discussed previously, Rebecca's initial response is indifference and irritation. This irritation, however, is not only caused by Amir himself, but also stems from the fact that Robert does not include her in his decision-making process. Although Rebecca expresses her objections, Robert, clarifying that her opinion does not count, says, 'Du kan tage på hotel, eller du kan lade være, men jeg agter at gøre det' [You can go to a hotel or stay here, but I have every intention of doing this] (14). When Robert informs Rebecca that Amir is supposed to stay with them until 'politikerne er mindre fjendtligt indstillede over for flygtningene' [the politicians are less hostile towards refugees], she fears that she cannot escape Amir's obtrusive alterity: 'Det kan [...] tage år, før vi igen slipper af med denne Amir' [It could [...] take years before we get rid of this Amir again] (16). It seems absurd that Robert would hide an undocumented migrant in their home until the political climate has changed at an indeterminable time in the future; at the same time, this absurdity brings the social reality of refugees into clear focus. Rebecca anticipates that exclusionary Danish immigration politics may interfere with her personal life, whereas actually, it is Amir's life that is most impinged upon. Construed as an 'illegal' immigrant by hostile politics, and treated with hostility by Rebecca, Amir is made to feel most unwelcome and held in a liminal status that only his deportation could end, the constant threat of which is looming large.

Robert, together with his friend Mark, hurls himself into activism that is supposed to provide assistance for Amir in his precarious situation. In fact, however, this activism is Robert and Mark's means to demonstrate their supposedly revolutionary left-wing politics, which they ostentatiously express with platitudes such as, 'Nu er det bare at håbe på, at hele skidtet kollapser, så vi kan starte noget nyt' [Now we just hope that the whole shit collapses so that we can start something new] (57). Mark, a writer, proposes the idea to collate some of his political, and, in his opinion, subversive, texts into a pamphlet, and to support Amir, he intends to link the purchase of the pamphlet to the condition that 'man forpligter sig til at give Amir en skærv eller en eller anden form for oplevelse. En tur i biffen, et måltid mad' [you commit to giving Amir some spare change, or some form of experience. A trip to the cinema, a meal] (114–15). While it is usually Rebecca who, with her scathing comments, underscores the hypocrisy in Robert and Mark's political activism, it is, in this case, Oskar's friend Florian who comments on Mark's plan, pointing out how ridiculous it is: 'Amir er under jorden, ikke? Så skal han da ikke gå på restaurant eller i biografen med alle mulige mennesker. Så er han jo ligesom ikke særlig hemmelig længere' [Amir is underground, right? So he shouldn't go to the restaurant or the cinema with all sorts of people. He just wouldn't be very hidden any more] (115). In addition, the teenager Florian demonstrates surprising acumen when he points out that Robert and Mark's activism, instead of increasing Amir's agency, takes decisions over his life out of his hands, and therefore patronises and disempowers Amir in the same way exclusionary immigration politics do: 'I har sgu umyndiggjort ham [...] Ligesom systemet før jer' [You have disenfranchised him [...] Just like the system before you] (116).

During the course of the complex interactions between these family members and their friends, the reader sees little of Amir other than him being the trigger for their contentions and becoming disempowered while they are fought out. Only in passing comments do we learn that Amir is a sophisticated man who reads Charles Dickens' *Bleak House* while he lives in the family's study, is educated in art history, and worked as a museum inspector before his flight, whereas in Rebecca's racist rhetoric, Amir is merely 'en halvgammel araber' [a middle-aged Arab] (35). It is hardly surprising that the reader is given little information about Amir himself, considering that all we know about him comes from Rebecca's standpoint of callous indifference, and that she, in line with exclusionary immigration politics and their marginalisation of refugees, would prefer Amir to be inaudible and invisible: 'For min skyld kunne han godt tilbringe mere tid på sit værelse med at glo på Al Jazeera' [For my sake, he could spend more time in his room and goggle at Al Jazeera] (62). As a consequence of her indifference, Rebecca has no interest in engaging with Amir's personal history, so that she does not want to know 'hvorfor Amir absolut må omtale sin søn i datid' [why Amir has to mention his son in the past tense] and is relieved when he falls silent. While Rebecca substantiates her callousness yet again, the children enter into contact with Amir without the adults' prejudices, so that it is eleven-year-old Sally who confronts the adults with details of Amir's son and his violent death: 'Det var et sandt slagtehus. Regeringshæren skød på alt, hvad der bevægede sig. Ingen blev skånet' [It was like a slaughterhouse. The government army shot everything that moved. Nobody was spared] (77). Nevertheless, Rebecca remains indifferent, whereas the knowledge about Amir's son explains why Amir appears depressed; why he mostly sits on the mattress in his room, smoking cigarettes.

To borrow Ahmed's term, Amir can be viewed as the 'melancholic migrant', who '"holds onto" an object that has been lost, who does not let go, or get over loss by letting go of it', and whose happiness is thus prevented. Additionally, Ahmed points out that, 'The sorrow of the stranger might give us a different angle on happiness not because it teaches us what it is like or must be like to be a stranger, but because it might estrange us from the very happiness of the familiar'.[49] Because of Rebecca's indifference, Amir's sorrow cannot touch her, and therefore, she resists learning what it must be like to be a stranger. Moreover, Rebecca is not happy in her familiar surroundings in the first place; or, as Oxfeldt puts it, 'Hun føler sig ikke lykkelig i de sammenhænge, hvor det forventes' [She does not feel happy in those contexts where it is expected], such as her partnership with Robert, or her relationship with her son Oskar, and thus, Amir's unhappiness cannot estrange her from her own supposed happiness.[50] On the contrary, Amir's sorrow for the loss of his son resonates with Rebecca's fear of losing Oskar, and hence, her indifference assists Rebecca in keeping her own anxieties at bay. Oskar's friendship with Amir, however, fuels Rebecca's trepidations, and when she finds a string of prayer beads in Oskar's room, she confronts her son and asks, 'Og hvad med Amir? [...] Han sætter ikke griller i hovedet på dig?' [And what about Amir? [...] He doesn't put any ideas in your head?]. Adding Islamophobia to the list of her prejudices, Rebecca gives voice to her fear that Oskar might be influenced to embrace religious extremism. Nevertheless, when Oskar answers her confrontational question with, 'Manden er ensom' [The man is lonely], and she responds with, 'Det er jeg også' [Me too] (120), Rebecca indicates that she is jealous that Oskar has a closer and less complicated relationship with Amir than with herself. Moreover, her response confirms that she is estranged from happiness, and that she, at least to a certain extent, considers Oskar already lost to her.

We can see that Robert's and Rebeca's affective responses to Amir focus predominantly on themselves instead of on Amir's needs, but this self-centredness also blinds them to their own children's health, so that Amir is the only one who understands what is wrong with Martha when she collapses in the bathroom. When Amir tells Rebecca, 'Hun er syg [...] Jeg hørte hende kaste op for lidt siden' [She's ill [...] I heard her throw up a while ago] (73), he identifies Martha's condition as anorexia, while Rebecca explained Martha's rapid weight loss to herself with 'et højt stofskifte' [a high metabolism] (75). Martha is committed to a hospital, where Robert, hugging Martha, 'begynder at småsnøfte igen' [begins to sniff again] (87), and Rebecca comments, 'Det er alt sammen meget rørende' [It's all very touching] (76), while she also states that she does not know 'hvad jeg skal gøre af mig selv' [what to do with myself] (86). This scene in the hospital substantiates Oxfeldt's observation that, in *Politisk roman*, 'de stereotype kønsroller er vendt på hovedet' [the stereotypical gender roles are turned on their head] insofar as Rebecca is hard, cynical and exclusive, while the men — at least on the surface — are open and inclusive: Robert expresses his emotions, whereas Rebecca is unable to cope with a situation that would require empathy with her partner and his daughter, and she reverts to cynical commentary.[51] Nevertheless, when Amir collapses in his room, it is Rebecca who saves his life, because she is the only one present who knows how 'at give hjertemassage og kunstigt åndedræt' [to give a cardiac massage and rescue breathing] (134), and she describes

> Mine læber er allerede samlet som en tragt, da jeg presser mit ansigt ned mod hans og blæser kraftige rytmiske pust af luft ned i hans lunger, mens jeg overvinder afskyen og ikke mindst det kejtede i at ånde en fremmed mand i munden.
>
> [My lips are already pursed like a funnel when I push my face down to his and blow strong rhythmic breaths of air into his lungs while I overcome the disgust and, not least, the awkwardness of breathing into the mouth of a strange man.] (135)

Seeing Amir poised between life and death suspends Rebecca's indifference momentarily, and it compels her to conquer such unprestigious feelings as disgust. Oxfeldt's analysis of this situation is to the point when she argues, 'I et kort øjeblik kan Rebecca ikke være indifferent, men tvinges til at handle og hjælpe. Hun kommer tæt på Amir i et sårbart øjeblik og erfarer hans menneskelighed' [For an instant, Rebecca cannot be indifferent, but is forced to act and help. She comes close to Amir in a vulnerable moment and experiences his humanity].[52] Amir's humanity enters through the cracks in Rebecca's hardened indifference, and she sidesteps her usual affective response to suffering. Like Amir Javadi and Mikkel in *Opphold*, Rebecca enters a space where the structures of her own subjectivity may be transformed. In much the same way that the encounter between Amir Javadi and Mikkel holds a micro-political potential when Mikkel's indifference becomes displaced, this moment between Rebecca and Amir Abdel allows for the forging of new alliances with a stranger whom Rebecca tried to ignore until this very moment.

In summary, the protagonists' relations with asylum seekers and refugees, as well as their affective responses to them, change when the contact to those 'others' is intensified. In *Politisk roman*, Rebecca's affective response changes in one crucial moment in which she is moved towards Amir, and when she cannot help but be affected by Amir's vulnerability in similar ways to Mikkel in *Opphold*, feeling stimulated to do something for the Javadi family when he beholds their distress. In Rebecca's case, her brief moment of affective responsibility saves Amir's life, but the question remains whether or not she can sustain this sense of responsibility, and if her indifference will be truly transformed, whereas in Mikkel's case, the question arises: in which ways can he convert his feelings into practice, or pro-social action? With regard to Miriam's changing attitude in *De fördrivna*, we have seen that Ashkan's provocations awaken her from her drug-induced indifference, and that closer contact with one (presumably) undocumented migrant instigates a sense of compassion in Miriam. When this compassion, however, becomes permeated by feelings of confusion and helplessness, Miriam is held in a state of affective ambiguity that curbs action, whereas her husband Filip remains entirely unmoved.

The Limits of Affective Responsibility

In *De fördrivna*, the text's dramatic ending is foreshadowed when Filip, in the beginning, gets lost in his car and ends up 'i ett labyrintisk industriområde i Catanias utkant' [in a mazy industrial area on the outskirts of Catania]. Filip realises that the area serves as, 'Arbetsplats för östra Siciliens prostituerade' [A workplace for the prostitutes of eastern Sicily] when he is approached by '[d]e afrikanska kvinnorna' [[t]he African women] (37) who work there. By means of the narrator's focalisation of Filip in this scene, the reality of these African women (presumably undocumented migrants) is seen through Filip's consciousness, and not further commented on, but only mentioned in passing. Filip's disconnection from the social and political reality of those refugees on the margins of his perception renders him unaware of the fact that these African women are socially marginalised, and, in addition, geographically segregated in an industrial area. Towards the end of the text, however, Miriam is on her way to the airport and makes the same mistake as Filip, and, taking a wrong turn, gets lost in the same industrial area. Remembering Filip's account, Miriam 'blir inte förvånad när hon ser fler och fler unga afrikanska kvinnor' [is not surprised when she sees more and more young African women]. Finding that all lanes in the area resemble each other, Miriam 'blir nervös av kvinnorna som står och ser på medan hon kör runt' [is made to feel nervous by the women standing and watching her while she is driving around] (170). Miriam's nervousness turns into outright fear when one of the young women knocks on her car window and offers help. Once the young woman — Lucy, as Miriam finds out — sits in the passenger seat, Miriam follows Lucy's demand and pays her fifty euros, but, 'När de når samma återvändsgränd som tidigare blir hon arg' [When they reach the same dead end as before, she gets angry]; Miriam has barely enough time to slow the car and turn towards Lucy 'förrän hon ser kniven' [before she sees the knife] (173). When Miriam sees herself threatened, she hands over her purse and mobile phone, and, when Lucy tries to grab the satnav from the floor, 'Miriam [...] sträcka sig för att hjälpa flickan med apparatens sladd' [Miriam [...] stretches to help the girl with the cord of the device] (174), which, in turn, seems to threaten Lucy, and she stabs Miriam. The reader is confronted with an open ending, in which both Miriam's and Lucy's fates remain unknown, and the text concludes with Miriam who, heavily bleeding, 'hör ambulansens tjut' [hears the wail of an ambulance] (175).

In a tripartite division of violence, Žižek identifies subjective violence as the most visible form of violence, and defines objective violence as consisting of '"symbolic" violence embodied in language and its forms', and of '"systemic" violence, or the often catastrophic consequences of the smooth functioning of our economic and political systems'.[53] 'Subjective violence is', as Žižek elaborates,

> experienced as such against the background of a non-violent zero level. It is seen as a perturbation of the 'normal', peaceful state of things. However, objective violence is precisely the violence inherent to this 'normal' state of things. Objective violence is invisible since it sustains the very zero-level standard against which we perceive something as subjectively violent. Systemic violence is thus [...] the counterpart to an all-too-visible subjective violence. It may be invisible, but it has to be taken into account if one is to make sense of what otherwise seem to be 'irrational' explosions of subjective violence.[54]

From this perspective, the fact that Lucy stabs Miriam in a seemingly irrational explosion of subjective violence has to be seen in the wider context of objective violence, against which Lucy's violent act is pitched. In accordance with Žižek's argument, it is necessary to investigate which forms of objective violence underpin this violent act, if one is to make sense of it; or, in other words, to ask which factors produce this subjective violence.

The scene between Miriam and Lucy is embedded in a wider context in which the non-violent zero level can be maintained when undocumented migrants are neither seen nor heard. The refugees are geographically, socially and politically excluded, and exist only on the margins of perception of native locals or more privileged migrants such as Miriam and Filip, and this invisibility and inaudibility renders the lives of these refugees precarious. To borrow Zygmunt Bauman's argument, the industrial area where Lucy sells her body can be viewed as the nowhere into which Lucy has been catapulted after she presumably fled her native country in fear, or was expelled by force, but was refused entry into another country. In this sense, Lucy has not changed places, but has lost her place on earth.[55] This nowhere is furthermore inscribed with exclusionary immigration policies that strip Lucy of civic rights — such as the right to work — and therefore, if Lucy wants to earn money, she has to prostitute herself. These political structures produce a precarity that jeopardises Lucy's survival, and she is displayed in the text as the figure 'that renders visible the exclusionary practices employed by the state in its attempt to maintain a territorial order' — practices which target the legally and economically least protected migrants.[56] This precarity, in turn, generates fear as the primary affect, as it hovers 'indistinctly but nonetheless insistently above and within' the situation in which Miriam and Lucy interact.[57] Fear, as the dominant affective quality in this scene, is corporeal, as it is equally embodied by Lucy and Miriam; it is relational as it passes as intensity between these two women; and it is situational as it is produced by the event of their encounter. Lucy sees herself threatened by Miriam's quick gesture in the same way as Miriam sees herself threatened by Lucy's knife. This irrational explosion of violence is thus effectuated by fear, but a fear that is closely related to, and generated by, the systemic violence inherent in the political and social marginalisation of refugees. When subjective and systemic violence become intricately entangled in this way, 'violence is not a direct property of some acts, but is distributed between acts and their contexts', which means that Lucy's violent act can be conceived of as one catastrophic consequence of exclusionary immigration politics.[58]

★   ★   ★   ★   ★

In *Opphold*, Mikkel begins to put his compassion into practice when he starts asking questions and listens to the answers, which, in line with Emily Beausoleil's argument, is the prerequisite for affective responsibility: 'to act responsibly towards others is at core to learn to hear what is at yet white noise'.[59] Mikkel, and with him the reader, learns about the past of the Javadi family, and about their health-related concerns in the narrative present, as well as about their legal situation. After four years in the country, the Javadi family would be entitled to a residence permit, but 'Javadiene har vært akkurat litt for kort tid i Norge. For *snart* fire år siden kom de hit' [The Javadis have not been in Norway quite long enough. They came here *almost* four years ago] (120, italics in original). Regardless of 'Afsoons blødende magesår' [Afsoon's bleeding stomach ulcer], a critical state of health is not enough reason for the Norwegian immigration authorities to grant the Javadi family a residence permit, because, 'Til det er helsevesenet for velfungerende i Iran' [The healthcare system in Iran is too good for that] (119). When Mikkel understands that the family are, despite their repeated appeals, 'i ferd med å få alle de avslagene som er å oppdrive' [about to get all the rejections you can possibly get] (119), he becomes aware of how strongly the individual family members are affected by their difficult situation, 'hvor mye stillere [Afsoon] har blitt. Og hun er bleik igjen, og bekymra' [that [Afsoon] is so much quieter. And she is pale again, and worried] (121); and Mikkel is concerned about Lila's reaction to their imminent deportation when he sees 'angsten. Panikkanfall. Antydning til spisevegring' [the anxiety. Panic attacks. Signs of anorexia] (123). Through Mikkel's perspective, we are given a detailed and intimate account of how the procedures of Norwegian immigration authorities and their concomitant arbitrariness can affect individual asylum seekers. Mikkel's account also underscores how, when the residence of the Javadi family in their host country is displayed as dependent on such procedures, their sense of belonging to Norway can only ever be contingent, despite an almost four-year-long process of integration.

While Mikkel actively engages with the vulnerability of the Javadi family by listening, he cannot 'resist the mental distancing of rationalization, defensiveness, or projection', which curbs his affective responsibility.[60] Therefore, Mikkel resorts to his own emotional strain as a defence mechanism, and despite his statement that it is 'umulig å holde avstand' [impossible to keep your distance], he asseverates and reiterates in ever shorter intervals that he has reached his breaking point; that 'det er for mye' [it's too much]; that he 'har ikke plass til Mitra og familien hennes' [has no room for Mitra and her family] (154); that he is 'skjør, sprø, bristeferdig, kaputt' [brittle, crumbling, breaking, kaput] (147); and that he cannot continue like this: 'Snart revner jeg. Jeg revner. Ungene mine revner' [Soon, I'll crack. I'll crack. My kids will crack] (168). When the immigration authorities interrupt this ever-intensifying strain with their final rejection of the Javadi family's asylum application, Mikkel sounds almost relieved when he says, 'Endelig avslag på søknad om oppholdstillatelse' [Finally, their last rejection of a residence permit] (173). In parallel plot developments, Mikkel's wife Sylvia is found dead by the police, and the Javadi family are picked up by the police to be deported. Afterwards, Mikkel reflects on the events with

> Afsoon og Nouri, Amir, Lila og Mitra ble kjørt vekk [...] Gata holdt pusten. Her skulle vært oppstandelse. Leven. Men folk sov, og mørket slo ut av vinduene da de ble henta. Snart er det jul. Politiet kom på en tid som gjorde det enklere. Eivind satt taus på armen min. Sa ikke et ord, men jentene gråt. De har ikke grått sånn over Sylvia.

> [Afsoon and Nouri, Amir, Lila and Mitra were driven away [...] The street held its breath. There should have been an uproar here. A rebellion. But people were asleep, and the windows stayed dark when they were picked up. Soon it's Christmas. The police came at a time that made it easier. Eivind sat on my arm in silence. Didn't say a word, but the girls cried. They haven't cried like this for Sylvia.] (184)

In *Borderlands*, Michel Agier asserts that 'everything that determines expulsion defines the border: discourses, laws, administrative measures and the police interventions that put it into operation'.[61] In the case of the Javadi family, the police function as the executives of exclusionary asylum policies which differentiate between inside and outside, and, when the Javadi family's deportation is viewed from the perspective of Agier's assertion, the family never left the liminality of the border zone, despite their almost four years in Norway and their gradual integration into Norwegian society. Being dependent on this state apparatus, the Javadi family are forcefully held in this liminal status, until they are, equally forcefully, evicted. This process illustrates that precarity is distributed differentially, and that systemic violence allows its agents to decide and enforce who belongs within this artificially constructed inside, and who does not.

Moreover, as Mikkel states, the police chose an opportune moment to deport the Javadi family: shortly before Christmas, when it is dark, and when the neighbours are sleeping. But what exactly has choosing this precise moment made easier? Reading the Javadi family's deportation through the same tripartite division of violence that served to analyse the ending of *De fördrivna*, there is no instance of subjective violence as such. The deportation of the Javadi family happens against their will, yet without any resistance; the forceful presence of the police certainly makes the systemic violence inherent in the Javadi family's deportation visible, but this visibility is calculated, so that it does not perturb the normal, peaceful state of the neighbourhood. The presence of the police in connection to asylum seekers disturbs the 'non-violent zero level' only ever so slightly, and, as Mikkel reflects, the neighbours maintain their indifference and hold their breath until the disturbance is over.[62] In the same way that Filip, in *De fördrivna*, disengages from refugees, the whole street where Mikkel lives practises Žižek's 'fetishist disavowal': the neighbours know exactly what is happening, but they refuse to assume any consequences, so that they can continue acting as if they do not know, and stay indifferent. Mikkel laments this indifference in his reflections when he says 'Her skulle vært oppstandelse' [There should have been an uproar here] (184), but the question remains: to what extent is he part of this neighbourhood and its indifference, or is his statement yet another attempt at deferring responsibility?

Mikkel's final reflections reveal that his affective responses to the Javadi family never ceased being focused on his own priorities. Although the deportation of the Javadi family is on a par with Sylvia's death insofar as it impacts Mikkel's family as strongly as the loss of Sylvia, this double loss is soon replaced with a kitten called Bruno. Apparently, the kitten easily helps Eivind to forget both Mitra and his mother, and Mikkel recognises with relief that, 'Bruno fyller huset med latter igjen' [Bruno fills the house with laughter again] (189–90). Nevertheless, Mikkel is active 'for å få dem til Norge igjen' [to get them back to Norway], and 'kampen [...] gir en viss energi' [the fight [...] gives a certain energy]. While this ending is depicted in positive terms, positivity is concentrated on Mikkel and his family: with a kitten in the house, and a struggle that helps Mikkel to regain some of his energy and makes him feel needed beyond his immediate family, the prospect for himself and his family is hopeful. With regard to the Javadi family's fate, the reader merely learns from Mikkel: 'vi holder i alle fall kontakt via Facebook' [we at least keep in touch via Facebook] (189). One can only speculate how much a Facebook contact actually helps, and it remains unknown what Mikkel's struggle for the Javadi family's return to Norway de facto entails. Instead of learning what becomes of the Javadi family, the reader is confronted once more with Mikkel's feeling of guilt, as he regrets his former indifference, and admits his impotence: 'Hver eneste dag tenker jeg på alt jeg kunne gjort annerledes. At jeg burde gjort mer for dem, mye mer. Det hjelper selvsagt ikke en dritt' [Every single day I think about everything I could have done differently. That I should have done more for them, much more. Obviously, this doesn't make the slightest difference] (189). As *Opphold* is solely rendered through Mikkel's narrative voice, the reader is granted detailed insight into his consciousness, and into the conflict that dominates Mikkel's affective engagement with the Javadi family. In this sense, the text invites the reader to empathise with Mikkel and his struggle; but when the reading of fiction requires 'that we step outside of ourselves and into "the shoes" of a character', a question emerges out of Mikkel's predicament which may instigate the reader's reflections on their own sense of affective responsibility: what would I have done if I had been in Mikkel's place?[63]

★   ★   ★   ★   ★

In the previous section, we have seen that in *Politisk roman*, a potentially transformative space opens between Rebecca and Amir, when the former saves the latter's life with mouth-to-mouth resuscitation out of an empathic reflex. Rebecca's way of managing the effects of this event, however, prevents her empathy extending beyond this moment, and blocks any affective responsibility that might result from it. When Rebecca states that 'væggene begyndte at komme nærmere' [the walls began to come closer] (137), she indicates that this event has unsettled her, and that its emotional and physical impact resembles some sort of breakdown. In a similar way to that by which Miriam, in *De fördrivna*, excludes the forbidding reality of the outside world with the help of prescription drugs and alcohol, Rebecca stops going to work and self-medicates with Diazepam to suppress the shock which the event with Amir caused her. Although Robert suggests that she 'skal holde op med at tage de piller og så se en psykolog' [should stop taking the pills and see a psychologist], Rebecca insists that there is nothing wrong with her or her overuse of Diazepam, and she reassures Robert, 'Jeg har det som sagt fint' [I am fine, as I said] (141). This reaction, together with her statement that she has 'så vidt muligt prøvet at undgå' [as far as possible tried to avoid] (138) Amir, allows her to remain indifferent despite the affective shock she experienced. In terms of happiness, Rebecca really seems to feel better for a brief moment, because her life-saving intervention brings her closer to her son Oskar. When Oskar leaves for a class trip to Berlin and waves farewell to her, Rebecca comments, 'Mon han overhovedet var klar over, hvor glad den simple bevægelse gjorde mig?' [Did he even realise how happy that simple gesture made me?], and she speculates optimistically that she and her son 'godt kunne være på vej et *okay sted* hen' [could be heading towards an *okay place*] (138, italics in original). Her hope, however, quickly evaporates when an agent from the Danish Security and Intelligence Service PET (Politiets Efterretningstjeneste), pays her a visit and informs Rebecca that Oskar has disappeared from his class trip, is wanted by the police, and will most likely be charged 'for overtrædelse af terrorloven' [for violation of the terror law] (142) once he is found. The agent then informs her that he has received an anonymous tip that an undocumented migrant lives hidden in the flat; he subsequently finds Amir with Rebecca's help, arrests him, and has him brought to the detention centre for asylum seekers in Ellebæk.

In her reading of the novel's ending, Oxfeldt points out that it offers insight into a connection between Rebecca and Amir, as they both have suffered the loss of a son. This connection, Oxfeldt suggests, 'kunne have knyttet dem sammen i solidaritet' [could have tied them together in solidarity], but instead, both characters remain in isolation from each other.[64] Since Rebecca is deeply shocked by the news about Oskar, Amir's fate is of no concern to her, and when the PET agent informs Rebecca about the prevailing legal norms, she comments to herself, 'Alt det kan han spare sig. Jeg hører alligevel ikke efter. Befinder mig i en døs, der langtfra er behagelig' [All this he can save himself. I'm not listening anyway. Am in a daze that's far from comfortable] (144). Rebecca's callousness to date enabled her to disguise her anxiety regarding the potential loss of her son, but when this loss eventually comes true, it does not jolt Rebecca from her indifference, but rather intensifies related affects when she feels a vague sense of unease and a dull stupor, which divests her of any other emotions and renders her hamstrung. In this sense, *Politisk roman* displays the indifference emerging out of Rebecca's personal predicament as the limits of her affective responsibility, in similar ways that *Opphold* presents Mikkel's individual struggle and affective disorientation as curbing his capacity to engage affectively with the Javadi family, and act.

Politisk roman, however, negotiates politics beyond the portrayal of the protagonists' personal affective responses to otherness, and therefore offers the reader a window into wider Danish political configurations in two ways. Firstly, Rebecca's reactionary political attitude is discredited by virtue of her hyperbolic, cynical narrative voice, and this voice and hyperbole distance the reader from the politics she represents. At the same time, this distancing also works in the opposite direction when Rebecca, with the same cynicism, debunks Robert and Mark's supposedly left-wing political activism as ridiculous and misguided. In this respect, the text criticises the two opposing poles of the Danish political spectrum, and, without clarifying its own political stance, reveals the flaws of both ideological mindsets. Secondly, the text contains dialogues between the characters in which Denmark 'fremstilles [...] som en yderst indvandrernegativ nation' [is presented [...] as a highly immigrant-negative nation].[65] In one of their rare conversations, Amir points out to Rebecca that he has relatives in France and England, and that they emigrated 'længe før det blev umoderne at være fremmed' [long before it became unfashionable to be a foreigner]. Rebecca corrects Amir's word choice by saying, 'I dag er det vist *personer med anden etnisk baggrund*' [Today, we say *people with a different ethnic background*], while she, in the same breath, recommends that Amir should go to France or England, because, 'Der er ingen fremtid her. Politikerne er ligeglade. Og det er størstedelen af danskerne sådan set også' [You have no future here. The politicians don't care. And the majority of Danes don't either] (123, italics in original). In her astute analysis of this conversation, Oxfeldt observes, 'Man er altså "politisk korrekt" i sin omtale af de Andre, men ønsker absolut ikke at huse dem indenfor nationens grænser' [So you are 'politically correct' in the way you talk about Others, but definitely do not want to have them living within the borders of the nation].[66] In this regard, the text brings Rebecca's right-wing political viewpoints into close correlation with those of the majority of Danes in general: Rebecca does not want to house a stranger in her flat in the same way that the Danish state is reluctant to welcome strangers within its national borders. This perspective of Denmark is even more cynical than Rebecca's cynical outlook on her own life, because it suggests that the Danish state and the majority of Danes are affectively disinvested in the question of asylum seekers and refugees, and because it denies both state and people the capacity for affective responsibility.

★   ★   ★   ★   ★

The Scandinavian protagonists in *De fördrivna*, *Opphold* and *Politisk roman* live in relatively privileged circumstances, particularly in comparison with those 'others' they encounter. These privileges may lead to a feeling of unease, or guilt, when the perceived poverty and suffering of underprivileged 'others' is brought close to the individual and is consequently compared to those Scandinavian privileges. However, the Scandinavians' understanding of themselves as rich and happy people does not quite apply to the protagonists portrayed in the three texts; they may be affluent, but they are certainly not happy: Miriam, in *De fördrivna*, is too worried about her daughter to feel happiness, and, moreover, she sees the need to soothe the possible affective impact of global injustices with prescription drugs and alcohol; Mikkel's life, in *Opphold*, is in crisis after the disappearance of his wife Sylvia; and Rebecca, in *Politisk roman*, is alienated from happiness in her partnership with Robert, and in her relationship with her son Oskar. In this respect, all three texts challenge the notion that the Scandinavian countries are the happiest countries in the world by portraying protagonists who do not live in the apparent state of happiness that is allegedly concomitant with Scandinavian privilege. By disengaging happiness from those factors which contribute to the perception of the Nordic model as successful, such as prosperity and equality, the three texts expose this Nordic model, and therefore Scandinavian exceptionalism, as a construct with inherent flaws, because the implied happiness is not applicable to everyone.

In terms of Scandinavian Guilt, we have seen what feelings of guilt, or a lack thereof, do: in Naseh's novel, Ashkan's challenging questions jolt Miriam from her self-centred indifference, but her ensuing compassion becomes diluted by helplessness and affective disorientation despite her newly awakened sense of guilt over her privileges, while her husband Filip reinterprets possible guilt feelings as pride, and refuses to feel guilty for privileges that he, in his view, has earned. In Linnestå's text, Mikkel's affective capacities are exhausted by his efforts to maintain his children's well-being, and, with regard to the Javadi family, he is torn between compassion emerging out of guilt, and indifference, so that his attempts to help them remain, at best, half-hearted. Rebecca, in Aburas's novel, does not feel guilty, but utilises her hardened indifference to protect her weakness — her fear of losing her son; and, although she saves Amir's life in a gesture of spontaneous compassion, she remains unmoved by his fate. Rebecca's partner, in contrast, displays signs of guilt which lead to pro-social action; this action, however, is satirised and exposed as hypocritical, and Robert's guilt feelings are portrayed as self-serving, because they centre on his aim to feel good about himself. None of the three texts depict protagonists who engage with 'others' on the basis of solidarity, or affective responsibility. Instead, the protagonists display various degrees of indifference, and use their individual preoccupations to abate, negate, or explain away, their sense of guilt, because these preoccupations justify their lack of affective responsibility in their own eyes.

Berlant argues that 'to feel compassion for people who struggle or fail is at best to take the first step toward forging a personal relation to a politics of the practice of equality'.[67] These politics entail two components which need to be considered in order for it to be practised successfully. The first component implies overcoming the inequality inherent in compassion, and its focus on the suffering or distress of someone who is in an object position in relation with the subject who is feeling compassion from a hierarchically elevated position. In terms of affective responsibility, the second component involves listening with care and attention, to be able to respond to the other's difference not on the basis of established norms, but by allowing oneself to be moved into an unknown terrain, where, potentially, this very difference, instead of creating mutually exclusive boundaries, can pave the way for new forms of solidarity. The Scandinavian protagonists are portrayed as failing to forge precisely those personal relations to a politics of the practice of equality that Berlant argues for, because they are too preoccupied with their own lives to have the affective capacities to engage with those 'others' whose alterity they experience as obtrusive, but with whom they are nevertheless compelled to enter into relations of proximity. As a result of excessive affective pressures, they react with indifference to the perceived intrusive difference of the asylum seekers or refugees they encounter, or who die in their vicinity. This indifference impedes the protagonists' affective engagement, as it prevents them from transcending the cognitive and emotional dissonance that separates them from those they perceive as radically other from themselves. Agier suggests that, 'The very existence of women and men in displacement, in migration [...] is their politics. A politics of life against the politics of indifference'.[68] By depicting protagonists who are unable to act within the parameters of a politics of the practice of equality, and who counterpoise the politics of life of the people in migration with their politics of indifference, the texts themselves highlight the effects of this politics of indifference, while simultaneously negotiating the protagonists' individual difficulties in practising affective responsibility.

Notes to Chapter 4

1. Butler, p. 34.
2. Aleida Assmann and Ines Detmers, 'Introduction', in *Empathy and Its Limits*, ed. by Assmann and Detmers (Basingstoke: Palgrave Macmillan, 2016), pp. 1–17 (p. 4).
3. Lauren Gail Berlant, 'Compassion (and Withholding)', in *Compassion: The Culture and Politics of an Emotion*, ed. by Berlant (London: Routledge, 2004), pp. 1–13 (p. 4, italics in original).
4. Ahmed, *Cultural Politics*, p. 192.
5. Butler, p. 36; Berlant p. 4.
6. Assmann and Detmers, p. 2.
7. Ibid., p. 6.
8. Ibid., pp. 6, 8.
9. Ngai, p. 6, italics in original.
10. Berlant, pp. 9–10.
11. Ngai, p. 14, italics in original.
12. Oxfeldt, 'Innledning', p. 9. Oxfeldt explains that the term 'Scandinavian Guilt', or 'ScanGuilt' in its abbreviated form, was coined, and served as a title for, an interdisciplinary research project at the University of Oslo between 2014 and 2018. I adopt the capitalised spelling of the term Scandinavian Guilt, to acknowledge that I refer to its conceptualisation as it is laid out by Oxfeldt.
13. Oxfeldt, 'Innledning', pp. 20, 12.
14. Ibid., p. 12.
15. Shelby Steele, 'White Guilt', *American Scholar*, 59 (1990), 497–506 (p. 501).
16. Sara Ahmed, 'Collective Feelings: Or, The Impressions Left by Others', *Theory, Culture and Society*, 21 (2004), 25–42 (pp. 26, italics in original; 27).
17. Ngai, p. 3.

18. Assmann and Detmers, p. 6.
19. Butler, p. 34.
20. I am indebted to Åsa Arping for some of these insights, which I gained from her excellent presentation at the DINO 2018 conference at the University of Oslo: Åsa Arping, 'Feeling Different, Acting Indifferently — Gender, Privilege and Vulnerability in Contemporary Swedish Fiction' (University of Oslo: Affects of Diversity in Nordic Literature Conference, 1–2 November 2018, Panel Presentation on 2 November 2018).
21. Pascal Bruckner, *The Tyranny of Guilt: An Essay on Western Masochism*, trans. by Steven Rendall (Princeton: Princeton University Press, 2010), pp. 98, 219.
22. Oxfeldt, 'Innledning', p. 23.
23. Butler, p. 36.
24. On the one hand, *gjennomtrekk* can be translated as 'draught', and, on the other, it denotes a turnover of people in the workplace or in a residential area: 'Gjennomtrekk', in *Bokmålsordboka* <http://www.ordbok.uib.no/GJENNOMTREKK> [accessed 13 June 2019].
25. Butler, p. 9.
26. Ngai, p. 6, italics in original.
27. Elisabeth Oxfeldt, 'Staten sa ja, så hva sier jeg?', in *Skandinaviske fortellinger om skyld og privilegier i en globaliseringstid*, ed. by Oxfeldt (Oslo: Universitetsforlaget, 2016), pp. 230–54 (p. 241).
28. Sara Ahmed, *The Promise of Happiness* (Durham, NC: Duke University Press, 2010), p. 26.
29. Steele, p. 502.
30. Oxfeldt, 'Innledning', p. 20.
31. Tobias Hübinette and Catrin Lundström, 'Sweden after the Recent Election: The Double-Binding Power of Swedish Whiteness through the Mourning of the Loss of "Old Sweden" and the Passing of "Good Sweden"', *NORA — Nordic Journal of Feminist and Gender Research*, 19 (2011), 42–52 (pp. 43, 50).
32. The book is *Bilal* by Fabrizio Gatti, an Italian investigative journalist, who travels the same routes of migration as a group refugees and documents these journeys.
33. Ngai, p. 14.
34. Devika Sharma, 'Doing Good, Feeling Bad: Humanitarian Emotion in Crisis', *Journal of Aesthetics and Culture*, 9 (2017), 1–12 (p. 3).
35. Slavoj Žižek, *Violence* (London: Profile, 2008), pp. 45–46.
36. Butler, pp. 7, 14, 29, 25.
37. Ibid., p. 34.
38. Ibid., p. 35.
39. Federica Mazzara, 'Subverting the Narrative of the Lampedusa Borderscape', *Crossings*, 7 (2016), 135–47 (pp. 137, 136).
40. Massumi, *User's Guide*, p. 106.
41. Rosi Braidotti, 'Nomadic Ethics', *Deleuze Studies*, 7 (2013), 342–59 (p. 356).
42. Berlant, pp. 4 (italics in original), 9.
43. Ibid., p. 9.
44. Ngai, p. 14.
45. Berlant, p. 10.
46. Butler, p. 50.
47. Berlant, p. 4.
48. Ibid., p. 1.
49. Ahmed, *Promise*, pp. 139, 17.
50. Oxfeldt, 'Staten', p. 241.
51. Ibid.
52. Ibid., p. 245.
53. Žižek, p. 1.
54. Ibid., p. 2.
55. Bauman, *Liquid Times*, pp. 44–45.
56. Squire, p. 3.
57. Tygstrup, 'Affective Spaces', p. 201.

58. Žižek, p. 180.
59. Beausoleil, p. 294.
60. Beausoleil, p. 308.
61. Agier, *Borderlands*, p. 52.
62. Žižek, p. 2.
63. Blake, p. 224.
64. Oxfeldt, 'Staten', p. 245.
65. Ibid., p. 244.
66. Ibid.
67. Berlant, p. 9.
68. Agier, *Borderlands*, p. 39.

CHAPTER 5

❖

Postmigrant Subjectivities in Senthuran Varatharajah's *Vor der Zunahme der Zeichen*, Pooneh Rohi's *Araben* and Zeshan Shakar's *Tante Ulrikkes vei*

I am now widening the comparative scope again by contrasting the Norwegian text *Tante Ulrikkes vei* (2017) by Zeshan Shakar and the Swedish text *Araben* (2014) by Pooneh Rohi with the German text *Vor der Zunahme der Zeichen* (2016) by Senthuran Varatharajah. These three texts depict protagonists whose journeys are over, or who never travelled in the first place, but whose parents migrated to the countries they now live in or were born into. My focus is on the texts' postmigrant protagonists, and by first discussing, and subsequently adopting, a postmigrant perspective for the critical analysis, I shall illustrate how the texts portray their protagonists' perceptions of themselves in relation to the societies in which they live, and how their self-understanding and sense of belonging are affected by their surroundings. In two of the texts, memory plays an undeniably strong role regarding the ways in which the protagonists negotiate their sense of belonging, and therefore, I am following two vectors of enquiry with regard to affect. Firstly, I am tracing the affects that emerge from the protagonists' processes of remembering with respect to the narrative present; and secondly, I am displaying the protagonists' conflicts and struggles as embedded into, and induced by, the societies in which they live.

The three texts' protagonists are postmigrant characters insofar as they have either not migrated themselves, or as their migratory journeys have come to an end because the destination has been reached. In this respect, the term 'postmigrant' can be understood as a temporal phrase, but, as Roger Bromley points out, it also holds an epistemological dimension in the sense that it encapsulates the question of when and how 'someone ceases to be thought of as a "migrant" or in terms of their supposed ethnicity'.[1] When, as Bromley suggests, the term 'migrant' is used to categorise someone from the outside, it becomes problematic, as it is 'often mobilised as part of aggressive identity-ascriptions and processes of othering'.[2] These identity ascriptions are particularly questionable considering that, as Regina Römhild contends, European societies in general are 'characterised through and through by the experiences and effects of coming, going and staying', so that migratory experiences shape not only the lives of those migrating and their descendants, but have an effect on any given society as a whole. Nevertheless, as Römhild argues further, 'in the established discourses, which revolve around "immigration" and "integration", migration is still treated as a separate problem as if the "majority society" (conceived as its opposite and automatically assumed to be national and white) had nothing to do with it'.[3] According to Römhild's observation, postmigrant societies do not consider migration and pluralisation normal or uncomplicated; rather the opposite in fact, as Riem Spielhaus clarifies when she identifies those societies as postmigrant which grapple with the effects of past and present migration movements, and 'mit der Pluralisierung ihrer Bevölkerung' [with the pluralisation of their population].[4] While Erol Yildiz and Marc Hill do not deny the challenges Römhild and Spielhaus address, they suggest that postmigrant societies hold the potential for producing spaces which allow for 'new strategies of assimilation and localisation, strategies that transcend the local, regional and national and connect our practice of everyday life with the world'.[5] Yildiz and Hill call these spaces 'transtopias', which implies that, while the creation of such spaces is highly aspirational, it is hardly viable in the current political and societal climates in Europe. In this light, I understand the term postmigrant, or postmigrant society, not as positively utopian, but as a term that implies all those negotiations and conflicts that arise in the whole of any society whose discourses insist on a separation between 'us' and 'them'. Rephrasing Bromley's earlier mentioned epistemological dimension of the term 'postmigrant', the question would then be why someone does not cease to be thought of as a migrant, and why people are continuously judged by their supposed ethnicity.

When migration is understood as integral to any society's structure, one would think that it is considered relatively unexceptional; yet, as the previous chapters have illustrated, human mobility and migration are by no means even playing fields: transnational mobility is not equally accessible to everyone, and migration, as well as migration experiences, are made problematic for some by the policies and practices which are employed to control state borders. Moreover, migrant and postmigrant experiences are rendered exceptional by those discourses that keep some people in a marginalised position by means of ethnic and racialised differentiation. One consequence of these forms of differentiation is that postmigrant societies are marked by an 'Obsession für Migrations- und Integrationsthemen' [obsession for migration and integration issues], which can lead to a so-called migrantisation.[6] This notion implies that issues become linked with migration that are not necessarily related to migration in the first place, while it, at the same time, obfuscates the fact that these issues usually tend to be of a more structural nature, or are caused by social power relations. Römhild, too, addresses the notion of migrantisation, or, as she calls it, 'this politics of ethnicisation', and she points out that critical (post) migration research developed in opposition to it by making migration not the object of critical study, but by employing it as a research perspective with the aim 'to observe society from the perspective of migration, in the sense of examining it from the margins it has itself created'.[7] In the same vein, Yildiz and Hill argue for a 'post-migrant view' which, when it is applied seriously as a critical lens, can serve as 'a discursive approach [...] against a discourse that continues to treat narratives of migration as specific, exceptional, historical phenomena and in which it is habitual to differentiate between native normality and "immigrant problems"'.[8] Moritz Schramm suggests that this critical lens can be adopted for the study of literature as a postmigrant perspective, and through this perspective, as he explains, 'lassen sich literarische und künstlerische Verarbeitungen von beispielsweise Ein- und Ausgrenzungsmechanismen, von Prozessen des *Othering*, von Selbst- und Fremdzuschreibungen und von Kämpfen um Teilhabe und Gleichheit beobachten und analysieren' [you can observe and analyse literary and artistic approaches to, for example, mechanisms of inclusion and exclusion, processes of othering, self-ascriptions and ascriptions from outside, and struggles about participation and equality].[9] This perspective makes it possible to view these dynamics and conflicts not as solely pertaining to migrant and postmigrant experiences and realities as they are depicted in fictional texts, but as phenomena that concern the whole of those societies into which the texts' characters are involved.

I endorse Römhild's point of view that (post)migration research is positioned in opposition to the problematic notion of migrantisation, and shall employ precisely the postmigrant perspective Schramm calls for, with two objectives in mind: firstly, the postmigrant perspective is a concept well suited to explore, as Bromley puts it, 'the conflicts and contradictions' and 'the dialectic of belonging and unbelonging' that are 'a feature of postmigrant belonging'.[10] In this respect, the postmigrant perspective allows me to illustrate how the texts portray their postmigrant protagonists' perceptions of themselves in relation to the societies in which they live, and how their self-understanding and sense of belonging are influenced from the outside. Secondly, when the struggles and conflicts of the texts' protagonists are analysed through the postmigrant perspective, they insist on being viewed as embedded in society as a whole. This begs the question of whether or not the three texts depict the protagonists' struggles as actually related to migration in any way, or whether they are portrayed as linked to political and social power relations, and therefore, as associated with systemic issues. With this in mind, these texts potentially hold a political dimension, because, as Erol Yildiz argues, 'Durch die Erzählung neuer Geschichten und die Umdeutung zugeschriebener Negativmerkmale werden einerseits Machtverhältnisse offengelegt und andererseits eine Anerkennung gleichzeitiger und widersprüchlicher Lebenswirklichkeiten gefordert' [Through the narration of new stories and the reinterpretation of ascribed negative characteristics, power relations become exposed on the one hand, and, on the other, these narratives demand recognition for simultaneous and conflicting realities of life]. This kind of storytelling, as Yildiz goes on to say, is politically provocative, because it challenges hegemonic national or cultural narratives by making those narratives visible which are usually marginalised within dominant discourses.[11] Assuming that the three texts are 'written from the affective experience of marginality', I shall probe them with regard to the politics underlying them: do they, by linking the protagonists' affective experiences of marginality to societal or political matters, create 'Räume des Widerstands' [spaces of resistance] which counterpoise this marginality?[12]

Pooneh Rohi's novel *Araben* weaves together two storylines: that of an elderly man who, for the most part, is only called 'the Arab', and who fled from Iran to Sweden, and that of Yasaman, a young woman who, as it turns out, is the Arab's daughter and who immigrated with him to Sweden as a child. Upon first inspection, the two strands of the text appear to be distinct from each other, as they are told from different narrative perspectives and follow diverging temporalities. Yasaman's parts of the text are dated and, without indicating years in which the narrative is set, encompass the time period from 15 November to 17 April, whereas the Arab's parts comprise of one single day. Yasaman's parts are told in her own voice, whereas the Arab's are rendered through the voice of a third-person narrator whose perspective is limited to that of the Arab's. Although temporally displaced, there are a few subtle parallels between the two storylines, and towards the end of the novel, the two storylines, ever so briefly and only narrated from Yasaman's perspective, merge. Senthuran Varatharajah's *Vor der Zunahme der Zeichen* is presented as a conversation between Senthil Vasuthevan and Valmira Surroi on Facebook. They initially befriend each other without ever having met in person, and the text consists of the stylised individual contributions to their week-long instant messenger conversation. Both protagonists are in their twenties and are studying for postgraduate degrees; they immigrated to Germany as children together with their parents, Senthil from Sri Lanka, and Valmira from Kosovo. Zeshan Shakar's novel *Tante Ulrikkes vei* captures the experiences of two Norwegian-born young men, Jamal and Mo (short for Mohammed), who live in the same housing block in Stovner, situated on the outskirts of Oslo. The text is presented as a fictitious research project, in which the senior researcher Lars Bakken of the NOVA group sets out to 'kartlegge hverdagen til ungdom med minoritetsbakgrunn i Groruddalen' [chart the daily life of young people with a migrant background in Grorud Valley] (5), with Jamal and Mo as two of the participants. Mo's contributions to the project consist of emails to Lars Bakken, written in the Bokmål standard of Norwegian, whereas Jamal does not feel comfortable with writing and thus, speaking in the multi-ethnolect typical for young people from his area, he uses a Dictaphone; his contributions are rendered as transcripts from the tape recordings that he sends to Bakken. The research project — as well as the text — follows Jamal and Mo over a period of five years, from July 2001 to October 2006.

As these brief synopses indicate, the three texts present the reader with time windows of different durations in the lives of their protagonists, and within the set frames of these time windows, the texts negotiate the dialectic of belonging and un-belonging by contrasting the protagonists' self-understanding with the perceptions that are brought to them from the outside, and by depicting the protagonists' conflicting relationships with the societies in which they live. Embedded in these time windows are analepses in which histories of marginalisation and othering unfold, which become related to the protagonists' realities in the narrative present. Acknowledging the significance of memory in the Arab's strand of the text in *Araben*, and in Senthil and Valmira's conversation in *Vor der Zunahme der Zeichen*, I shall first detail the role of the past in the protagonists' present, and then relate the protagonists' postmigrant subjectivities to the societies in Sweden and German. Therefore, the first part of the present chapter will mainly focus on the Arab's parts of *Araben* and *Vor der Zunahme der Zeichen*, while the second and third part will primarily engage with *Tante Ulrikkes vei* and Yasaman's narrative strand in *Araben*. However, all three sections of this chapter share the general goal of seeking to compare, to paraphrase Römhild, the societies in which the protagonists live, and to observe these societies from the margins they have themselves created — through the prism of the past as well as the present, and to bring to light how these three texts negotiate the political and social power relations at the root of the protagonists' conflicts.

Postmigrant Societies: Through the Prism of the Past

In *Vor der Zunahme der Zeichen*, Senthil and Valmira present themselves as intelligent young people who have strong affiliations with German places such as Marburg and Berlin, but also with places such as New York, Tokyo, Oslo, London, Toronto, Boston and Montreal, where they visited their diasporic families, or spent periods of time. Navigating their mobile lives confidently, Senthil and Valmira state their belonging to Germany, while they, simultaneously, transnationalise a perceived notion of a homogeneous German national identity. Looking back on similarities and dissimilarities between their respective lives, Senthil and Valmira compare their experiences of settling into German society in a process of remembering that consists of conscious and deliberate acts, as memory is constructed and, at the same time, questioned, in dialogue. In Varatharajah's text memory is presented as the workings of attention and focus, whereas in Rohi's novel, memory occurs as a force with very different dynamics from those of a conscious reconstruction. The Arab is overwhelmed with a flood of memories that he, although he would like to, cannot control, and the reiteration of similar phrases such as, 'Han [...] känner det strömma till honom' [He [...] feels it flowing to him] (155), or that the memories are 'som en iskall dusch' [like an ice cold shower] (28), shows that the force of these memories is irrepressible. Nonetheless, these memories invoke conscious reflections in which the Arab makes connections between his life in the present and his past. Although these two processes of remembering are so different in nature, memories are, in both cases, instantiated from the vantage point of the narrative now to make sense of present realities through reflections on past events. Before discussing in more detail how memories emerge or are constructed, and how they affect the protagonists' self-understanding, I shall first turn to the question of where remembering takes place. These spaces are more than just a backdrop, as they facilitate the production of particular affects, and hence, they become themselves imbued with affect; in an adaption of Frederik Tygstrup's term 'affective spaces', they become mnemonic affective spaces.[13]

As previously stated, the Arab's parts of *Araben* comprise of one single day. Outwardly, nothing much happens on this wintry Tuesday just before Christmas; from morning until evening, the Arab travels through Stockholm, changes from commuter trains to the underground and back to the train, and looks out of train windows onto the snowy cityscape, without an obvious purpose or destination. Within this apparently arbitrary outward journey, an inward journey unfolds in the form of memories which, seemingly without any order or control, overwhelm the Arab. The train journey becomes an inward journey of reminiscence, and the anonymous public spaces of the trains turn into one single mnemonic space that gives these memories room to surface. Although the Arab appears turned inwards and towards the memories of his past when he sits '[f]örsjunken, nästan okontaktbar' [absorbed, almost inapproachable] (20), the first paragraph of the text, introducing the Arab through free indirect discourse, suggests otherwise:

> Araben, som nog egentligen är en turk eller kurd eller pers, kan liknas vid en avfallsprodukt. En felmarginal som ingår i beräkningarna [...] tänker han själv där han sitter på sitt säte. [...] Han är ett misslyckande, ett någonting som aldrig blev, en tabbe eller en gudomlig flopp. [...] Han ler för sig själv vid tanken. Han har inte sett det på det sättet tidigare.

> [The Arab, who is probably a Turk or a Kurd or a Persian, is like a waste product. A margin of error included in the calculations [...] he thinks to himself while sitting on his seat [...] He is a failure, a something that never came to anything, a howler or a magnificent flop. [...] He smiles to himself at the thought. He hasn't seen it like that before.] (7)

The Arab's reflections reveal a complex and intricate entanglement of past and present, self-attributions and ascriptions by others. The Arab considers himself a failure while he is involuntarily flooded with memories, which suggests that this self-perception is triggered by his past. However, the Arab distances himself from this perception when he finds this thought ridiculous, which implies that he does not necessarily see himself as a failure, but that he instead engages with the ways in which he assumes he is perceived from the outside. The Arab's state of mind is redolent of W. E. B. Du Bois's famous term 'double consciousness', which, he explains, is 'this sense of always looking at one's self through the eyes of others, of measuring one's soul by the tape of a world that looks on in amused contempt and pity'.[14] The outside world, as it is presented through the Arab's consciousness, sees him not only as a failure, a piece of garbage even, but expresses its contempt by viewing him as one of many, as a man without a name and an identity, as one of an undifferentiated mass of 'Arabs'. This view is reminiscent of dominant exclusionary discourses that tend to stereotype and construct anyone as 'other' by way of racialised differences. In the anonymous space of the trains, we see an anonymised man, whose anonymity, however, is undercut, since he is singled out for his anonymised otherness, and who, moreover, is acutely aware of being othered despite his absorption.

I consider Gabriel Zoran's spatial approach to narrative text pertinent for an assessment of the mnemonic space that the trains constitute for the Arab. Zoran differentiates between the topographical level of a text, and, with reference to Bakhtin, the chronotopic level.[15] The topographical level signifies the static 'container for all sites mentioned in the story', while the chronotopic level pertains to 'the emplotment of narrative space through movement', which links the narrative sites into a network. Furthermore, '[t]he movements that connect the sites of a narrative network are not only physical but mental; a character "thinking" of a place can make this place a significant part of the story, even if it is not physically accessible'.[16] On the topographical level, the container for the sites of the Arab's story — the anonymous space of the trains — is not static but in motion. It is a transitory and contingent space, a liminal zone, which highlights not only the contingency of memory itself, but the uncertainty that the Arab experiences while he is confronted with his relation to the past, and his surroundings in the present. While, within the Arab's outward journey on the topographical level, time follows the linear temporal sequence of changing trains, and precise arrival and departure times, on the chronotopic level, the linearity of time is suspended. The Arab's remembered past unfolds in associative leaps without linear order or coherence, so that present and past become juxtaposed, and can be read next to each other. In the Arab's, and also in the reader's perception, they exist simultaneously in the same time zone, and past events come into view, 'tydligare än perrongen han går på' [clearer than the platform he walks on] (55). Hence, the places and events of the Arab's past spread into a network before our eyes, and we can follow closely how failure is produced in the intersections of past, present, self-perception and ascriptions from the outside.

The windows into the past further reveal that the Arab's sense of failure is generated inter-relationally, and that it is closely linked to a hegemonic notion of masculinity, which Raewyn Connell defines as 'the configuration of gender practice [...] which guarantees (or is taken to guarantee) the dominant position of men and the subordination of women'.[17] In a conversation between Yasaman and her mother (in one of Yasaman's parts of *Araben*), the mother tells Yasaman: 'Din pappa tjänade jättebra med pengar när han ledde fabriken. Vi levde ett jättebra liv. Hus, bil, pengar [...] Varje vecka kom han hem och la hela lönen på soffbordet [...] Sen fick jag använda pengarna som jag ville' [Your dad earned good money when he managed the factory. We lived a great life. House, car, money [...] Every week he came home and put the entire salary on the coffee table [...] And I could use the money as I wanted] (218). Yasaman's mother bemoans the loss of a time in which she lived a comfortable life because of the money her husband earned and placed at her disposal. For the Arab, being 'Herr ingenjör' [Mr. Engineer] (133) entails what can be called a 'patriarchal dividend' in the sense that he, as the breadwinner, gains 'a dividend from patriarchy in terms of honour, prestige and the right to command'. However, as this role is socially, culturally and inter-relationally constructed, it 'will come under pressure when it becomes impossible for men to win the bread'.[18] Indeed, when the Arab is sent to prison in consequence of his involvement with the Communist Party, he loses his job as an engineer, which, concomitantly, jeopardises his marriage because he cannot provide for his family any longer, and it precipitates a crisis for his masculinity: 'Han klarade inte av att hon såg på honom så där. Att hon såg på den här mannen som han var. Som han hade blivit' [He couldn't bear that she looked at him like that. That she saw him for the man he was. That he had become] (135). Failure emerges here in the tension between husband and wife, when the Arab is not only emasculated in his own eyes, but also when he sees his perceived loss of masculinity mirrored in the eyes of his wife. In his view, which is confirmed by her gaze, he has failed his wife as a man.

Through yet another window into the past, we learn that the Arab's emigration to Sweden is motivated by the aspiration to recuperate his masculinity, which, for the Arab, correlates with status: 'Där borta skulle allting börja om. Ett annat liv, en andra chans. Ett hus, en bil. Friheten [...] Han skulle ge det till henne. Han skulle ge henne det han inte kunde ge henne i det gamla landet' [Over there, everything would start afresh. Another life, a second chance. A house, a car. Freedom [...] He would give this to her. He would give her what he couldn't give her in the old country] (131). By regaining his masculinity and the status that he has lost in Iran, the Arab hopes to win back the love of his wife by proving to her that he can be the provider that she expects him to be. However, the Arab's new reality in Sweden is not congruent with his dreams: his engineering degree is not recognised in Sweden, and although he studies engineering at the KTH Royal Institute of Technology in Stockholm and subsequently finds work with the telecommunications company Ericsson, he is eventually made redundant, even though, as the Arab says to himself, 'du är en med mest kompetens' [you're the most qualified] and 'både Olsson, Petter, Moberg och Ålind [kom] in efter dig' [Olsson, Petter, Moberg and Ålind were all employed after you] (256). Examining the intersections between masculinities and immigration, Raymond Hibbins and Bob Pease propose, 'With pressures on men to be the main breadwinner in the societies in which they are settled [...] they face a range of personal, cultural, educational and systemic barriers that hinder their ability to realise their expected role as "men"'.[19] Considering the fact that the names mentioned by the Arab are all stereotypically Swedish, his dismissal from Ericsson seems to be the result of discriminatory racist practices rather than personal failure, and systemic barriers, upheld by racism, impede the Arab's chances to realise his expected role as the breadwinner.

Irrespective of his dismissal, however, the Arab recognises that his relocation to Sweden has changed him: 'Magen putade ut på honom och spände mot bältet. Han hade blivit äldre. Slapp. Huvudet var kalt mitt på. [...] Han var en annan här. En annan slags man' [His belly bulged out and strained against his belt. He had become old. Flabby. The crown of his head was bald. [...] He was someone else here. Another kind of man] (163). In comparison, Yasaman describes the Arab's former self from a photograph of her father from the 1970s, and we see '[s]tora starka armar, håriga underarmar. Trygga händer mot den korniga bakgrunden. En lång stark man med stadig blick. Muskulösa lår. [...] principfast och målmedveten' [[b]ig strong arms, hairy forearms. Hands inspiring confidence against the grainy background. A tall strong man with a steady gaze. Muscular thighs. [...] steady in both his principles and purpose] (269) — in short, a handsome, physically strong man with equally strong principles. Through the changes in his physique, the Arab comes to realise that he has lost his erstwhile sense of masculinity on an embodied and an inter-relational level, and, with regard to his wife, he understands that he has nothing to offer her any more, and that she will leave him, 'Förr eller senare' [Sooner or later] (163), because of this; indeed, the Arab's wife does divorce him once it becomes clear that he cannot provide for her and their two children any more. During his reflections on the train, the Arab comes to understand that even his life-long credo, 'Den som offrar mest och lever svårast får utdelningen på slutet' [The one who sacrifices most and lives the hardest life reaps the profit in the end] (96), is a fallacy. Divorced and alone, estranged from his children, unemployed and on benefits, there is no profit to reap, and all the Arab is left with is 'skammen som han dragit över sig och sitt namn' [the shame that he has brought upon himself and his name] (202). This shame is increased by the Arab's attempt to keep up appearances, as he travels with a briefcase that 'endast rymmer några vita ark' [contains nothing but a few white sheets of paper] (86). While we learn that the train journey's purpose is to make it look like the Arab is on his way to, or back from, work, he questions himself: 'Hans ansikte reflekteras tillbaka. Han ser sig själv. Så gammal nu. Så sliten. [...] Kan det vara så att han haft fel?' [His face is reflected back. He sees himself. So old now. So worn out. [...] Is it possible that he was wrong?] (192). The Arab's life is mirrored back at him in the same way that he sees his face reflected in the dark train window, and he admits to himself that he sees himself as a failure; that his whole life is a fake. Through the network of sites, created by the analepses into the Arab's past, we can follow the trajectory of failure: we can see how failure is produced, and how it dominates the Arab's reflections in the narrative present. Hence, the affect of failure helps to build the narrative architecture of the Arab's part of *Araben*, and through this affective structure, contextual configurations become evident for the reader in the clash between restrictive exclusionary immigration policies (at least, at that time) and possible racist exclusionary work practices, and a particular perception of masculinity.

Moreover, these contextual configurations are made visible in the ways that the Arab establishes relations between his own life experiences, now remembered, and those of the (native, white) Swedes around him on the trains. In the beginning of the text, the Arab feels stereotyped by his surroundings, and towards the end of the text, he 'stereotypes back':

> De här människorna som inte sett diktaturer, fängslade ungdomar och oändliga korridorer med isoleringsceller eller hört skriken från torterade studenter [...] de som istället sett välfärdsstater och pensioner, ställt sig i kö utan att trängas [...] Haft tilltro och varit trygga. Är detta verkligheten?

> [These people who haven't seen dictatorships, imprisoned teenagers and endless corridors lined with isolation cells, or heard the screams of tortured students [...] who instead have seen welfare states and pensions, stood in queues without any pushing [...] Had faith and felt safe. Is this reality?] (189)

This direct comparison between the Arab's violent past and a contemporary Sweden highlights that, at least in the Arab's perception, his reality deviates to a great extent from a perceived typical native Swedish one. Moreover, in the Arab's view, his reality remains unrecognised by those Swedes whom he stereotypes, and instead, he is seen as a threat to the welfare state that he describes so cynically.

This is implied when the Arab, again in a state of double consciousness, assumes the viewpoint of a derogatory perception of 'others' that he ascribes to the woman opposite him on the train: 'Lisa Perssons blick faller på honom över tidningen: han, potentiell kvinnomisshandlare och våldtäktsman som även är en potentiell högpratare på biblioteket och kan tänkas medha matsäck på kafé och vara parasiterande bidragstagare' [Lisa Persson's gaze catches him over the top of her newspaper: a potential wife-beater and rapist who also quite possibly talks too loudly in the library and probably brings his own packed lunch to the café and is likely to be a scrounging benefits recipient] (9). Lisa Persson comes to stand for the majority of white, native Swedes who, in the Arab's anticipation, construct him as someone who does not know the rules, exploits the Swedish welfare state and is potentially a criminal.

The Arab juxtaposes this discriminatory perspective with his own opinion of Sweden, according to which Sweden, and, by extension, all the Nordic countries, seem like 'en inskränkt liten byhåla i det stora Europa. Hela Norden kändes så för den delen. Som en liten avkrok. Som de där fiskarna som bodde i dyngan vid strandkanten och trodde att det var havet' [a narrow-minded, lousy little town in the European expanse. For that matter, so did the rest of the Nordic countries. Like a remote backwater. Like those fish who lived in the muck along the shoreline and thought it was the sea] (253). From the Arab's viewpoint, the ostensible remoteness of the Nordic countries is responsible for the insularity of the Swedes, who, with their supposed lack of experience and diverging realities, will never be able to understand him, and the incompatibility of these conflicting realities interferes with the Arab's sense of belonging. The narrator's focalisation of the Arab and the use of free indirect discourse allow us to share the Arab's reflections and emotions; and, when the Arab distances himself, and simultaneously the reader, from the perceptions he presumes the outside have of him, the text invites us to assess the Arab on his own terms. At the same time, this grants a view on Swedish society from the Arab's marginalised position.

Through the prism of the Arab's disillusioned perspective of himself and his life in Sweden, the trains are transformed into one liminal zone that is suspended in time, and the train journey becomes a metaphor for a life pending in non-belonging. When, as Sara Ahmed asserts, 'being-at-home is a matter of *how one feels or how one might fail to feel*', and when being-at-home is equated with belonging, the fact that the Arab feels, and is made to feel, a failure, would explain that he does not feel he belongs.[20] Nonetheless, the ending of the text points to something different. Ahmed argues that home, as 'the lived experience of a locality', is experienced with all senses as it 'involves the enveloping of subjects in a space which is not simply outside them: being-at-home suggests that the subject and space leak into each other, *inhabit each other*'.[21] While the Arab travels through Stockholm, he repeatedly comments on the weather, and insinuates that the appreciation of the Swedish winter is yet another national cliché that he is supposed to adopt: 'Man måste älska vintern i detta land' [You have to love the winter in this country] (200). This comment distances the Arab from a stereotyped Swedish appreciation of winter, but when his train journey comes to an end, the Swedish winter inhabits the Arab on his walk home, and he, in turn, fully inhabits his own appreciation of it. The Arab's body and the space around him leak into each other:

> Han vet att han sviker alla dem som åkte lastbil om natten och åker än idag och kippar efter andan och bor i någon håla i detta kalla land med barn utan namn och kvinnor utan pengar till tamponger, men. Men men men det är så härligt att se på snön och älska den [...] Kylan tränger in utan att märkas. [...] Han känner det ta över hela hans kropp.

> [He knows that he is betraying all those who travelled by truck at night and are still travelling today and are gasping for air and live in some hole in this cold country, their children without names and their women without money for tampons, but. But but but it is so wonderful to look at the snow and love it [...] The cold seeps in unnoticed. [...] He feels how it takes over his whole body.] (281)

The Arab's elation with regard to the Swedish winter is elicited by a direct comparison of his life with that of other refugees who were less lucky than he was. The sense of failure, which hovered affectively like an atmosphere over the Arab's train journey and his memories, yields now first to a feeling of guilt about his privilege, and then to a feeling of gratitude. At least in this instance, failure, guilt and shame are transcended in the Arab's sense of connectivity and embodied fusion with the cold, and, when the cold is seen as a synecdoche for Sweden, the narrator confirms the Arab's reconciliation with his life in Sweden by concluding, 'Han är i detta ögonblick en tacksam man' [In this moment, he is a grateful man] (281).

★   ★   ★   ★   ★

The mnemonic affective space in which Senthil and Valmira construct their memories in *Vor der Zunahme der Zeichen* is also, although in different ways, a liminal and contingent space: it is virtual, their encounter is not embodied, and their conversation is non-committal insofar as they could leave it at any moment without any consequences. Weighing up the advantages and disadvantages of both the online and the offline world, Zygmunt Bauman argues that in the offline world, 'I am *under control*' because I am 'expected [...] to obey, to adjust, to negotiate my place, my role', whereas in the online world I am '*in control*'. In addition, the advantages of an online existence are, as Bauman identifies them, 'the promise and expectation of liberation from the discomforts, inconveniences and hardships' that characterise the offline world.[22] Still, as Susannah Radstone points out,

> the senses and sensibilities that we bring *to* the web are woven through with our locatedness in histories, in place, in culture — all of which play their part in producing the never random associative leaps that constitute the rhetorics of memory.[23]

The online world grants Senthil and Valmira the freedom to share the hardships of their respective pasts without the regulating forces of the offline world, and with remoteness from the exclusionary discourses which the Arab negotiates in direct contact with his surroundings. While the Arab turns inwards towards his past, and outwards to engage with these discourses, Senthil and Valmira turn towards each other; they are in control, as they can manage and direct their memories in this alternative online space. However, Valmira stating, 'Wir können nur aus dieser Entfernung zueinander sprechen' [We can only talk to each other from this distance] (120), and Senthil confirming this with 'ich weiß' [I know] (121), suggests that it is not only the remoteness from an exclusionary society, but also from each other, which grants them the freedom to share and work through memories that are, potentially, painful.

Senthil alludes to the advantages of the online world when he, in a direct reference to Ludwig Wittgenstein's limits of language, says, 'niemand wird wissen, von welchen rändern wir aus sprechen' [nobody will know from which edges we speak] (30).[24] These edges can be viewed as the margins of society from which Senthil and Valmira observe this very society; and this reference also reflects Senthil's doubts about being able to capture the significance of their memories with words. At the same time, Senthil uses language to express the contingency of these memories when he repeats the word *vermutlich* [probably] three times on one page, and *vielleicht* [maybe] four times on another, or when he says, 'ich erinnere mich' [I remember], only to correct himself immediately afterwards to, 'ich glaube mich erinnern zu können' [I think I can remember] (210). This suggests that the events Senthil is recalling might have taken place in the way he recounts them — or perhaps with slight differences. Discussing the social function of narrative memory, Mieke Bal asserts that the meaning-making process happens in dialogue, in the exchange of responses and reactions to the witnessed memories, and that hence, 'narrative memory offers some form of feedback that ratifies the memory'.[25] Senthil and Valmira reiterate particular phrases and images to define their memories, in this way making use of this function: they give their memories form in their own imagination, and also in that of their interlocutor, and thus, they ratify their memories and increase their reliability in dialogue. Senthil and Valmira's mutual reassurances also imply that there is a certain knowledge of truth within these contingent memories that does not require words anyway. Senthil says, 'du weißt es' [you know it] (129), when he assumes that Valmira knows what he means without him having to explain it, and she echoes this notion with, 'Du kennst es, ich muss es Dir nicht sagen' [You know it, I don't need to tell you] (191). This knowledge of truth is that, although their experiences differ, they produce the same affects. Words might be insufficient to express their experiences accurately, but the unspoken understanding of shared affects grants their memories veracity. Not every detail of what they remember might be correct, whereas the affects are: the truth lies in what these experiences felt like.

In the same way that their initials — S.V. and V.S. — mirror each other, Senthil and Valmira compare not only their own experiences, but also reflect on their parents' professional histories. Valmira says about her mother, 'Sie wollte Neurologin werden. Seit dreizehn Jahren arbeitet sie in zwei Arztpraxen als Putzfrau' [She wanted to become a neurologist. For thirteen years, she has been working in two doctor's surgeries as a cleaner] (75), and Senthil responds with, 'seit fast fünfundzwanzig jahren arbeitet meine mutter als putzfrau' [for almost twenty-five years has my mother been working as a cleaner] (84). Senthil tells Valmira that his father, although he was once awarded a talent grant in Sri Lanka, has worked 'seit fast fünfundzwanzig jahren [...] in einer fabrik' [for almost twenty-five years [...] in a factory] (78), whereas Valmira's father studied law in Prishtina, but works as a translator now, because his degree was not recognised in Germany. This is reminiscent of the way in which the Arab's engineering degree was not recognised in Sweden, and there seems to be a tacit understanding that their parents' careers did not become diverted through lack of ambition, but rather because of exclusionary politics which consider asylum seekers such as their parents only fit for unskilled work. Returning to their own experiences of arrival and education in Germany, Senthil talks about the 'sozialwohnung' [council flat] that they 'beziehen durften' [were allowed to move into] (90), and Valmira remembers the time when she 'die Schule besuchen durfte' [was allowed to go to school] (74). The reiteration of the verb *dürfen* [to be allowed to] emphasises that Senthil and Valmira consider themselves to be at the mercy of the German state, because their parents' work, and where they live and what they learn, is contingent on German immigration regulations. Harald Welzer asserts that:

> 'Communicative memory' denotes a wilful agreement of the members of a group as to what they consider their own past to be, in interplay with the identity-specific grand narrative of the we-group, and what meaning they ascribe to this past.[26]

From this perspective, Senthil and Valmira seek agreement on their respective pasts in communication and relate their memories to the we-group, in their case German society. In consideration of Astrid Erll's argument that 'memories are never a mirror image of the past, but rather an expressive indication of the needs and interests of the person or group doing the remembering in the present', Senthil and Valmira's way of remembering serves a particular purpose in their lives in the narrative present: in dialogue, they find recognition for a past that is usually disregarded or marginalised by the predominantly white majority in their so-called host country.[27]

In *Araben*, it is the devaluation of the Arab's degree, the loss of his wife and job, and the ensuing unemployment which produces a sense of failure and shame, whereas in Senthil and Valmira's case, shame emerges in the generational gap between the protagonists and their parents. Valmira remembers 'die Scham' [the shame] (92) about her mother's lack of German when she was speaking to the officials in the Home Office, and Senthil relates that he would turn a corner before reaching 'das haus, das meine mutter putzte' [the house that my mother cleaned] (243) when he walked home from school with friends. In these instances, shame becomes tied to a perceived lack of (linguistic) integration, and to social status, despite the fact that the cause for this shame (the cleaning job) is possibly brought about by discriminatory policies and practices. Shame, however, is not only produced affectively with regard to Senthil and Valmira's parents; it also inscribes their own experiences. Recounting a memory from nursery, Senthil describes how he once drew 'menschen mit dunkler haut' [people with dark skin], and how the nursery teachers pressed a pink crayon between his fingers, instructing him, 'diese farbe nenne man *hautfarbe*, sie wiederholten es, *diese farbe nennen wir hier hautfarbe*' [this colour is called *skin colour*, they repeated it, *this colour we call skin colour here*] (94–95, italics in original). In this context of institutional racialised discrimination, the nursery teachers speak for the whole of German society with using *wir* [we] and *hier* [here], and they assume this society to be overwhelmingly and normatively white. Senthil's racialised difference is pitched against this norm, and negated: his difference is recognised, but merely as an aberration from the norm, while he, simultaneously, is asked to accept it as the status quo and abide by its rules despite his difference.

Valmira describes the centre for asylum seekers where she lived with her family as situated 'in einem Wald hinter einem hohen Zaun mit Stacheldraht darauf' [in a forest behind a high fence with barbed wire on it] (47), and, she continues, everyone in her class knew 'wo und wie wir wohnten, aber sie wussten es nicht von mir' [where and how we lived, but they didn't know it from me] (53–54). Valmira's classmates do not talk with her directly, but assume they have some knowledge about her, and, as a result, she becomes excluded from the we-group of German school children, and ostracised. Senthil and Valmira are marginalised not only geographically, but also socially, because they are the children of asylum seekers. In Senthil and Valmira's peers, the intersection of this form of social marginalisation and their being othered for outward appearances finds its expression in a racialised xenophobic rhetoric. Thinking of her class in school, Valmira remembers that she was called '*dreckige Bettlerin* und *schmutziges Asylantenkind*' [*filthy beggar* and *dirty asylum seeker*] (93, italics in original), and Senthil recalls how some children referred to him and his brother as 'die söhne des schwarzen mannes' [the sons of the bogeyman] because there is 'schmutz' [dirt] on their skin 'der abfärbt, wenn man uns berührt' [that rubs off when you touch us] (94). These practices of othering mark Senthil and Valmira as different, and when this difference is associated with dirt that could potentially 'contaminate' the we-group, 'the threat posed by strange bodies to bodily and social integrity is registered on the skin': the skin is the boundary between 'us' and 'them', and the separation between 'us' and 'them' works affectively via the skin.[28] Seen this way, Senthil and Valmira are made into Julia Kristeva's abjects, for 'what is *abject* [...] is radically excluded'. Abjection, as Kristeva argues further, is not caused by 'lack of cleanliness or health [...] but [by] what disturbs identity, system, order'.[29] The association of otherness with dirt is used to construct Senthil and Valmira as a threat to the immediate members of the white, German we-group, and, by extension, of the whole German body politic. On their path through nursery and school, Senthil and Valmira are purportedly integrated into German society, while, in truth, they are stigmatised, and remain excluded because of their embodied otherness.

When Senthil and Valmira change from the past tense to the present tense, we realise that their lives in the narrative now are still affected by exclusionary discourses and practices, although they state their belonging to a predominantly native German student community. Valmira tells Senthil that her lecturers at university often take her for 'eine Austauschstudentin' [an exchange student], and further, that one lecturer complimented her on her '*fehlerfreien Deutsch*' [*flawless German*] (192, italics in original), while Senthil comments on the lecturer's patronising attitude with, 'nur gebrochenes deutsch wird uns zugestanden' [we are only granted broken German] (191). With regard to this exchange, Armin Nassehi's notion of a 'Paradoxie des Sichtbaren' [paradox of the visible] is instructive. Nassehi defines this paradox as a conscious oversight, which, although it seems contradictory, leads to an explicit way of seeing, as visible differences produce a particular kind of attention that is usually mistaken for information from which conclusions are drawn: because someone is visibly different, it is impossible, for instance, that they have a full grasp of the German language. Summarising his observations, Nassehi argues that it makes no difference whether those perceived as 'other' are 'positiv oder negativ diskriminiert' [positively or negatively discriminated].[30] This paradoxical way of seeing can be understood as one technique of othering that fetishises Senthil and Valmira: despite both being part of German society, they are recognised as strangers, and thus, they become fixed in a juxtaposition of proximity and distance. Within this 'ontology of strangers', their otherness becomes ontological, because their beings are determined from the outside by their status as 'strangers', although they have lived in Germany most of their lives.[31]

This form of stranger fetishism is further accentuated when, in Senthil and Valmira's conversation, the past slides into the present, and when we come to realise that discriminations similar to those which marked their pasts are still prevalent in the narrative present. Senthil relates an event from his past school days in which his geography teacher, in the lesson on India, asks him 'wann ich wieder zurückgehen würde, in *dein heimatland*' [when I would go back, to *your home country*] (186, italics in original), and Valmira responds almost verbatim with the observation that people ask her repeatedly 'wann ich wieder zurückgehe, zurück in *meine Heimat*' [when I would go back, back to *my home country*] (191, italics in original). Yildiz and Hill argue that those who are perceived as migrants, or their descendants, are often accosted by '"natives" who act as self-appointed experts on their origin', and who, by insisting on the question of return, make it clear 'that the migrants do not really belong'.[32] While Senthil and Valmira see themselves as part of German society with a rich history of German and international popular culture, as indicated by their exchange about literature, films and music, the outside world picks out their origins as a central theme, and make it known to them that they do not belong. The reiteration of the past in the present emphasises the continuity of such discourses and practices of othering, with a somewhat bleak outlook for the future, as it suggests that these practices, clichéd as they may appear, will not cease, and that Senthil and Valmira will always be thought of in terms of their supposed otherness.

We have seen how, in the Arab's parts of *Araben* and in *Vor der Zunahme der Zeichen*, histories of marginalisation and othering unfold within the protagonists' memories, and how such histories work affectively, because they produce a sense of failure, and of shame. For the Arab, this failure is transcended when he feels grateful in a moment of reconciliation with the Swedish cold, and Senthil and

Valmira's conversation equally ends on a positive note. Towards the end of the text, Valmira states, 'Wir sind am Ende angekommen' [We have arrived at the end] (240). In a temporal sense, they have worked their way backwards through their memories until they arrived at the moment of their respective departures; and, within the context of their conversation, they have arrived at the point where they can accept the shame (and pain) inherent in their memories. When Bal discusses traumatic memory, she argues that the threatening quality of memory can be alleviated when another person bears witness, and that listening, or dialogue, can be of help to 'narratively integrate what was until then an assailing spectre'; and, as Bal continues, 'a second person is needed for the first person to come into his- or herself in the present, able to bear the past'.[33] Disregarding the question of whether Senthil's and Valmira's memories qualify as traumatic or not, Bal's words help us to understand their need for each other to state the truthfulness of their affectively shared experiences. With the reiteration of phrases such as 'Du wirst es wissen' [You'll know it] (192), they validate their own interpretations of past and present events, and they ascribe meaning to their histories. By stating what their pasts felt like, and having it confirmed by their interlocutor, the shame does not necessarily disappear, but Senthil and Valmira find recognition, at least vis-à-vis each other, which allows them to come into themselves. It is not surprising that in both texts, marginalised memories can only emerge in similarly marginal, or liminal, spaces, considering that they run contrary to those discourses which usually sustain this kind of marginalisation. However, Senthil and Valmira verify their knowledge of past events and the affective impact of these events, while the Arab negotiates his past in direct confrontation with his surroundings. In this sense, the protagonists set their histories against what Yildiz calls 'das vorherrschende Wissen der Dominanzgesellschaft' [the prevailing knowledge of the dominant society],[34] and the liminal zones of the online world in *Vor der Zunahme der Zeichen*, and the trains in *Araben*, are transformed into spaces of resistance in which histories of marginalisation find recognition. The texts reveal these processes of marginalisation and othering, and in this way, they grant us not only insight into the workings of these processes, but also a view on German and Swedish society, respectively, from the margins these societies have themselves created.

Postmigrant Societies: From within the 'Ghetto'

While the previous section arrived at a postmigrant perspective on Swedish and German society through the prism of the protagonists' pasts, the following two sections turn to the question of how Jamal and Mo, in *Tante Ulrikkes vei*, and Yasaman, in her narrative strand of *Araben*, perceive themselves in relation to the Norwegian and Swedish societies in the narrative present. In the previous section, I utilised the term 'liminal zones' to refer to those spaces where remembering takes place from the vantage point of the present, whereas, for the purpose of the following discussion, I conceive of liminal zones as the 'multiple localities and spatialities of state and society' where boundaries of sameness and otherness are contested in negotiations of inclusion and exclusion.[35] Then, liminal zones are not only recognisable in physical locations, but also tangentially in the protagonists' conflicts; in their 'Kämpfen um Teilhabe und Gleichheit' [struggles for participation and equality].[36] Through the postmigrant perspective, I ask whether these conflicts are actually related to what Yildiz and Hill mark as 'immigrant problems',[37] or whether they are depicted as linked to societal, political and economic power relations. From the angle of affect, the postmigrant perspective serves to explore those affects that inscribe the protagonists' experiences of marginality, and, at the same time, to make the connection between these affective experiences of marginality and the power structures that complicate the protagonists' sense of belonging. The protagonists' conflicts, and their sense of marginality, are closely tied to particular spaces, and therefore it is relevant to consider where these struggles are played out. As we have seen in the previous section, these spaces are more than just a backdrop; they become affective spaces, because they facilitate the emergence of particular affects, and thus themselves become imbued with affects.

I am drawing on Ahmed's notion of 'affect aliens' to illustrate the ways in which the conjunctions or disjunctions between the protagonists and Swedish, or Norwegian, society work affectively. Ahmed claims that personally felt emotions are social in the sense that they 'involve different movements towards and away from others', and that therefore the ways in which 'we feel about others is what aligns us with a collective'.[38] In Ahmed's view, one of the most prominent emotions that aligns individuals with a collective is happiness: some objects gain affective value through their circulation as happy objects, and when 'we feel pleasure from such objects, we are aligned'; in contrast, we 'become alienated — out of line with an affective community — when we do not experience pleasure from proximity to objects that are attributed as being good'. Becoming alienated from a community on an affective level does not necessarily entail that someone feels different affects, but rather, that 'an affect alien might experience the same affect but in relation to different objects' than those the dominant majority feels happy about. In the context of migration, the integration of migrants and their descendants is, as Ahmed argues, considered a national ideal, and serves as a means for 'imagining national happiness'. Hence, migrant and postmigrant individuals are subject to 'the happiness duty', which implies, in positive terms, speaking only of good experiences, and, in negative terms, not speaking of those histories or present realities which are not happy. When migrant or postmigrant individuals 'speak out of consciousness of such histories, and with consciousness of racism', despite this injunction, they become affect aliens. We have already seen how the Arab, in *Araben*, and Senthil and Valmira, in *Vor der Zunahme der Zeichen*, become precisely such affect aliens in the sense that they seek recognition for their marginalised histories and experiences of racism against the dominant discourses of the German and Swedish nations into which they are ostensibly happily integrated. With regard to Yasaman's experiences in *Araben*, and Jamal's and Mo's in *Tante Ulrikkes vei*, I am interested in the ways in which they become alienated from themselves or the societies in which they live, 'by virtue of how they are affected by the world or how they affect others in the world'.[39]

In *Tante Ulrikkes vei*, the two Norwegian-born young men Mo and Jamal live in Stovner, a satellite town that Mo describes as having a, 'Høy tetthet av innvandrere. Høy ungdomskriminalitet. Høy andel skoledropouts. Høy andel kassamedarbeidere, hjelpepleiere, vaskepersonale og trygdemottakere' [High density of immigrants. High rate of youth crime. High proportion of school dropouts. High percentage of cashiers, care workers, cleaners and benefits recipients] (8). Mo's description resonates with a conversation between Yasaman and her best friend Tove, in which Tove, with reference to one of Stockholm's suburbs, says, 'Jag menar, bo i fucking jävla Alby och gå på SFI och bli behandlad som om man har pesten' [I mean, live in fucking Alby and go to SFI and get treated as if you've got the plague] (49).[40] These two urban districts, Stovner in Oslo and Alby in Stockholm, strongly resemble each other; but while Mo's description merely states facts, Tove adds qualifiers to areas such as these, and thus indicates how they are perceived in the dominant public view, namely as highly undesirable. In addition, Tove suggests that living in an area such as Alby is concomitant with being treated in particular ways, and, when she uses the plague as a simile, the threat of contagion becomes affectively associated with the inhabitants of Alby. Earlier, we have seen how Senthil and Valmira are made into abjects and are excluded for their embodied otherness; in the case of Alby (and Stovner, too), the inhabitants of a whole area are seen as abjects who have to be excluded because they could contaminate the perceived homogeneity of Swedish (or Norwegian) society. In Tabish Khair's words, Tove addresses a form of xenophobia which 'entails the construction of a stranger or a strangeness to be detested or feared in ways that enable or sustain institutionally uneven power relations': when affects such as fear and threat circulate and stick to the inhabitants of particular areas, affect bolsters these uneven power relations and allows for the ghettoisation and stigmatisation of racialised 'others' despite the assumption that the majority of them are born in the countries in which they live.[41] The protagonists of both *Araben* and *Tante Ulrikkes vei* take a stand with regard to areas which are marked by what the sociologist Loïc Wacquant calls 'territorial stigmatization', and which are perceived as points of contention where the boundaries between 'us' and 'them' are staked out, reinforced or questioned.[42] However, while Mo and Jamal position themselves in relation to such an area and its stigma from within its boundaries, Yasaman does so from the outside, which suggests that geographical and social marginalisation plays a more significant role in Jamal's and Mo's negotiations of belonging or un-belonging than in Yasaman's.

This notion is confirmed when Yasaman and Tove, in the same conversation, discuss degrees of sameness and difference. Tove asks, 'Hur många riktiga blattar hänger vi med ens en gång?' [How many proper *blattar* do we actually hang out with even once?], and answers her own rhetorical question immediately afterwards with, 'Noll om vi räknar bort såna svennebanan-invandrare som du' [Zero, if we discount Superswede-immigrants like you] (49).[43] Tove operates within a class system in which she differentiates between white Swedes, integrated postmigrants such as Yasaman, and those Ahmed calls 'other others' — the residents of Alby.[44] Tove distinguishes Yasaman from those people of colour whom she derogatorily calls *riktiga blattar*, and, when Tove uses hyphenation to emphasise Yasaman's

Swedish-ness, instead of denoting an ethnicity in combination with the name of the country of residence, she attests Yasaman's belonging to Sweden. In addition, with the use of the pronoun *vi* [we], Tove makes Yasaman her equal by including her as part of the native Swedish we-group. While the inhabitants of Alby remain excluded from Swedish society because they are discredited on the basis of their place of residence, Yasaman is included because she is assimilated, and belongs to the group of those who are, in Tove's jesting words, 'svarta utanpå, vita inuti' [black on the outside, white on the inside] (49). Yasaman endorses her assimilation, and states that she has to thank her father for it: 'Det första min pappa gjorde när vi flyttade hit var att skaffa en lägenhet där svenskarna bodde. [...] Så att vi skulle växa upp med svenskar, var tanken. Lära oss svenska, bli assimilerade' [The first thing my dad did when we moved here was to get a flat where the Swedes lived. [...] So that we would grow up with Swedes — that was the idea. Learn Swedish, become assimilated] (50).

From the outset, the Arab provided Yasaman and her brother Pedram with a position of privilege in the sense that he spared them the social and geographical marginalisation, as well as the humiliation, which Senthil and Valmira had to suffer, and which were tied to racialised differences, and to their status as children of asylum seekers. While the Arab, in his parts of the text, does not acknowledge his success, Yasaman's perspective modifies the Arab's sense of failure somewhat when we learn that he accomplished his dream: in Sweden, the Arab thought his children to 'bli människor som han aldrig haft möjligheten att bli' [become people that he never had the chance to become himself]; he gave them the opportunity to attend university, and '[l]ära sig tänka som fria människor' [[l]earn to think like free people] (131). For Yasaman, this privilege correlates with her assimilation, and it entails that those boundaries that simultaneously confine and exclude Alby's residents do not concern her. However, the Norwegian equivalent of these boundaries, those constructed discursively and politically around Stovner, are a reality for Jamal and Mo which concerns them directly, and as they live within Stovner's confines, they are compelled to position themselves in relation to these boundaries.

To recapitulate, *Tante Ulrikkes vei* is presented as a research project with Mo and Jamal as participants, in which they are encouraged to talk about their daily lives in school, and their relationships with parents, friends and partners. While Alby, as it is depicted by Tove, is a secluded unit with boundaries set from the outside, this fictitious research project seeks to penetrate precisely such boundaries. Within the framework of this research project, the researcher Lars Bakken submits an intermediate report to the funding body, and, summarising the provisional results of the project, points towards particular challenges that distinguish the experiences of his respondents from those of young people in other parts of Oslo: '*Dette handler i en del tilfeller om levekår og økonomi, samt at enkelte opplever at deres bakgrunn kan virke tyngende, særlig i møte med eksterne*' [*In some cases, it is about living conditions and financial means, but also that some individuals experience their background as problematic, particularly in relation to people who are not from Stovner*] (261, italics in original). As the research project focuses exclusively on young people with a migrant background, Bakken's comment shows that he, and by extension the project, conflates issues of financial means and social standing with matters of migration. In addition, Bakken's comment points towards a degree of migrantisation, or, to paraphrase Spielhaus, towards the project's obsession with issues of migration and integration. With this focus, the project runs the risk of deflecting attention away from the structural, economic and political inequalities which are at the core of Mo's and Jamal's struggles. Moreover, when Bakken uses the term *eksterne* [people who are not from Stovner], he uncritically addresses an inside and an outside, or an 'us' and 'them'. Within this binary, Bakken marks Mo and Jamal as belonging to a particular group and to a certain area, while they are simultaneously excluded from other groups and areas. However, Bakken observes that this belonging is not solely a construction from the outside, but that the young people themselves *'I sterkere grad enn ungdommer i andre bydeler i Oslo oppfatter seg selv som å tilhøre bydelen sin [...] fremfor å være Oslo-borger eller nordmann'* [to a greater extent than young people from other areas of Oslo perceive themselves as belonging to their area [...] rather than to Oslo or Norway] (261–62, italics in original). According to Bakken's observations, there are, as he puts it, *'noen motstridende trekk'* [some contradictory aspects] in this belonging. Being granted access to the participants' thoughts and opinions by virtue of his research project, Bakken is able to state that they, to the outside, *'beskriver oppveksten sin i positive ordelag'* [describe their upbringing in positive terms] and *'villig forsvarer sin bakgrunn'* [willingly defend their background], while they, internally, *'uttrykker et ønske om å flytte på sikt'* [express a wish to move away in the long run] (262, italics in original).

This dichotomy between a sense of belonging to Stovner and the wish to break away from it is exemplified in Mo's and Jamal's diverging attitudes towards their district, and in their bifurcating 'strategies of coping and escape'.[45] Mo learns early in his life that he is categorised as belonging to the group of the territorially stigmatised, and when he recalls a conversation between two teachers at his school, he remembers that, 'Det de snakka så opphissa om, var oss' [What they were all getting so worked up about was us] (10). The teachers clarify that the social and ethnic composition of this group is bound to a particular area, and Mo, paraphrasing them, says that, 'Så mange utlendinger det hadde blitt [...] Evnesvake elever. Foreldrene som ikke forsto noe. Nabolagene som var slum' [There were so many foreigners now [...] Incompetent pupils. Parents who didn't understand anything. Neighbourhoods that were slums] (10); for Mo, it becomes unequivocally clear 'hvor sterkt de mislikte oss' [how strongly they disliked us] (11). In her sociological study of Furuset — an area in Oslo contiguous with Stovner and similarly stigmatised — Monika Grønli Rosten suggests that the negative public discourses about the place 'skaper en kollektiv opplevelse av uverdighet og skam blant beboerne' [create a collective experience of unworthiness and shame among the inhabitants].[46] Mo feels the shame concomitant with this stigma individually, yet keenly, and as a child, he hoped that the issue 'kom til å forsvinne om jeg bare holdt kjeft' [would disappear if I just shut up] (11). However, instead of disappearing by way of keeping it a secret, the issue expands:

> Jeg fant ut at lærerne ikke var alene. De snakka om oss på nyhetene og skrev om oss i avisa. Om ungdomsgjenger som tvang nye rekrutter til å slå ned tilfeldig

forbipasserende. Hvor dårlig skolene var. Om attenåringer som ikke kunne lese engang, og hvert fall ikke skrive skikkelig norsk [...] Jeg husker de begynte å si integrere.

[I found out that the teachers were not alone. They talked about us on the news and wrote about us in the newspaper. About gangs of teenagers who forced new recruits to knock down random passers-by. How bad the schools were. About eighteen-year-olds who couldn't even read, let alone write proper Norwegian [...] I remember they started to use the word integration.] (12)

Mo engages with a discourse and politics of ethnicisation which relates a set of problems to questions of migration and integration, while they, particularly when considering that Mo and his peer group are all Norwegian-born, are actually connected to social and economic inequalities, and territorial stigmatisation. When these discourses and politics defer responsibility to those they brand as *utlendinger* [foreigners], migration, to paraphrase Römhild, is treated as a separate problem as if the majority of Norwegian society has nothing to do with it. Concomitantly, as Juliane Karakayali and Paul Mecheril rightly point out, integration is viewed as 'einseitig als von Migrant_innen zu erbringende Anpassungsleistungen' [demands to assimilate which have to be unilaterally fulfilled by migrants], and the success or failure, the acceptance or refusal, of this assimilation is solely dependent on the migrants or postmigrants themselves.[47] Mo's embodied reaction to this rhetoric of stigmatisation invades his adolescent life and becomes established as a permanent feature: 'Det jeg vokste opp med, forandra seg til noe fremmed, voksent og stygg [...] Alt blanda seg sammen til et ubehag som satt i magen' [Everything I grew up with became strange, grown-up and ugly [...] Everything got tangled together into a knot of unease that sat in my stomach] (13). Mo's words demonstrate that he, as a result of these discourses, is made into an affect alien, because he is excluded from the supposed happiness of the affective community of Norwegian society on the basis of his migrant background and his place of residence.

As a coping strategy, Mo chooses to escape Stovner in the hope of aligning himself practically and affectively with the majority of Norwegian society. This attempt, however, complicates his sense of belonging, because an affiliation with the dominant affective community is impeded by said discourses, and Mo's academic ambitions distinguish him from his peers in a way that alienates him: 'Jeg er den rare gutten, jeg vet de tenker det. Som dem, men ikke. Norsk 1, ikke norsk 2. Et språk med flere ord fra skolebøkene inne på rommet enn fra gata utafor' [I'm the weird boy, I know they think this. Like them, but not. Norwegian 1, not Norwegian 2. Using a language with more words from the schoolbooks in the classroom than from the street outside] (26). Nevertheless, Mo mobilises the only resources available to him — his talent and his intellectual capacities — as a way out of Stovner, which indicates that he holds the place responsible for his double alienation, and not the politics that stigmatise it: 'jeg pugger til prøver som om det står om livet, for det er liksom det jeg veit om for å komme meg ut fra skogen på Stovner' [I cram for the tests as if it's a matter of life or death, because it's like the only way I know to get out of Stovner] (23). Mo's ambition is supported by his parents, who repeatedly advise him to 'gå på et universitet, få en grad, bra jobb, stort hus, fin bil, pen kone' [go to university, get a degree, good job, big house, nice car, beautiful wife] (21); in short, Mo's parents urge him to achieve all those materialistic values that would allow him to align himself with the dominant majority. Mo's strategy proves successful, as he finishes school with excellent results and begins to study economics at the University of Oslo. As a boy, Mo dreamed of girls, but '[i]kke jenter fra Stovner, men sånne norske jenter' [[n]ot girls from Stovner, but proper Norwegian girls] (21); in other words, white girls without the stigma of the 'ghetto'. When Mo meets Maria at university and enters into a relationship with her, his dream has come true, and through his proximity to those objects that the Norwegian majority considers good, he feels less alienated from this majority when he becomes ostensibly aligned with the Norwegian affective community.

Mo's university studies are made possible with the help of a scholarship which is part of a governmental support package for Grorud, and, conspicuously excluding female teenagers from higher education, aimed at 'ungdom fra ressurssvake familier' [teenagers from low-income families] and intended 'å øke gutter med innvandrerbakgrunns deltakelse i høyere utdanning' [to increase the participation of boys with a migrant background in higher education] (96, italics in original). The other part of the support package is 'verdens største lampe' [the world's biggest lamp] (252) — a giant street lamp that only works for a short period of time, and, once darkness secludes the area around it after it has stopped working, it is used by teenagers as a meeting point to smoke cannabis. When Rosten polemically argues that, 'Både det norske velferdsnivået og velferdsstatens vilje til å sørge for sine borgere skulle kanskje tilsi at territoriell stigmatisering ikke var et problem i Norge' [Both the level of Norwegian welfare and the will of the welfare state to provide for its citizens might suggest that territorial stigmatisation is not a problem in Norway],[48] her polemic can be brought in direct relation to the way in which *Tante Ulrikkes vei* portrays these governmental measures. On the one hand, the text ridicules these measures, because the lamp is not only not working, but also useless in the first place, and thus a waste of public money. On the other hand, and although the scholarship appears as if tailored for Mo, these measures are depicted as exclusively supporting those (male) 'others' who demonstrate ambition and potential to align with the norm. Thus, the text exposes the Norwegian welfare state as only providing for those citizens who are recognisable within frames of likeness, or who adapt to these frames by way of assimilation, whereas those who do not adapt to this normative frame remain territorially and socially stigmatised.

Be that as it may, Mo's studies and his relationship with Maria are his means to venture out of the narrow confines of Stovner, and he explores parts of Oslo that were hitherto unknown to him, enjoying 'å gå rundt og oppdage størrelsen på byen' [to walk around and discover the size of the city] (230). However, when international events such as 9/11, and local events such as the murder of the young Muslim woman Farah in Stovner, intersect with racism, this newly discovered size of Oslo shrinks back to Stovner, and Mo is reminded of the stigma he carries because of his place of residence, and because of his appearance, which marks him as 'other'. At first, Mo tries to ignore any news coverage in relation to 9/11, because, as he states when he watches President Bush on TV declaring war on terror, 'Jeg klarer det ikke [...] Jeg har bestemt meg for at det er nok nå. Jeg kan ikke ha mer av sånt' [I can't cope with this [...] I have decided that enough is enough. I can't take any more of this] (64). Bush's declaration results in polarisation, with local ripple effects also in Norway, and Mo knows, when President Bush talks about 'kampen mellom godt og ondt' [the fight between good and evil] (64), that he will be stereotyped as 'evil' despite his assimilation, which jeopardises his wish to escape Stovner. In the same way that Mo could not avoid being stigmatised as a child by keeping quiet, his deliberate ignorance cannot prevent these dynamics. When Farah is shot dead by her brother in Stovner, Stovner is spotlighted in the media as, 'Hatets hovedkvarter' [The Headquarters of Hate], and articles appear which feature headlines such as 'Drabantbyen som dreper? Vitner forteller: Æreskultur utbredt på Stovner' [The Ghetto that Kills? Witnesses Reveal: Honour Culture Widespread in Stovner] (276, italics in original). These events have an immediate impact on Mo's life: Maria's mother, who had treated him without prejudice to date, sees herself now compelled to ask, 'er ikke du fra stedet der hun stakkars Farah ble drept?' [aren't you from the place where poor Farah was killed?] (286); Maria's friends just want to ask whether Mo knew Farah, and volunteer their opinions on Muslims, headscarves and stories where someone's brother 'ble rana av utlendinger' [was mugged by foreigners] (289), always with the disclaimer, 'Ikke noe stygt ment' [No offence] (288). This Islamophobia, the prejudiced and racist focus on 'immigrant problems', or rather, white Norwegians' problems with racialised 'others', makes Mo uncomfortable, so that he can only half-heartedly agree with Maria when she tells him, 'Glem det nå' [Forget about it now] (291).

When Mo's affective alignment with the majority becomes ruptured, it demonstrates that he, through the circulation of hate and its attachment to particular others, 'comes to stand for, and stand in for, a group of others', and, as hate 'functions to substantiate the threat of invasion and contamination', it results in Mo's exclusion from the affective community that included him before.[49] The newspaper headlines show that Mo is perceived as the representative of a group, and also of a place: in the jargon of the journalists, it reads as if the place Stovner itself fired the shot that killed Farah. When Mo describes that it is for him, 'Som om skuddet som ble avfyrt, fortsatte inn i meg' [As if the shot that was fired went straight into me] (266), he acknowledges the power of this kind of representation; he knows that, when one other stands in for the group, the negative impact will necessarily also affect the whole group. Or, in other words, the deed of one is a crime committed by all of those who, in the public view, are complicit by proxy. In consequence of this transference, Farah's murder is not treated as an isolated case, and Oslo City Council implements measures for tackling violence in Stovner in general, so that Mo's family receive an invitation from Oslo City Council 'til gruppesamtale med en barnepsykolog om gode holdninger i barneoppdragelse' [to a group discussion with a child psychologist about positive attitudes for bringing up children] (277). When Mo's mother reacts with, 'Tror de virkelig jeg kan drepe mitt eget barn?' [Do they really think I could kill my own child?] (277), her question highlights that these measures cause more harm than they solve problems, and how misguided and prejudiced such means are when they are applied in a generalising way.

For Mo, this negative representation is epitomised when he arrives at Oslo Airport on return from a holiday in Spain with Maria. While Maria goes speedily through passport control, Mo is held back by policemen and kept waiting for hours, on suspicion of 'ulovlig innvandring' [illegal immigration] (317), as he is informed curtly. Eventually, the police ask Mo a list of questions such as, 'Hvor har du lært språket så godt?' [Where have you learned the language so well?], or whether he can quote the national anthem. When Mo's Norwegian citizenship is thus called into question by exclusionary and racist practices, he loses his composure and shouts, 'Hvem faen tror dere egentlig at jeg er a?!' [Who the fuck do you actually think I am?!]. By way of explanation, the police tell him, 'Må bare sjekke noen ganger vettu. Sånn har det blitt' [Just have to check sometimes, you know. That's how it is now] (319). They trivialise their attitude, and normalise the implicit racism by describing their actions as a natural development that is outside their control. In reply to this event, Mo devours any national or international news coverage on immigration, asylum seekers and integration, or, as he has it in a gesture of identification with those who are similarly othered as he is, 'Alt som handler om meg' [Everything that is about me] (334). Mo's growing anger estranges him from his studies and Maria, and when he says, 'det glipper' [it's slipping] (226), he acknowledges that all those values that aligned him affectively with the Norwegian majority have lost their valence for him. As a result, Maria and Mo drift apart and eventually separate, and Mo misses the deadline for his bachelor's thesis. Finding himself repeatedly racialised and marginalised, Mo realises, to paraphrase Bromley, that it will never cease that he is thought of as a 'migrant', or in terms of his supposed ethnicity, no matter how educated or integrated he perceives himself to be — a fact which only increases his anger: 'Men noen ganger klarer jeg ikke roe meg likevel, for jeg vet at det alltid er der i bakgrunnen' [But sometimes I don't manage to calm down, because I know that it's always there in the background] (429). Ahmed's insights provide a cogent explanation for the reasons of Mo's anger: 'Tolerance', as Ahmed argues,

> offers its own promise of happiness: as if the world is open to you, as if you can do what you want in the world that you are in. Your experience of living in the world exposes this openness as a fantasy. Anger fills the gap between the promise and what happens.[50]

Through his living in the world, in Norwegian society, Mo comes to realise that the openness which, for him, held the promise that he could leave Stovner and the concomitant stigma behind, is false, and he understands that his hope of affectively aligning himself with those objects that guarantee the majority's happiness has become disappointed. In this moment of realisation, Mo has become an affect alien, because he is estranged from himself and his dreams, and from the community that, seemingly, promised the fulfilment of these dreams.

★   ★   ★   ★   ★

Jamal, the other correspondent in Bakken's research project, employs a coping strategy in relation to Stovner and its territorial stigmatisation which is diametrically opposed to Mo's. Jamal states his belonging to a particular ethnic, religious and local group which is distinct from the white Norwegian majority when he introduces himself to Bakken with, 'Men ok, jeg er Jamal. Svarting, muslim, fra Stovner' [But ok, I'm Jamal. A black guy, Muslim, from Stovner] (15). In addition, Jamal demonstrates a keen awareness of the rhetoric of stigmatisation that is attached to the multi-ethnic composition of Stovner when he complains about the 'skada folka [...] [som] går på tv og sånn og snakker dritt og så har dem aldri har vært på Stovner eller shaka hånda med en svarting engang' [crackpots [...] [who] go on TV and talk shit and then they've never even been to Stovner or shook hands with a black guy] (18); and, summarising the problem concisely, Jamal says, 'Liksom, vi alle er svartinger på en hvit land, skjønner du?' [Like, we are all black guys in a white land, you know?] (17). Rosten observes that young people living in such stigmatised areas 'benytter seg mer eller mindre konsekvent av identitetskategorien "utlending" som betegnelse for sitt skjebnefellesskap' [use more or less consistently the identity category 'foreigner' for their community of fate] and, in this way, '"tar de tilbake" en kategori som en del majoritetsnordmenn benytter for å definere etniske og religiøse minoriteter ut av det nasjonale fellesskapet' [they 'take back' a category that a number of the majority of Norwegians use to define ethnic or religious minorities as outside the national community].[51] Jamal does not use the term *utlending* [foreigner], but *svarting* [black guy] to acknowledge his exclusion from the national community, and to reclaim with defiance and pride a category that is meant to stigmatise him. Jamal turns the negative attributions concomitant with this stigmatisation on their head, and reinterpreting them as positive values, confirms from within the boundaries that are drawn around Stovner from the outside:

> Men vi folka her, vi er sånn nå, fuck dem som snakker dritt, skjønner du? [...] Glem dem andre folka på den landen her a. Vi trenger ikke dem. Vi har det her, skjønner du hva jeg mener? [...] Liksom, ikke la dem gjøre sånn at du tenker du er dårlig. Nei ass. Du er schpaa, mann.
>
> [But we here, we are like, fuck them who talk shit, you know? [...] Forget them other people in this country here. We don't need them. We have this here, know what I mean? [...] Like, don't let them get you down and think you are bad. No way. You are cool man.] (18)

When Ahmed discusses national identity, she argues that it can be viewed as 'a site of social conflict' where nationhood is staked out in relation to and against those who are constructed as strangers. These negotiations, as Ahmed goes on to say, utilise the '*proximity of that which cannot be assimilated into a national body*' to demarcate the national body by way of defining boundaries within the confines of the nation.[52] Jamal reverses this perspective, and reappropriates its mechanisms of demarcation when he defines his identity against his construction and fetishisation as a stranger within the Norwegian national space. On a legal level, Jamal is part of the Norwegian state, but by reclaiming and defending his belonging to Stovner, Jamal clarifies that, on an affective level, he is in the Norwegian national space, but not of it.

In Wacquant's words, Jamal's coping strategy is one of 'material and symbolic distancing', when he validates 'negative outside perceptions of the neighbourhood',[53] and thus reverses their exclusionary dynamics. In addition, Jamal is doing what Rosten calls 'å "leke getto"' [to 'play ghetto'], which she describes as a way to cope with 'territoriell stigmatisering gjennom å bekrefte, overdrive og "leke med" fordommene knyttet til "den farlige innvandrergettoen"' [territorial stigmatisation via confirming, exaggerating and 'playing with' the prejudices associated with 'the dangerous immigrant ghetto'].[54] Jamal actively engages with Bakken as the recipient of his contributions, or the intended reader/listener, and, by extension, with the actual reader. While Jamal's engagement primarily emphasises the reader's limited social knowledge, it gives Jamal the opportunity to portray the 'ghetto' from his own point of view, and to use his superior position of insider knowledge to explain the 'ghetto' to the reader. These explanations serve Jamal simultaneously as a means to distance himself from the norm, when he, for instance, sets himself apart from white Norwegians whom he derogatorily calls *poteter* [potatoes]: 'Men vi hilser sånn. Sånn, går bra elle? [...] Så shaker vi hender sånn kjapt. Alltid shaker hender. Må det. Poteter gjør ikke det så mye' [But this is how we say hello. Like, wassup? [...] Then we shake hands, like, quickly. Always shake hands. Have to. The potatoes don't do it that much] (97). With a certain hyperbole, Jamal claims that Stovner 'er en av dem heftigste ghettostedene i Oslo' [is one of the coolest ghettos in Oslo] (269), of which he is a proud part: 'jeg er ghetto som faen' [I'm so fucking ghetto] (75); and, confirming prejudices, he states, 'Ja, jeg keefer liksom' [Yeah, I smoke hash, like] (29). Jamal suggests that his openness towards Bakken could have legal consequences, and therefore, he reminds Bakken, 'Ikke start å skrive sånne ting som Jamal røyker hasj og sånn på den forskinga, ok? Plutselig bausersen kommer til meg og sånn' [Don't write stuff like Jamal smokes hash or something in this research, okay? Suddenly I get a visit from the busies, like] (32). While this reminder serves Jamal to play with and reinforce the image of the 'bad boy', his repeated requests for discretion make Bakken, and the reader, complicit in his contraventions. This complicity disrupts Bakken's, and the reader's, otherwise impassive, voyeuristic observer position when they become instrumentalised by Jamal in creating and maintaining his image.

Concealed in Jamal's play with this image, however, is a social and economic reality that throws his personality into an entirely different light. Describing his family situation, Jamal states that he lives with his mother and his younger brother Suli, while his father 'er borte, han tisharen der' [is away, that scumbag] (15). We learn that Jamal's mother suffers from depression and spends most days on the sofa, while Jamal takes on responsibilities that would usually be considered those of a parent: Jamal does the shopping for the household, he takes his brother to nursery and later to school, he cleans his brother and washes his clothes when Suli, despite being of school age, regularly wets the bed, and he attends the parent–teacher meetings at school because his mother deems herself unable to go. Moreover, the family's financial situation is strained, because, as Jamal depicts it, his mother has applied for disability allowance, but, 'Trygdekontoret sier nei hele tida ass [...] Så hun får sånn, hva sier dem, midlertidige greier, og det er jævlig lite [...] Kroppen er ikke syk og sånn, sier dem' [The Social says no all the time [...] She gets like, what do they call it, temporary stuff, and that's not fucking much [...] Her body isn't ill, like, is what they say] (27). Laying out his financial situation in detail, Jamal states that he receives a stipend, the same as Mo, 'for elever fra lavinntektshusholdninger, 1000 kroner i måneden' [for pupils from low-income households, 1000 kroner per month] (57), but unlike Mo, Jamal has to support the household financially, and, as he does not have enough money for public transport, he dodges the fare; and, when Jamal drops out of school, his mother reminds him that she is dependent on his support. Jamal finds illicit employment in a garage where he washes cars for 'femti spenn timen' [fifty an hour] (113), and sharing his meagre monthly wages with his mother fills him with pride: 'Først jeg gir moren min to lapper. [...] jeg legger flusa på borden, liksom: "Vær så god". Det var så bra følelse da' [First I give my mother two notes [...] I put the dosh on the table, like: 'There you go'. It was such a good feeling] (119).

Despite Jamal's efforts, however, he is told by his brother's teachers that Suli is not sociable enough, that his clothes are not warm enough, that he sometimes smells of urine, and that, 'Matpakkene hans er dårlig. [...] Han trenger mer frukt og grønt og grove kornsorter' [His packed lunches are not good enough. [...] He needs more fruit and vegetables and wholemeal bread] (143). Considering that Jamal is glad to be able to afford 'sånne pizza som koster 19 spenn' [those pizzas for 19 kroner] (101), the teachers' demands seem preposterous, and Jamal rightly wonders, 'Liksom, hva veit dem om livet vårt?' [Like, what do they know about our lives?] (143), and he admits, 'jeg blir sliten liksom [...] Jeg klarer ikke alltid ta alle tinga og fikse alle tinga' [I get tired like [...] I can't always take it all and fix it all] (284). Instead of seeing a mere 'ghetto bad boy', we are granted detailed insights into the life of a young man who carries an amount of responsibility that exceeds his capacities. When Jamal identifies the gap between his actual reality and a lack of knowledge on the part of authorities as part of the problem, the text exposes structural deficiencies, such as lack of support for single and ailing parents, as the cause of Jamal's struggles: because of the politics underpinning territorial stigmatisation, Jamal is denied equal opportunities.

Before the incident that prompts Jamal to drop out of school, he reports a confrontation with one of his teachers who, when Jamal complains about being cold on a school trip in winter, replies, 'Sånn er det her i Norge. Fryser du, må du kle deg bedre' [That's what it's like here in Norway. When you are cold, you have to wear warmer clothes]. Insinuating a lack of knowledge on Jamal's part, the teacher excludes him from the national body of Norway, and, condemning the teacher's racist attitude, Jamal conveys his anger to Bakken: 'Sånn er det i Norge liksom? Som jeg ikke veit? Hva faen? Du skal lære meg om å bo her liksom? Fuck han, og jeg sier det til han ass' [That's what it's like in Norway like? As if I don't know? What the fuck? You want to teach me about living here like? Fuck him, and I say it to him. I just snapped] (66). The teachers consider Jamal a problematic pupil with little motivation or talent, whereas, when economic destitution intersects with systemic and institutional racism, the teachers themselves are the problem, and the strain on Jamal's life becomes exacerbated. These dynamics grow more acute and, during three minutes of silence in his class for the victims of 9/11, Jamal loses his temper again: 'Det her er bullshit ass [...] Dere veit ikke en dritt ass. Hvor er tre minutter for alle på Palestina a? [...] Hadde det her skjedd med svartinger, dere hadde gitt så faen' [This here is bullshit [...] You don't know shit. Where are the three minutes for all the Palestinians, eh? [...] If this had happened to black guys, you wouldn't have given a fuck]. The teacher's reaction to Jamal's outburst is to ask him to leave the classroom, to which he replies, 'Fuck ut på gangen, bitch, jeg skal ut av skolen' [Fuck out of the room, bitch, I'll be out of the school] (67). Jamal becomes an affect alien not in terms of happiness, but in terms of solidarity: in Jamal's view, the Norwegian solidarity with the American victims of 9/11 is hypocritical and mediated by norms of likeness, and, realising that divisions of 'us' and 'them' function on a transnational level, Jamal shows his solidarity with others who are equally marginalised as he is, also across national boundaries. His anger emerges in the gap between 'us' and 'them', in the unequal distribution of solidarity, and, instigated by the mourning of his white Norwegian classmates, he confirms his affective alienation and concludes, 'liksom dem der og meg, nei ass, vi er ikke det samma' [like, them there and me, nah, we are not the same] (66).

Jamal, in similar ways to Mo, finds himself compelled to position himself in relation to the entanglement of international events, local incidents and the racism implicit in territorial stigmatisation. With regard to the murder of Farah in Stovner, Jamal points out that it is ignorance which leads to misguided and disproportionate governmental measures, and he ridicules the fact that since the killing, Oslo City Council has reinforced police patrols in Stovner:

> Hele tida dem kjører rundt [...] som dem vil skremme folk eller no [...] Liksom, som andre folk som tenker å blæste noen, når dem sjofer ut av vindua, dem ser bauers, og da dem tenker, nei, bauers jo, da jeg skal ikke gjøre det.

> [The whole time they are driving around [...] like they want to scare people or something [...] Like, as if other people who want to finish someone, when they look out of the window and see the cops, and think like, wait a minute, the cops, then I won't do it.] (280)

Although Jamal makes fun of these governmental measures, he finds it necessary to correct the biased picture that the media has painted of Farah and her boyfriend as the innocent victims of an honour killing, and therefore, he presents Bakken with his version of the events. In Jamal's view, Farah 'var kæbe' [was a slag] (270) who knew that 'hun dissa familien sin så jævlig heftig med han søpla [kjæresten sin]' [she dissed her family so fucking much with this piece of shit [her boyfriend]] (271), which, however, does not justify retribution in his opinion. Calling Farah's boyfriend *skitten* [nasty], Jamal distances himself from people like him: 'vi har gjort ting [...] men vi har ikke gjort sånne skitne ting' [we've done stuff [...] but we haven't done such nasty stuff] (271), which substantiates the notion that Jamal is merely 'playing ghetto' without doing any actual harm. When Jamal mimics the rhetoric of journalists and says, ' "Disse innvandrere. De forstår ingenting. De synes det er helt greit med vold mot kvinner". Nei ass, mann' ['These foreigners. They don't understand anything. They think it's alright to physically abuse women'. No way, man] (273), he highlights the myopic and ignorant view which characterises public discourses, and simultaneously objects that he is discredited by way of geographical marginalisation and such racist generalisations.

Jamal and Mo live in the same housing block, and yet, their paths rarely cross because of their diverging strategies to cope with Stovner's stigmatisation. We have seen that Jamal identifies with Stovner and a playful image of the bad boy in the ghetto, whereas Mo does not feel a sense of belonging to the area to the same degree; in Jamal's words, Mo 'er svarting som meg og sånn, men han er litt, jeg veit ikke ass, liksom, potet eller no' [is a black guy like me, but he is a bit, I dunno, potato] (110), which makes Mo, in Jamal's view, the Norwegian equivalent of a *svennebanan-invandrar* [Superswede-immigrant]. When the paths of these two young men do cross, Mo tells Jamal about his anger and disillusionment in a heart-to-heart, and Jamal comments with, 'karen har skjønt masse ting nå' [the guy has understood a lot of stuff now]. The things Mo realises — the tight, inescapable discursive and political boundaries around Stovner, processes of racialised othering and marginalisation — have always been in Jamal's awareness, and a reality in his life. Nevertheless, Jamal is of the opinion that Mo 'klager litt for mye ass' [moans a bit too much], because Jamal 'har alle problemene til han, pluss hundre flere' [has all his problems, plus a hundred more] (402). Jamal alludes to the fact that Mo's parents, despite their limited financial means, support their son and his studies, with the result that Mo excels, whereas Jamal does not receive the same support, but on the contrary, has to contribute to the family's upkeep practically and financially. In his discussion of social structures in the so-called ghetto, Wacquant argues that 'scattered islets of relative economic and social stability persist, which offer fragile but crucial launching pads for the strategies of coping and escape of its residents'.[55] Mo's family is such an islet, and, at least initially, his parents' support does serve Mo as a launching pad to escape Stovner, but this support cannot prevent his marginalisation and stigmatisation. Towards the end of *Tante Ulrikkes vei*, both protagonists are equally alienated from their country of birth and its society, Mo's and Jamal's actions in the world are impeded instead of assisted, and as they speak 'with consciousness of racism', they have become affect aliens.[56]

Postmigrant Societies: From outside the 'Ghetto'

Yasaman, in *Araben*, is not exposed to the same degree of social and territorial marginalisation as Jamal and Mo in *Tante Ulrikkes vei*, because her father ensured that she did not grow up in a stigmatised area, and thus, one would assume, her conflicts with Swedish society are less acute than Mo's and Jamal's with Norwegian society. Yet, in Yasaman's view, her assimilation comes at a price: 'Vi lärde oss ju också svenska och bryter när vi pratar persiska istället. Varken jag eller min bror kan snacka med en iranier-iranier på ett vettigt sätt. Man fastnar mellan två världar' [We did learn Swedish, and stumble over the words when we speak Persian. Neither me nor my brother can talk properly to an Iranian-Iranian. You get stuck between two worlds] (50). An Iranian-Iranian, for Yasaman, is someone who lives in Iran and speaks Persian, and, as neither applies to her, she denotes her territorial and linguistic un-belonging to her country of birth with hyphenation, whereas Tove, as previously discussed, emphasises Yasaman's belonging to Sweden with hyphenation. It is misleading, however, that Yasaman uses language, and a territorial concept of belonging, as tropes to position herself on a 'bridge "between two worlds"' which is 'designed to keep discrete worlds apart'.[57] In practice, the Iranian and Swedish worlds are not kept apart, and Yasaman does not establish her belonging or un-belonging to Swedish culture and society in relation to something outside it. Instead, as I shall illustrate shortly, she negotiates multiple forms of cultural affiliations with Sweden and Iran simultaneously, from within Sweden and in Swedish, thus bringing these two seemingly discrete worlds together, albeit in tension. Nonetheless, Yasaman's following remark suggests that these negotiations are pervaded by a sense of liminality, which, as she highlights, is not necessarily self-generated, but produced by her surroundings. In an imagined conversation with her cousin who lives in Iran, she wishes she could tell her, 'Att du aldrig kan bli en av de här människorna. Man kommer ut men man kommer liksom aldrig in någon annanstans' [That you can never become one of these people here. You get out, but you never get in anywhere else] (48–49). While Yasaman can avoid the immediate stigma of a particular territory, she underscores that boundaries are nevertheless intact, and tangible for her in discursive locations where inclusion or exclusion are staked out in conversations, or on her behalf.

With a keen awareness that these boundaries hinge on frames of sameness and difference, Yasaman observes the people around her on the bus, and reflects:

> Här kommer blatten från någon dammig by i Afghanistan och har aldrig sett civilisation förut. Vi har ju svart på vitt att folk är rassar häruppe numera. Det är inte rättvist, jag vet, att du ska representera oss alla och att vi alla ska bli dömda efter ditt beteende [...] Det är inte rättvist att de vita bara representerar sig själva medan du representerar mig och dig och min morsa som sen blir rasistisk bemött på jobbet.

> [Here comes *blatten* from some dusty village in Afghanistan who has never seen civilisation before. We have it in black and white that people up here are racists these days. I know that it's not fair that you will have to represent all of us and that we will all be judged on the basis of your behaviour [...] It's not fair that the whites only represent themselves while you represent me and you and my old mum who then gets racially abused at work.] (260)

In similar ways to Mo and Jamal, Yasaman acknowledges the power of representation: when others are constructed as strangers by way of racialised differentiation, one will always stand in for all of them, and, from the viewpoint of the Swedish normative majority, will be judged and excluded through a racist lens. When these mechanisms of inclusion and exclusion serve as a means to negotiate national identity, the nation, as Ahmed argues, becomes an imagined and embodied space, 'defined as close to some others (friends), and further away from other others (strangers)'.[58] Yasaman's position within such negotiations is one of relative marginalisation: by the people around her, she is identified as other, yet familiar because of her assimilation; internally, she fears to be excluded from the national body, or Swedish society, when she is perceived as an other other by proxy. In Edward Said's words, Yasaman assumes a 'plurality of vision [that] gives rise to an awareness of simultaneous dimensions'.[59] Yasaman demonstrates awareness of exclusionary derogatory discourses, and of the racially motivated violence such discourses may lead to. She adopts the rhetoric of such discourses, and, in the same breath, critically distances herself from it by calling it unfair and racist. At the same time, however, Yasaman distances herself from those other others, because she fears that Swedish society's harsh judgment of them will reflect badly on herself. Yasaman's state of mind is reminiscent of her father's double consciousness, as she looks at herself through the eyes of others and tries to gauge by which measure the world will judge her. In her imagination, Yasaman says to the man driving the bus, 'Så nästa gång du behöver ringa din brorsa och snacka om *bademdjon* och *ghorme sabzi* kan du väl göra det när du inte kör buss!' [So next time you have to call your brother to talk about *bademdjon* and *ghorme sabzi*, why don't you do it when you're not driving the bus!] (260). When Yasaman advises against drawing attention to one's otherness, she adopts the racist viewpoint she criticises earlier, so much so that she deems it inappropriate to display a language other than Swedish in public. Yasaman aligns herself with the Swedish affective community and rules out her solidarity with others who are othered. In Yasaman's view, and although she considers it unfair, it is better to assimilate and deny one's mother tongue than being ostracised and excluded.

Yasaman's self-understanding in relation to the Swedish affective community, however, is continuously questioned and displaced in personal conversations with her mother, her partner Peter, Tove, or random strangers. Therefore, to adapt Trinh T. Minh-ha's assertion to Yasaman's situation, the latter's 'boundaries of identity and difference are continually repositioned in relation to varying points of reference'.[60] A stranger in the university cafeteria first points out to Yasaman how homogeneous Swedish society and culture appear to him, only to then ask her, 'Känner du verkligen att du passar in här?' [Do you really feel that you fit in here?]. Finding herself compelled to defend her own and her interlocutor's Swedish-ness despite their mutual ethnic backgrounds, Yasaman replies, 'Jag är svensk, du är också svensk [...] Vi är representative båda två' [I am Swedish, you are Swedish too [...] We are both representative] (144). Previously, we have seen that Yasaman regards negative representation as threatening her affective belonging to the Swedish we-group when one 'other' comes to stand for all of 'them' in the public eye. In a form of counter-representation, Yasaman contends now that she represents a new Swedish-ness: by means of assimilation, she demonstrates that she can align herself with Swedish values despite her outward 'otherness', and in turn, she is met with tolerance for cultural and ethnic multiplicity, which offers 'its own promise of happiness', because she is granted the same opportunities as everyone else.[61] Another stranger in a different conversation confirms this notion when he points out to Yasaman that it is easy to embrace difference and multiplicity in her case, because, as he says,

> Det är ju skillnad på folk som du, som pratar svenska utan brytning. Jag menar du är ju precis som jag. Men de här andra som kommer hit och låser in sina döttrar och tvingar dom att gifta sig och allt det där.

> [It's different with people like you who talk Swedish fluently. I mean, you are just like me. But these others who come here and lock their daughters in and force them to marry and all that.] (187)

This stranger does not embrace difference, but sameness; from his viewpoint, Yasaman is the 'right' kind of immigrant because she is assimilated, and her outward difference negligible. In Ahmed's terms, the view of Yasaman's interlocutor involves 'a double and contradictory process of incorporation and expulsion': Yasaman's difference can be incorporated into the nation, because she does 'fit into a standardised pattern' despite her difference, whereas 'those stranger strangers' are excluded because their 'difference may be dangerous to the well-being of even the most heterogenous of nations'.[62]

We have already seen that Yasaman defends her assimilated Swedish-ness against others who, potentially, could make her an excluded 'other' by proxy; and, as Yasaman repeatedly sets herself apart from them, she has internalised this differentiation between others and other others. In the queue in the tax office, Yasaman does not view herself as part of the people around her when she says to Peter, 'Inte en svenska så långt ögat kan nå. Afrikaner och asiater, blattar hela bunten' [Not a Swede as far as the eye can see. Africans and Asians, *blattar* the lot of them] (169). Peter exposes her hypocrisy when he facetiously replies, 'Alla förutom jag då menar du eller?' [You mean, everyone apart from me, right?] (172). Yasaman's ostentatious outward assurances of her Swedish-ness correlate with an inward questioning of the Iranian cultural values and traditions which her mother represents. When Yasaman reprimands her mother for cooking too much food for a dinner party with Peter's parents, her mother reminds her, 'Men vi är inte svenskar [...] Så gör vi. Det här är vår tradition' [But we aren't Swedes [...] This is how we do it. This is our tradition] (110–11). In comparison, while Yasaman worries that there will be too much food, Jamal, in *Tante Ulrikkes vei*, describes what it feels like to eat the only food he can afford to buy, for instance cornflakes: 'du blir ikke bra mett [...] Du blir sånn, jeg veit ikke, magen din blir bare full med luft, og hard og sånn, og du blir bare heftig sulten halvtime seinere. Det er dritt ass' [it doesn't make you properly full [...] You get like, I dunno, your stomach just gets full with air, and you're super hungry half an hour later. That's shit like] (55). From Jamal's perspective, Yasaman's worries are problems that only privileged people can have. Obviously, these two instances are only tangentially related, because Yasaman negotiates cultural belonging, and Jamal precarity. However, Yasaman can afford to stake out her cultural affiliations in relation to Iranian traditions, whereas Jamal cannot — his concern is whether or not he can put food on the table at all.

Nonetheless, seeing her mother prepare food reminds Yasaman of Iranian traditions, and she reflects, 'Alltid i sällskap av sina systrar, svägerskor, kusiner, väninnor. [...] Generation efter generation har mammorna lärt sina döttrar' [Always in the company of their sisters, sisters-in-law, cousins, female friends. [...] For generations, mothers have taught their daughters]. When Yasaman says, 'Här går en grens [...] Här tar det slut' [I'm drawing a line under this [...] This is where it ends] (111), she distances herself from these all-female traditions, and emphasises by means of reiteration that she is resolved not to conform to the gender norms which these traditions entail. Instead, Yasaman aligns herself with the happy objects of Swedish society, which are, in the words of one of her conversational partners, 'Skaffa lägenhet, skaffa barn, ta på sig samma kläder som alla andra. Tjäna pengar, åka på resor, älska andra kulturer men ändå veta att Sverige är bäst' [Get a flat, have kids, wear the same clothes as everyone else. Earn money, go travelling, love other cultures but always know that Sweden is best] (143–44). The adaptation to the standardised patterns of Swedish culture and society, however, disconcerts Yasaman when she feels the pressure within these homogenising tendencies, and she reflects in relation to the thought of having a child, 'Det känns som att man måste bara för att man är trettio' [It feels as if I simply have to because I'm thirty] (115). Subsequently, Yasaman realises, 'att jag alltid har vetat att vi inte kan ha barn ihop' [that I have always known that we can't have kids together] (265). While she refuses fervently the gendered traditions her mother has to offer, Yasaman recognises that everything which is Iranian about her in terms of tradition and cultural heritage would cease to exist with this child:

> Plötsligt väller det fram. [...] Jasmindoften och den fuktiga luften och saffransriset. Språket, de där gamla orden som jag inte förstår [...] Min farmors traditioner, hennes hand på koranen [...] Alla mina minnen, allt det där som jag har inom mig.

> [All of a sudden, it wells forth. [...] The scent of jasmine and the moist air and the saffron rice. The language, those old words that I don't understand [...] My grandmother's traditions, her hand on the Koran [...] All my memories, all the things that are within me.] (265–66)

In light of this, it is not necessarily a refusal of a stereotyped role of woman- or motherhood when Yasaman decides against having a child, but an acknowledgement of a deeply felt connection with two cultures simultaneously. When she says, 'Allting dör med mig, med våra framtida barn' [Everything dies with me, with our future children] (266), it begs the question, why? Yasaman finds it 'så charmigt att han [Peter] var så omacho' [so charming that he [Peter] was so un-macho] (69), which suggests that he would not prevent her from reviving these traditions and memories for their child, or rather that it would be in her hands to do so. Yet, as she has set her boundaries against such traditions, she has lost the ability to do so. In this sense, these traditions do not become lost with her future child, they are lost already, and Yasaman is merely bemoaning this loss. She holds on to nostalgic and clichéd images remote from her lived reality, so that the fragrance of 'basilika, mynta och koriander' [basil, mint and coriander] encapsulates the essence of Iran for her when her mother cooks with these herbs: 'Jag drar in lukten av Iran' [I inhale the scent of Iran] (13). In fact, however, Yasaman has to admit, 'Jag vet inte ett skit om Iran' [I don't know shit about Iran] (32).

When Yasaman cannot agree to having a child with Peter, the couple separate, and afterwards Yasaman receives confirmation that her application to study for a PhD was successful. While this is not presented as an alternative to motherhood, it demonstrates that her choices actually never had anything to do with Iranian traditions, or the social pressure to be a mother at thirty: 'Jag har velat det så länge och så mycket. Det var som gjort för mig. Det var vad alla sa. En självklar fortsättning' [I have wanted it so much and for so long. It was as if made for me. That's what everyone said. A natural continuation]. Yasaman follows a different standardised pattern from that of becoming a mother, and she also follows a personal choice when she says that a PhD seems tailored for her, which implies that, in her view, motherhood is not, at least not at this moment in her life. In addition, she clears a debt with this choice: 'Skulden är återbetalt. Språket, landet, kulturen. Sjukvård, tandställning, svensk standard och gratis skolmat' [The debt is paid off. The language, the country, the culture. Healthcare, dental braces, Swedish standards and free school meals] (276), and 'friheten framför allt' [freedom, above all]. Yasaman contrasts these achievements with 'Dina år och dina rynkor längs med munnen och utmed dina ögon. [...] Din böjda rygg över köksbänken' [Your years and the wrinkles around your mouth and eyes. [...] Your bent back over the kitchen counter] (277), and it becomes clear that her debt is to her parents. As Yasaman is estranged from her father, she conspicuously excludes him when she expresses a sense of indebtedness towards her mother alone, but her mother corrects her when she says, 'Det var din pappa som hade drömmar [...] Det var han som ville komma hit. Inte jag' [It was your dad who had dreams [...] It was him who wanted to come here. Not me] (220). Being thus reminded, Yasaman informs her father of her success, and at last, the Arab learns that some of his dreams and ambitions have come true. The Arab's immigration to Sweden frustrated his own aspirations, and therefore, he expected the promise of happiness, which migration may imply, to be kept with a generational slide; and indeed, while the Arab's life is pervaded by a sense of failure, he provided his daughter with the opportunity to align herself with the affective Swedish community. This proved successful, because Yasaman, despite her struggles and conflicts, has the freedom to make her own choices.

★　★　★　★　★

To sum up, the spaces in which the protagonists' conflicts and struggles are fought out are more than mere backdrops: they are affective spaces insofar as they facilitate the emergence of particular affects, and as they become themselves imbued with affect. In Rohi's novel, and in Varatharajah's text, remembering takes place in liminal zones which are characterised by contingency, and in these contingent spaces, histories of othering and marginalisation unfold, and become related to the protagonists' current realities. The protagonists' reflections on their present lives are pervaded by a sense of failure and shame, and past processes of othering and marginalisation have never actually ceased in their contemporary lives. These memories are produced from the affective experience of marginality, and therefore it is unsurprising that they unfold in equally marginal, or liminal, spaces. Considering that these memories run contrary to those discourses that tend to sustain this kind of marginalisation, the spaces themselves can be viewed as 'Räume des Widerstands' [spaces of resistance] which counterpoise this marginality, and, simultaneously, these discourses.[63]

Focusing on Yasaman's narrative strand in *Araben*, and *Tante Ulrikkes vei*, has illustrated how similar processes of othering and marginalisation, as well as racist and exclusionary discourses, are at the root of the protagonists' conflicts within the societies in which they live. The comparisons of Yasaman's, and Mo's and Jamal's, social realities, and the similar or different ways in which the protagonists relate to the territorial stigmatisation that is attached to particular areas, have shed light on those exclusionary discourses and practices which allow or do not allow the protagonists to align themselves with affective communities. Mo and Jamal relate their stories from within the boundaries of Stovner; therefore they cannot escape the stigma of this area, and, by virtue of this territorial stigmatisation and their racialised otherness, both protagonists are affectively alienated from Norwegian society. Yasaman had the privilege to grow up outside the limits of such a stigmatised area, and that is why her affective alienation is not as acute as Mo's and Jamal's. While Yasaman also experiences processes of racialised marginalisation, she, because of her integration into Swedish society, has the chance to make her own life choices. However, when those postmigrant protagonists who are considered assimilated (Yasaman, Mo, and Senthil and Valmira) experience racialised othering because of their ostensible otherness, the outlook for the future is not too hopeful: the texts draw attention to the fact that when someone appears different from the white majorities in Germany, Norway and Sweden, these individuals will tend to be othered, no matter how integrated they are. These individuals will always be thought of as migrants, and remain judged by their supposed ethnicity, because of their perceived otherness.

In comparison with Mo and Jamal, Yasaman's attitude, her integration into a Swedish norm, has first and foremost to do with class privilege, or with financial means and social standing, despite the discursive boundaries which Yasaman experiences as restricting. The conflicts which are deemed 'immigrant problems' in discourses supportive of such migrantisation are, more often than not, caused by social and financial disparities. By highlighting the ways in which these conflicts become related to migration in the public view, and also how this public view affects the protagonists, the texts foreground how territorial stigmatisation is politically produced, and is not a matter of immigration, but of spatial, economic and political dynamics, or rather, inequalities. By revealing not only processes of othering, but also the political, social and economic structures underpinning them, the three texts grant the reader a view on German, Norwegian and Swedish societies, respectively, from the margins these societies have created. In this sense, the reader can critically reflect on the ways in which the protagonists' struggles are politically effectuated, and the texts prompt us to ask: what would have to change on a structural level for the protagonists to be able to live their lives with as much freedom and as many opportunities as any other member of their societies? Thus, it is not only the critical reader who employs a postmigrant perspective to reading those texts, but the texts themselves support such a perspective, because they shift the focus from 'immigrant problems' and migrantisation to issues that concern any society as a whole by depicting how mechanisms of migrantisation work, and how they affect the protagonists on an individual basis.

Notes to Chapter 5

1. Roger Bromley, 'A Bricolage of Identifications: Storying Postmigrant Belonging', *Journal of Aesthetics and Culture*, 9 (2017), 36–44 (p. 36).
2. Anne Ring Petersen and Moritz Schramm, '(Post-)Migration in the Age of Globalisation: New Challenges to Imagination and Representation', *Journal of Aesthetics and Culture*, 9 (2017), 1–12 (p. 6).
3. Regina Römhild, 'Beyond the Bounds of the Ethnic: For Postmigrant Cultural and Social Research', *Journal of Aesthetics and Culture*, 9 (2017), 69–75 (p. 69).
4. Riem Spielhaus, 'Studien in der postmigrantischen Gesellschaft: Eine kritische Auseinandersetzung', in *Kongressdokumentation 4. Bundesfachkongress Interkultur, Hamburg 2012*, ed. by Marius Koniarczyck and others (Hamburg: Kulturbehörde der Freien und Hansestadt Hamburg, 2014), pp. 96–100 (p. 97).
5. Erol Yildiz and Marc Hill, 'In-between as Resistance: The Post-migrant Generation Between Discrimination and Transnationalization', *Transnational Social Review*, 7 (2017), 273–86 (p. 280).
6. Spielhaus, p. 97.
7. Römhild, p. 69.
8. Yildiz and Hill, p. 277.
9. Schramm, 'Jenseits', p. 90.
10. Bromley, 'Bricolage', p. 36.
11. Erol Yildiz, 'Ideen zum Postmigrantischen', in *Postmigrantische Perspektiven*, ed. by Naika Foroutan and others (Frankfurt a.M.: Campus, 2018), pp. 19–34 (p. 29).
12. Roger Bromley, *Narratives for a New Belonging: Diasporic Cultural Fictions* (Edinburgh: Edinburgh University Press, 2000), p. 1; Yildiz, p. 28.
13. Tygstrup, 'Affective Spaces', p. 204.
14. W. E. B. Du Bois, *The Souls of Black Folk: The Oxford W. E. B. Du Bois*, 1st edn (Oxford: Oxford University Press, 2010), p. 3.
15. Gabriel Zoran, 'Towards a Theory of Space in Narrative', *Poetics Today*, 5 (1984), 309–35 (p. 315).
16. Marie-Laure Ryan, Kenneth E. Foote and Maoz Azaryahu, *Narrating Space/Spatializing Narrative: Where Narrative Theory and Geography Meet* (Columbus: Ohio State University Press, 2016), p. 21.
17. Raewyn Connell, *Masculinities*, 2nd edn (Cambridge: Polity Press, 2005), p. 77.
18. Connell, pp. 82, 90.
19. Raymond Hibbins and Bob Pease, 'Men and Masculinities on the Move', in *Migrant Men: Critical Studies of Masculinities and the Migration Experience*, ed. by Mike Donaldson and others (London: Routledge, 2009), pp. 1–19 (p. 5).
20. Ahmed, *Strange Encounters*, p. 89, italics in original.
21. Brah, p. 192; Ahmed, *Strange Encounters*, p. 89, italics in original.
22. Bauman, *Strangers*, pp. 103 (italics in original), 104.
23. Susannah Radstone, 'What Place Is This? Transcultural Memory and the Locations of Memory Studies', *Parallax*, 17 (2011), 109–23 (p. 111, italics in original).
24. Senthil consistently writes German with lower-case initials, thus self-consciously flouting orthographical conventions.
25. Mieke Bal, 'Introduction', in *Acts of Memory: Cultural Recall in the Present*, ed. by Bal and others (London: University Press of New England, 1999), pp. vii–xvii (p. x).

26. Harald Welzer, 'Communicative Memory', in *A Companion to Cultural Memory Studies*, ed. by Astrid Erll and Ansgar Nünning (Berlin: De Gruyter, 2008), pp. 285–98 (p. 285).

27. Astrid Erll, *Memory in Culture* (Basingstoke: Palgrave Macmillan, 2011), p. 8.

28. Ahmed, *Strange Encounters*, p. 46.

29. Julia Kristeva, *Powers of Horror: An Essay on Abjection*, trans. by Leon S. Roudiez (Oxford: Columbia University Press, 1982), pp. 2 (italics in original), 4.

30. Armin Nassehi, 'Namenlos glücklich', *Zeit Online* (30 January 2014) <http://www.zeit. de/2014/06/herkunft> [accessed 15 August 2018] (p. 2).

31. Ahmed, *Strange Encounters*, p. 3.

32. Yildiz and Hill, p. 278.

33. Bal, p. xi.

34. Yildiz, p. 29.

35. Rajaram and Grundy-Warr, p. x.

36. Schramm, 'Jenseits', p. 90.

37. Yildiz and Hill, p. 277.

38. Ahmed, *Cultural Politics*, p. 209; 'Collective Feelings', p. 27.

39. Ahmed, *Promise*, pp. 41, 171, 158, 164.

40. 'Alby', in *Botkyrka kommun* <http://www.botkyrka.statistikportal.se/omradesfakta> [accessed 22 July 2019], is a suburb in the Botkyrka Municipality within Stockholm, and, according to their statistics from 2017, 84 per cent of Alby's inhabitants have a migrant background; SFI stands for *Svenska för invandrare* (Swedish for immigrants).

41. Tabish Khair, 'Old and New Xenophobia', in *The Culture of Migration*, ed. by Sten Pultz Moslund and others (London: I. B. Tauris, 2015), pp. 59–68 (p. 61).

42. Loïc J. D. Wacquant, *Urban Outcasts: A Comparative Sociology of Advanced Marginality* (Cambridge: Polity Press, 2008), p. 5.

43. *Slangopedia*, <http://www.slangopedia.se/ordlista/?ord=blatte> [accessed 15 August 2019], explains that *blatte* (*blattar* in the plural) is a derogatory term denoting Swedes with a migrant background, usually of colour and not of Western European descent, who behave 'som en gangster-stereotyp' [like a gangster stereotype]. The term is retained in the translation, because there is no appropriate equivalent in English, and because similar terms in English carry postcolonial connotations which do not apply to a Scandinavian context. The same slang dictionary defines *Svennebanan* as a 'vidare påbyggnad av "svenne"' [further extension of 'svenne'] and denotes a person who is very stereotypically Swedish.

44. Ahmed, *Strange Encounters*, p. 25, italics in original.

45. Wacquant, p. 169.

46. Monika Grønli Rosten, 'Territoriell stigmatisering og gutter som "leker getto" i Groruddalen', *Norsk sosiologisk tidsskrift*, 1 (2017), 53–70 (p. 54).

47. Juliane Karakayali and Paul Mecheril, 'Umkämpfte Krisen: Migrationsregime als Analyseperspektive', in *Postmigrantische Perspektiven*, ed. by Naika Foroutan and others (Frankfurt a.M.: Campus) 2018, pp. 225–36 (p. 231).

48. Rosten, p. 67.

49. Ahmed, *Cultural Politics*, p. 53.

50. Ahmed, *Promise*, p. 157.

51. Rosten, p. 60.

52. Ahmed, *Strange Encounters*, pp. 101, 100, italics in original.

53. Wacquant, p. 184.

54. Rosten, p. 59.

55. Wacquant, p. 49.

56. Ahmed, *Promise*, p. 158.

57. Leslie A. Adelson, 'Against Between: A Manifesto', in *Zafer Şenocak*, ed. by Tom Cheesman and Karin Yeşilada (Cardiff: University of Wales Press, 2003), pp. 130–43 (p. 132).

58. Ahmed, *Strange Encounters*, p. 100.

59. Edward Said, 'Reflections on Exile', in *Reflections on Exile and Other Literary and Cultural Essays* (London: Granta, 2012), pp. 173–86 (p. 186).

60. Trinh T. Minh-Ha, *Elsewhere, within Here: Immigration, Refugeeism and the Boundary Event* (London: Routledge, 2011), p. 39.
61. Ahmed, *Promise*, p. 157.
62. Ahmed, *Strange Encounters*, pp. 96, 97.
63. Yildiz, p. 28.

CONCLUSION

❖

In the introduction, it was Jonas Hassen Khemiri's question to Beatrice Ask which paved the way for the discussion of the power relations underpinning the characters' conflicts and struggles: 'När blir en personlig upplevelse en rasistisk struktur? När blir den diskriminering, förtryck, våld? Och hur kan ett "helhetsperspektiv" utesluta en stor del av medborgarnas personliga upplevelser? Vilka upplevelser räknas?' [When does a personal experience become a structure of racism? When does it become discrimination, oppression, violence? And how can looking at 'the big picture' rule out so many personal experiences of citizens? Which experiences count?].[1] In a similar way to that in which Khemiri makes his own experiences of marginalisation and othering count by offering them to Ask for an imagined re-experiencing, this study homed in on those experiences of fictional characters which are usually marginalised in dominant discourses of exclusion and discrimination, and made them count. Instead of ruling out the personal experiences of citizens, and also of characters hoping to become citizens, I utilised the perspectives of these personal experiences, and the related emotions, to gain deeper insight into 'the big picture'. Emotions, as we have seen, regulate the relationship between an individual and a social body, because how 'we feel about others is what aligns us with a collective', or, equally, alienates us from this very collective.[2] Therefore, affect has proven to be ideally suited to analysing the characters' emotional and embodied lived experiences, and how they, in turn, 'deeply connect [...] to the contextual social and political world'.[3] I have complemented the theoretical angle of affect with the employment of a postmigrant perspective, which aided me in exploring the ways in which the characters' experiences become related to this contextual and political world. Through this perspective, I have been able to show that the Scandinavian and German societies, as they are depicted in the twelve texts, by no means consider pluralisation as normal or uncomplicated. Instead, these societies are presented as marginalising those they perceive as not really belonging, and as treating those problems as related to immigration which, in fact, are caused by structural or economic inequalities. When the texts' characters are othered and excluded by means of outside ascriptions, and when their conflicts are, moreover, 'treated as a separate problem as if the "majority society" [...] had nothing to do with it', they do not cease to be thought of as migrants, 'or in terms of their supposed ethnicity'.[4]

Following the different steps of the migratory journey from departure and travel to an uncertain arrival, and examining the problematic notions of belonging and integration, I have illustrated that a sense of liminality pervades every single step of the depicted migratory journeys. Even before the Kallay family, in Akos

Doma's novel, and P, in Johannes Anyuru's text, reach their respective destinations, Germany and Sweden, they are forcibly held in liminal zones such as centres for asylum seekers and refugee camps. Although the protagonists' violent childhood experiences have, at first glance, nothing to do with their migrations, later similarly violent experiences amplify the protagonists' affective reactions and shatter their lives in a way that jeopardises their well-being in their desired destinations: we never know whether the Kallay family actually reach Germany; and P, presumably, would have never felt safe, no matter where he migrated. Karim and Miki in Abbas Khider's and Alen Mešković's narratives are held in similarly liminal zones after they have arrived in their potential host countries, Germany and Denmark. Because the outcome of their applications for asylum is uncertain, these liminal zones are marked by a sense of prolonged indeterminacy. Being held in these geographically marginalised zones means for the characters that their lives are put on hold, and because they are, in addition, socially and politically marginalised, they are deprived of any chance for self-realisation, and find themselves in 'a state hardly perceptible, hardly audible and "voiceless"'.[5] This liminality, however, also pertains to those postmigrant characters in Sweden, Norway and Germany whose migratory journeys came to an end, or who are descendants of migrants without immediate migration experiences of their own: the Arab and his daughter Yasaman in Pooneh Rohi's novel, Jamal and Mo in Zeshan Shakar's text, and Senthil and Valmira in Senthuran Varatharajah's novel. In their cases, the liminality that characterises the spatial boundaries of the nation-state extends into the social and cultural sphere: liminal zones can be recognised tangentially in all those areas or situations where notions of belonging and integration, of inclusion and exclusion, are negotiated and fought out, while the characters themselves remain similarly marginalised as those who are in the process of crossing borders and trying to settle into their so-called host countries.

We have further seen that these liminal zones are always inscribed with unequal power structures. By virtue of this power imbalance, binaries such as rich and poor, black and white, privileged and underprivileged, acquire stability, and examining the conditions of their formation has shown that these dichotomies do not exist in isolation from each other, but, more often than not, become conflated. This means that asylum seekers, refugees and marginalised postmigrants are simultaneously depicted as poor, underprivileged and of colour, whereas those characters they encounter, native Scandinavian and German citizens, are portrayed as affluent, privileged and white. For the most part, the unequal power relations depicted in the twelve texts become apparent in personal encounters between individuals; but when 'these signifiers slide into one another in the articulation of power', the inequalities within these power relations become consolidated, and the affects emerging from these encounters grant insight into the ways in which inequalities between individuals are related to wider political and societal frameworks.[6] The Kallay family, P, Karim and Miki are subject to the immigration politics and policies in their respective host countries, and while their asylum claims are pending, and even after they had gained refugee status, their lives are characterised by precarity. This precarity exposes them differentially to violence, exploitation, racialised processes of othering and marginalisation; and, although these aspects come into play in personal encounters, they are displayed as politically effectuated. Obviously, the affects produced by this precarity are negative; the characters' experiences, and some of their encounters, change their bodies, and instead of causing them 'to grow, enlighten, transform, strengthen', they 'mutate, freeze, rupture, break, traumatize'.[7] Accordingly, the characters feel isolated, lonely, disillusioned and angry, and through these emotions, they begin to question their self-understanding. I have also shown that the Arab and his daughter Yasaman, Senthil and Valmira, and Mo and Jamal, are exposed to similar processes of othering, marginalisation and ghettoisation, despite having lived most of their lives in their so-called host countries, or being born in Germany, Norway or Sweden as descendants of migrants. Those postmigrant characters find themselves excluded for their embodied and racialised otherness although they have lived in Scandinavia or Germany as lawful citizens all, or most of, their lives, and those boundaries which define the liminal zones of the border-crossing experience become expanded into the nation-state when they serve to delimit who does and does not belong on a social and cultural level.

Selecting, in addition, the texts *Snakk til meg, Tilfældets gud, Opphold, De fördrivna* and *Politisk roman*, which focus on the white native Scandinavian characters Ingeborg, Ana, Mikkel, Miriam and Filip, and Rebecca and Robert, and comparing their affective reactions to those they encounter and construct as 'other', allowed me to explore the notions of affective responsibility and Scandinavian Guilt. Analysing Mikkel's, Miriam's and Filip's, and Rebecca's and Robert's affective engagement with, or disengagement from, the 'others' they come up against, has brought to the fore the Scandinavian characters' difficulties in 'resist[ing] the mental distancing of rationalization, defensiveness, or projection', because they use their own affective dispositions to make excuses for not engaging with 'others'.[8] In this sense, affective responsibility becomes thwarted by various degrees of indifference, and, although most of the characters feel the moral obligation that they should do something, they are unable to loosen the hold of their own personal agendas, and remain inactive, or impassive. In the gap between this felt moral obligation and the characters' inaction, and also between their own privileges and the others' precarity, emerges a feeling of guilt, or unease, 'overfor en global, lidende Annen' [towards a global, suffering Other].[9] Especially when global suffering is contrasted with the perception that the Scandinavian countries are the happiest countries in the world in terms of prosperity, equality and social security, Elisabeth Oxfeldt identifies this feeling of unease as a distinctly Scandinavian form of guilt. In none of the discussed texts has this form of guilt been depicted as inspiring altruistic, or pro-social, action; rather, we have seen how Rebecca suppresses guilt, how Filip reinterprets it as pride in his own achievements, how Miriam and Mikkel explain it away, and how Robert, and, in particular, Ana and Ingeborg, utilise it as a self-serving mechanism to feel good about themselves. However, as the texts simultaneously refute the notion of Scandinavian exceptionalism by portraying characters who might be affluent and privileged, but who are not at all happy, the texts implicitly suggest that the characters' feelings of guilt are more of a general, and less of a particularly Scandinavian, nature.

Moreover, I have challenged the perceived happiness of the Scandinavian countries in two different ways: firstly, by scrutinising the ways in which migrant and postmigrant characters are received and accepted in Denmark, Norway and Sweden; and secondly, by comparing these aspects with texts from German literature, and how they depict the reception and acceptance of 'others'. This close comparison of Scandinavian and German texts has shown that the notion of Scandinavian happiness is, when it is attributed to the Scandinavian countries in a generalising way, a construct with inherent flaws, because it is not equally applicable to all Scandinavians. It is especially not applicable to newcomers to the Scandinavian countries, or to those who have lived there most of their lives and are marked as 'other' due to their outward appearance. We have seen that particularly the Arab and Yasaman, and Mo and Jamal, are excluded from a national sense of happiness by way of marginalisation, and, when they cannot be part of the societies they live in because they are not allowed to align themselves affectively with them, they become affectively alienated from these very societies. Comparing processes of othering and marginalisation, as they are depicted in Scandinavian texts, with texts from German literature, revealed that they exist in very similar ways in Germany to their existence in Scandinavia: Senthil and Valmira are exposed to and affected by marginalisation and othering in the same way as the Scandinavian characters. In addition, the political structures and public discourses enabling and maintaining these processes differ only in minor details. In conclusion, when (native white) individuals lack the affective responsibility to listen with care and attention to someone they perceive as different from themselves; to recognise difference for its own sake without the immediate urge to draw boundaries; and when personal conflicts and struggles become related to issues of immigration, instead of being identified as effected by structural economic, political and social deficits, it remains challenging to transcend national, territorial and personal borders and boundaries. Or, in Khemiri's words, this study has evidenced that whether it is in personal encounters, or in confrontations between individuals and the state, 'det är omöjligt att vara en del av gemenskapen när Makten ständigt förutsätter att en är en Annan' [it's impossible to be part of a community when Power continually assumes that you are an Other].[10]

From a transnational perspective, this is certainly a somewhat bleak outlook; and yet, the twelve texts can be viewed as supporting a transnational incentive by visualising the undiminished ascendancy of borders, including their policies and practices, and of embodied boundaries, and by making evident 'the urgency of issues of belonging, inclusion and exclusion, citizenship, [...] status and privilege'.[11] This transnational incentive gains political prominence through the role of affect as it is depicted in the texts, or, as Carrie Smith-Prei asserts, through 'social impulses resulting from the appearance of affect in the text's aesthetic architecture, [and] in the depiction of embodied affect (including also the effect of affect) to uncover or destabilize power structures'.[12] In the same vein, I have illustrated how particular aesthetic choices produce affects and how these narrative strategies help to build the structure of the texts; which affects are generated by precarious life situations, in embodied encounters, and through policies and practices of inclusion or exclusion; and the effects of these embodied affects, to shed light on how the texts work politically. Or, in other words, in which ways the texts resist their characters' marginalisation.

Accordingly, in chapter 1 we have seen how affects resulting from violence concatenate with long-lasting ripple effects in the characters' personal lives; but, as Doma's and Anyuru's texts display violence as embedded into political structures, the texts critically highlight the origins of violence, and not just its causes. The comparison of Khider's *Ohrfeige* and Mešković's *Enmandstelt* in chapter 2 has underscored the importance of political agency in the context of seeking asylum. While Mešković's novel emphasises that political agency is tantamount to self-realisation, Khider's novel demonstrates that it is possible to resist exclusionary structures which deny political agency, albeit in imaginary form. Jumping to chapter 5, which focused on Varatharajah's *Vor der Zunahme der Zeichen*, Rohi's *Araben* and Shakar's *Tante Ulrikkes vei*, we have seen that the literary realms of the texts themselves can be viewed as 'Räume des Widerstands' [spaces of resistance], because they give room to memories and histories that are usually disregarded, and therefore counterpoise the characters' marginalisation; and they depict characters who 'speak out of consciousness of such histories, and with consciousness of racism', which opposes exclusionary discourses which often support and sustain racism and marginalisation.[13] Chapter 3 discussed two texts which centre on white, native Scandinavian characters, Kirsten Thorup's *Tilfældets gud* and Vigdis Hjorth's *Snakk til meg*, and demonstrated how, in the context of tourism, liminal zones can be interpreted as areas open to experimental freedom, because they offer the tourist a suspension from everyday obligations. Through the lens of affective economies, I have illuminated that these zones, because of their inherent freedom, and because of the economic disparity between the Scandinavian characters and the 'others' they encounter, enable the exoticisation and fetishisation of the others' desired difference. By exposing the fetishisation of exoticised otherness as problematic, and by highlighting the fatal effects of a politics of appropriation on those who become fetishised for their otherness, these two texts were shown as activating the reader's political consciousness. In a similar vein, chapter 4 concentrated on the white Scandinavian characters of Lone Aburas's *Politisk roman*, Aasne Linnestå's *Opphold*, and Negar Naseh's *De fördrivna*, and revealing the characters' lack of affective responsibility has simultaneously highlighted the effects of a politics of indifference on those who are marginalised, and proposed that the texts might potentially inspire a sense of affective responsibility in the reader. In sum, we can establish that, first and foremost, those texts focusing on asylum seekers, refugees and marginalised postmigrant characters, give them a literary platform, and therefore refute the notion that they are rendered invisible and inaudible. Moreover, all the twelve texts, by defamiliarising the reader from potentially stereotyped preconceptions, may foster 'a greater aesthetic-political reflexivity and sensitivity' in the reader.[14]

When affect enhances the reader's political reflexivity, parallels can be drawn between the ways in which affect has been identified as the conjunction between the characters' lived experiences and their social world, and how it, potentially, connects the texts with the reader's own reality. In this respect, I have pointed towards certain narrative techniques and aesthetic choices, which may invite the reader's affective engagement with the twelve texts. In chapter 1, we have seen that Doma and Anyuru treat the unspeakability of trauma differently, yet with the similar effect of highlighting its causes: Doma employs a third-person narrator, who, by virtue of temporal delays in the linear chronology of the narrative and selective focalisation, leaves gaps and ambiguities, which can be filled by the reader with empathy for Teréz, and an understanding for her desperate situation. Anyuru makes use of a framing device, in which P's son reveals how he reimagines his father's history from a narratorial position of empathy, and the son's understanding and concern are tacitly extended to the reader as an invitation to feel with P. Chapter 2, by utilising the concept of ironic realism, assessed the first-person narrative voices of Karim in Khider's novel, and of Miki in Mešković's text, and has illustrated that the use of irony affectively distances the reader from the depicted harsh realities of asylum seekers. At the same time, this distancing spotlights the political constellations depriving the characters of political agency, and when the narrative voices change from irony to gratitude in Miki's case, and to anger in Karim's, these affective changes underscore with urgency the necessity of political agency with regard to self-realisation. Comparing the voice of the third-person narrator in Thorup's novel with that of the first-person narrator in Hjorth's novel in chapter 3 has shown that the narrator's distance from, and commentary about, Ana, in *Tilfældets gud*, together with the narrator's oscillation between Ana and Mariama, undermines Ana's supposed confidence; Ingeborg, in *Snakk til meg*, undercuts her own credibility when it becomes obvious to the reader that she is utilising Enrique and her narrative for the purpose of eliciting a response from her son. These formal choices complicate the reader's immediate affective engagement with the Scandinavian characters, which, in turn, brings to the fore how questionable the politics underlying the characters' intended appropriation of desired otherness are. In chapter 4, we have seen that the third-person narrator in Naseh's novel focalises mainly Miriam and Filip, and while this highlights the tensions in their relationship, it also illustrates the couple's self-centredness. Through the introduction of the character Ashkan and his interest in refugees, however, juxtapositions are built into the text which contrast Miriam and Filip's privileged lifestyle with the refugees' precarity. In Linnestå's novel, Mikkel's first-person narrative voice, as it centres on his immediate concerns, dominates the entire narrative, and only when the Javadi family's predicaments manage to penetrate Mikkel's indifference is the reader granted a glimpse into their lives. Rebecca's caustic first-person narrative voice similarly dominates Aburas's novel, but while Rebecca continuously underscores her indifference, the text itself, by means of hyperbole and irony, satirises Rebecca's racist position, and also Robert's supposedly liberal stance, thus distancing the reader from both political attitudes. While all three texts emphasise their Scandinavian characters' indifference, they simultaneously expose the degree to which this lack of affective responsibility eclipses those who might be in need of it. In chapter 5, we have seen that the privacy of the Facebook conversation in Varatharajah's novel seemingly excludes the reader while, at the same time, it makes the reader a witness to Senthil and Valmira's marginalised histories, in similar ways to Shakar's text granting the reader access to a research project in which the characters reveal their histories of racism and discrimination. In Rohi's novel, meanwhile, it is the third-person narrator's focalisation of the Arab which exposes the ways in which he is othered. By way of the authors' structural decisions, all three texts give the reader an unfiltered view into the characters' lives, inviting them to assess the characters on their own terms, connect with them affectively, and show recognition for their otherwise disregarded histories and realities.

These aesthetic choices can be seen as invitations for the reader to engage with fictional characters affectively, whereas the political and ethical reach of these twelve texts can only be understood as a potential, or an impulse. In this sense, I shall end on a hopeful, yet slightly speculative note, precisely because 'the contract of fictionality' does not require immediate pro-social action of the reader in their real world, and because it is left to the individual reader to decide whether or not 'to convert their emotional fusion with the denizens of make-believe worlds into actions on behalf of real others'.[15] While Keen's argument may give the impression that it is a somewhat futile undertaking to investigate the affective power of literature in the reader's real world without the necessary empirical evidence, she makes one concession that revaluates this undertaking. With reference to Larry P. Nucci's research on the ways in which social and moral awareness can be developed in and through education, Keen argues that 'the development of social and moral understanding requires *discussion*',[16] and, following on from this, she suggests that the reader's affective engagement with fictional texts can only be effective when it is cultivated in such discussion. Only then, Keen proposes, can the analysis of affects generated by texts 'point toward the potential for novel reading to help citizens respond to real others with greater openness and consciousness of their shared humanity'.[17] With regard to the twelve texts analysed here, the affective and political impulses these texts have to offer can be taken up by the reader and into their social and political environments. Because the texts guide the reader's affective engagement to feel with marginalised characters and their life situations, and, moreover, because they invite the critical assessment of the social and political power relations that cause these situations, these impulses may, potentially, develop into interventions — interventions in discussions on exclusionary discourses on migration and postmigration. These discussions, or conversations, as Zygmunt Bauman has it, are both unavoidable and necessary, because, 'Whatever the obstacles, and however immense they might seem, conversation will remain the royal road to agreement and so to peaceful and mutually beneficial, cooperative and solidary coexistence'.[18] Advocating the concept of affective responsibility, I propose that the obstacles Bauman mentions can be overcome with mindful listening, and this fine adjustment of attentiveness, in turn, may inspire receptivity, and, ultimately, responsible acts in support of others. In this sense, when conversations are held in the awareness of affective responsibility, they may yield an answer to Butler's question of what 'our responsibility toward those we do not know' actually is.[19]

Notes to the Conclusion

1. Khemiri, p. 130. Khemiri's last question, 'Vilka upplevelser räknas?', is missing in Rachel Willson-Broyles' translation, and, as I consider it relevant, I have included it in the translation here.
2. Ahmed, 'Collective Feelings', p. 27.
3. Smith-Prei, p. 70.
4. Römhild, p. 69; Bromley, 'Bricolage', p. 36.
5. Agier, *Borderlands*, p. 36.
6. Brah, p. 185, italics in original.
7. Richardson, p. 35.
8. Beausoleil, p. 308.
9. Oxfeldt, 'Innledning', p. 20.
10. Khemiri, p. 138.
11. Herrmann and others, p. 4.
12. Smith-Prei, p. 80.
13. Yildiz, p. 28; Ahmed, *Promise*, p. 158.
14. Bromley, 'Politics of Displacement', p. 20.
15. Keen, p. 168.
16. Ibid., p. 146, italics in original.
17. Ibid., p. 147.
18. Bauman, *Strangers*, p. 116.
19. Butler, p. 36.

BIBLIOGRAPHY

❖

Aburas, Lone, *Politisk roman* (Copenhagen: Gyldendal, 2013)

Adelson, Leslie A., 'Against Between: A Manifesto', in *Zafer Şenocak*, ed. by Tom Cheesman and Karin Yeşilada (Cardiff: University of Wales Press, 2003), pp. 130–43

Agamben, Giorgio, *Homo Sacer: Sovereign Power and Bare Life*, trans. by Daniel Heller-Roazen (Stanford: Stanford University Press, 1995)

Agier, Michel, *Borderlands*, trans. by David Fernbach (Cambridge: Polity Press, 2016)

——*On the Margins of the World: The Refugee Experience Today*, trans. by David Fernbach (Cambridge: Polity Press, 2008)

Ahmed, Sara, 'Affective Economies', *Social Text*, 22 (2004), 117–39

——'Collective Feelings: Or, The Impressions Left by Others', *Theory, Culture and Society*, 21 (2004), 25–42

——*The Cultural Politics of Emotion* (Edinburgh: Edinburgh University Press, 2004)

——*The Promise of Happiness* (Durham, NC: Duke University Press, 2010)

——*Strange Encounters: Embodied Others in Post-Coloniality* (London: Routledge, 2000)

Ahmed, Sara, and others, 'Introduction', in *Uprootings/Regroundings: Questions of Home and Migration*, ed. by Ahmed and others (Oxford: Berg, 2003), pp. 1–20

'Alby', in *Botkyrka kommun* <http://www.botkyrka.statistikportal.se/omradesfakta> [accessed 22 July 2019]

Anyuru, Johannes, *A Storm Blew in from Paradise*, trans. by Rachel Willson-Broyles (London: World Editions, 2015)

——*En storm kom från paradiset* (Stockholm: Norstedts, 2011)

Arping, Åsa, 'Feeling Different, Acting Indifferently — Gender, Privilege and Vulnerability in Contemporary Swedish Fiction' (University of Oslo: Affects of Diversity in Nordic Literature Conference, 1–2 November 2018, Panel Presentation on 2 November 2018)

Assmann, Aleida, and Ines Detmers, 'Introduction', in *Empathy and its Limits*, ed. by Assmann and Detmers (Basingstoke: Palgrave Macmillan, 2016), pp. 1–17

Atkinson, Meera, and Michael Richardson, 'At the Nexus', in *Traumatic Affect*, ed. by Atkinson and Richardson (Newcastle upon Tyne: Cambridge Scholars Publishing, 2013), pp. 1–21

Bal, Mieke, 'Introduction', in *Acts of Memory: Cultural Recall in the Present*, ed. by Bal and others (London: University Press of New England, 1999), pp. vii–xvii

Bauman, Zygmunt, *Liquid Times: Living in an Age of Uncertainty* (Cambridge: Polity Press, 2007)

——*Strangers at Our Door* (Cambridge: Polity Press, 2016)

Beausoleil, Emily, 'Responsibility as Responsiveness: Enacting a Dispositional Ethics of Encounter', *Political Theory*, 45 (2017) 291–318

Benjamin, Walter, *Gesammelte Schriften*, ed. by Rolf Tiedemann and Hermann Schweppenhäuser, I.2 (Frankfurt a.M.: Suhrkamp, 1972)

——*Illuminations*, ed. and intro. by Hannah Arendt, trans. by Harry Zohn (London: Fontana, 1973)

Berlant, Lauren Gail, 'Compassion (and Withholding)', in *Compassion: The Culture and Politics of an Emotion*, ed. by Berlant (London: Routledge, 2004), pp. 1–13

BJÖRKLUND, JENNY, and URSULA LINDQVIST, 'Introduction', in *New Dimensions of Diversity in Nordic Culture and Society*, ed. by Björklund and Lindqvist (Newcastle upon Tyne: Cambridge Scholars Publishing, 2016), pp. viii–xx

BLAKE, THOMAS, 'Affective Aversion, Ethics, and Fiction', in *The Palgrave Handbook of Affect Studies and Textual Criticism*, ed. by Donald R. Wehrs and Blake (Basingstoke: Palgrave Macmillan, 2017), pp. 207–34

'Blatte', in *Slangopedia*, <http://www.slangopedia.se/ordlista/?ord=blatte> [accessed 15 August 2019]

BOOTH, WAYNE C., *The Rhetoric of Fiction*, 2nd edn (Chicago: University of Chicago Press, 1983)

BRAH, AVTAR, *Cartographies of Diaspora: Contesting Identities* (London: Routledge, 1996)

BRAIDOTTI, ROSI, 'Nomadic Ethics', *Deleuze Studies*, 7 (2013), 342–59

BROMLEY, ROGER, 'A Bricolage of Identifications: Storying Postmigrant Belonging', *Journal of Aesthetics and Culture*, 9 (2017), 36–44

——'Displacement, Asylum and Narratives of Nation: Giving Voice to Refugees in the Film "La Forteress"', in *The Culture of Migration*, ed. by Sten Pultz Moslund and others (London: I. B. Tauris, 2015), pp. 41–58

——*Narratives for a New Belonging: Diasporic Cultural Fictions* (Edinburgh: Edinburgh University Press, 2000)

——'The Politics of Displacement: The Far Right Narrative of Europe and its "Others"', *From the European South*, 3 (2018) 13–26

BRUCKNER, PASCAL, *The Tyranny of Guilt: An Essay on Western Masochism*, trans. by Steven Rendall (Princeton: Princeton University Press, 2010)

BUTLER, JUDITH, *Frames of War: When Is Life Grievable?* (London: Verso, 2009)

CONNELL, RAEWYN, *Masculinities*, 2nd edn (Cambridge: Polity Press, 2005)

DAIGLE, MEGAN, *From Cuba with Love* (Oakland: University of California Press, 2015)

DELEUZE, GILLES, *Spinoza: Practical Philosophy*, trans. by Robert Hurley (San Francisco: City Lights Books, 1988)

DELEUZE, GILLES, and FÉLIX GUATTARI, *A Thousand Plateaus*, trans. by Brian Massumi (London: Bloomsbury, 2013)

'Dissensus, n', *Oxford English Dictionary Online* (Oxford: Oxford University Press, June 2019) <http://www.oed.com/view/Entry/242116> [accessed 16 August 2019]

DOMA, AKOS, *Der Weg der Wünsche* (Hamburg: Rowohlt, 2016)

DONNAN, HASTINGS, 'Borders, Anthropology of', in *International Encyclopedia of the Social and Behavioral Sciences*, ed. by James D. Wright (Amsterdam: Elsevier, 2015), pp. 760–64

DU BOIS, W. E. B., *The Souls of Black Folk: The Oxford W. E. B. Du Bois*, 1st edn (Oxford: Oxford University Press, 2010)

'Dublin Convention', in *A Dictionary of Law*, ed. by Jonathan Law (Oxford: Oxford University Press, 2018)

ERLL, ASTRID, *Memory in Culture* (Basingstoke: Palgrave Macmillan, 2011)

FARRIER, DAVID, *Postcolonial Asylum: Seeking Sanctuary before the Law* (Liverpool: Liverpool University Press, 2011)

FIFIELD, PETER, 'The Body, Pain and Violence', in *The Cambridge Companion to the Body in Literature*, ed. by David Hillman and Ulrika Maude (Cambridge: Cambridge University Press, 2015), pp. 116–31

FOUCAULT, MICHEL, *Security, Territory, Population: Lectures at the Collège de France, 1977–78*, ed. by Michel Senellart, trans. by Graham Burchell (Basingstoke: Palgrave Macmillan, 2007)

GARTON, JANET, 'Afterword', in *The God of Chance*, by Kirsten Thorup (London: Norvik Press, 2013) pp. 289–94

GATES, HENRY LOUIS, JR, 'Introduction', in *'Race,' Writing and Difference*, ed. by Gates, Jr (Chicago: University of Chicago Press, 1986) pp. 1–20

GIBBS, ANNA, 'Apparently Unrelated: Affective Resonance, Concatenation and Traumatic Circuitry in the Terrain of the Everyday', in *Traumatic Affect*, ed. by Meera Atkinson and Michael Richardson (Newcastle upon Tyne: Cambridge Scholars Publishing, 2013) pp. 129–47

'Gjennomtrekk', in *Bokmålsordboka* <http://www.ordbok.uib.no/GJENNOMTREKK> [accessed 13 June 2019]

GREGG, MELISSA, and GREGORY J. SEIGWORTH, 'An Inventory of Shimmers', in *The Affect Theory Reader*, ed. by Gregg and Seigworth (Durham, NC: Duke University Press, 2010), pp. 1–26

HANSEN, HOLGER BERNT, 'Uganda in the 1970s: A Decade of Paradoxes and Ambiguities', *Journal of Eastern African Studies*, 1 (2013), 83–103

HARDT, MICHAEL, 'What Affects are Good For', in *The Affective Turn: Theorizing the Social*, ed. by Patricia Ticineto Clough and Jean Halley (Durham, NC: Duke University Press, 2007), pp. ix–xiii

HEITMANN, ANNEGRET, 'Female Tourists Going Global: Danish Travel Narratives between Happiness and Guilt', *Scandinavian Studies*, 89 (2017), 512–29

HERLIHY, JANE, and OTHERS, 'Just Tell Us What Happened to You: Autobiographical Memory and Seeking Asylum', *Applied Cognitive Psychology*, 26 (2012), 661–76

HERMAN, JUDITH LEWIS, *Trauma and Recovery* (London: Pandora, 1997)

HERRMANN, ELISABETH, and OTHERS, 'Introduction', in *Transnationalism in Contemporary German-Language Literature*, ed. by Herrmann and others (Rochester: Camden House, 2015), pp. 1–16

HIBBINS, RAYMOND, and BOB PEASE, 'Men and Masculinities on the Move', in *Migrant Men: Critical Studies of Masculinities and the Migration Experience*, ed. by Mike Donaldson and others (London: Routledge, 2009), pp. 1–19

HILLMAN, DAVID, and ULRIKA MAUDE, 'Introduction', in *The Cambridge Companion to the Body in Literature*, ed. by Hillman and Maude (Cambridge: Cambridge University Press, 2015), pp. 1–9

HJORTH, VIGDIS, *Snakk til meg* (Oslo: Cappelen Damm, 2010)

HOOKS, BELL, *Black Looks: Race and Representation* (Boston, MA: South End Press, 1992)

——*We Real Cool: Black Men and Masculinity* (London: Routledge, 2004)

HÜBINETTE, TOBIAS, and CATRIN LUNDSTRÖM, 'Sweden after the Recent Election: The Double-Binding Power of Swedish Whiteness through the Mourning of the Loss of "Old Sweden" and the Passing of "Good Sweden"', *NORA — Nordic Journal of Feminist and Gender Research*, 19 (2011), 42–52

HUGGAN, GRAHAM, *The Postcolonial Exotic* (London: Routledge, 2001)

ISIN, ENGIN F., and KIM RYGIEL, 'Abject Spaces: Frontiers, Zones, Camps', in *The Logics of Biopower and the War on Terror: Living, Dying, Surviving*, ed. by Elizabeth Dauphinee and Christina Masters (Basingstoke: Palgrave Macmillan, 2007), pp. 181–203

KARAKAYALI, JULIANE, and PAUL MECHERIL, 'Umkämpfte Krisen: Migrationsregime als Analyseperspektive', in *Postmigrantische Perspektiven*, ed. by Naika Foroutan and others (Frankfurt a.M.: Campus, 2018), pp. 225–36

KEEN, SUZANNE, *Empathy and the Novel* (Oxford: Oxford University Press, 2007)

KHAIR, TABISH, 'Old and New Xenophobia', in *The Culture of Migration*, ed. by Sten Pultz Moslund and others (London: I. B. Tauris, 2015), pp. 59–68

KHEMIRI, JONAS HASSEN, 'Bästa Beatrice', in *Jag ringer mina bröder* (Stockholm: Bonnier, 2013), pp. 129–41

——'An Open Letter to Beatrice Ask', *Asymptote*, trans. by Rachel Willson-Broyles,

<http://www.asymptotejournal.com/nonfiction/jonas-hassen-khemiri-an-open-letter-to-beatrice-ask> [accessed 26 March 2019]

KHIDER, ABBAS, *Ohrfeige* (Munich: Hanser, 2016)

——*A Slap in the Face*, trans. by Simon Pare (London: Seagull Books, 2018)

KRISTEVA, JULIA, *Powers of Horror: An Essay on Abjection*, trans. by Leon S. Roudiez (Oxford: Columbia University Press, 1982)

KUNDERA, MILAN, *The Art of the Novel*, trans. by Linda Asher (New York: Perennial-Harper, 1988)

LAWRENCE, BRUCE B., and AISHA KARIM, 'Introduction', in *On Violence: A Reader*, ed. by Lawrence and Karim (Durham, NC: Duke University Press, 2007), pp. 1–15

'Limen, n', in *Oxford English Dictionary Online* (Oxford: Oxford University Press, June 2019) <http://www.oed.com/view/Entry/108451> [accessed 16 August 2019]

LINNESTÅ, AASE, *Opphold* (Oslo: Aschehoug, 2014)

LORRAINE, TAMSIN, 'Lines of Flight', in *The Deleuze Dictionary*, ed. by Adrian Parr (Edinburgh: Edinburgh University Press, 2010), pp. 147–48

'Lov om midlertidig opholdstilladelse til visse personer fra det tidligere Jugoslavien m.v.', in *Onlaw*, 933 (28 November 1992) <https://onlaw.dk/lov/lov-nr-933-af-28-11-1992> [accessed 24 August 2019]

MASSUMI, BRIAN, 'The Future Birth of the Affective Fact: The Political Ontology of Threat', in *The Affect Theory Reader*, ed. by Melissa Gregg and Gregory J. Seigworth (Durham, NC: Duke University Press, 2010), pp. 52–70

——*Parables for the Virtual: Movement, Affect, Sensation* (Durham, NC: Duke University Press, 2002)

——*A User's Guide to Capitalism and Schizophrenia: Deviations from Deleuze and Guattari* (London: MIT Press, 1992)

MAZZARA, FEDERICA, 'Subverting the Narrative of the Lampedusa Borderscape', *Crossings*, 7 (2016), 135–47

MBEMBE, ACHILLE, 'Necropolitics', *Public Culture*, 15 (2003), 1–40

McCORMICK, JOHN, *European Union Politics* (Basingstoke: Palgrave Macmillan, 2011)

MERLEAU-PONTY, MAURICE, *Phenomenology of Perception*, trans. by Colin Smith (London: Routledge & Kegan Paul, 1962)

MEŠKOVIĆ, ALEN, *Enmandstelt* (Copenhagen: Gyldendal, 2016)

NASEH, NEGAR, *De fördrivna* (Stockholm: Natur & Kultur, 2016)

NASSEHI, ARMIN, 'Namenlos glücklich', *Zeit Online* (30 January 2014) <http://www.zeit.de/2014/06/herkunft> [accessed 15 August 2018]

NGAI, SIANNE, *Ugly Feelings* (Cambridge, MA: Harvard University Press, 2007)

O'CONNELL DAVIDSON, JULIA, and JACQUELINE SANCHEZ TAYLOR, 'Fantasy Islands: Exploring the Demand for Sex Tourism', in *Men's Lives*, ed. by Michael S. Kimmel and Michael A. Messner, 6th edn (London: Allyn & Bacon, 2004) pp. 454–66

OXFELDT, ELISABETH, '"I Come from Crap Country and You Come from Luxury Country": Ugly Encounters in Scandinavian Au-Pair Novels', *Scandinavian Studies*, 89 (2017), 468–86

——'Innledning', in *Skandinaviske fortellinger om skyld og privilegier i en globaliseringstid*, ed. by Elisabeth Oxfeldt (Oslo: Universitetsforlaget, 2016), pp. 9–31

——'Staten sa ja, så hva sier jeg?', in *Skandinaviske fortellinger om skyld og privilegier i en globaliseringstid*, ed. by Oxfeldt (Oslo: Universitetsforlaget, 2016), pp. 230–54

PEDERSEN, CAMILLA, 'Venteland — bosniske flygtninge i Danmark', in *Folkedrab*, <http://www.folkedrab.dk/artikler/venteland-bosniske-flygtninge-i-danmark> [accessed 20 April 2017]

PELLEGRINI, ANN, and JASBIR PUAR, 'Affect', *Social Text*, 27 (2009), 35–38

PETERSEN, ANNE RING, and MORITZ SCHRAMM, '(Post-)Migration in the Age of

Globalisation: New Challenges to Imagination and Representation', *Journal of Aesthetics and Culture*, 9 (2017), 1–12

PRATT, MARY LOUISE, *Imperial Eyes: Travel Writing and Transculturation* (London: Routledge, 2008)

RADSTONE, SUSANNAH, 'What Place Is This? Transcultural Memory and the Locations of Memory Studies', *Parallax*, 17 (2011), 109–23

RAJARAM, PREM KUMAR, and CARL GRUNDY-WARR, 'Introduction', in *Borderscapes: Hidden Geographies and Politics at Territory's Edge*, ed. by Rajaram and Grundy-Warr (Minnesota: University of Minnesota Press, 2007), pp. ix–xl

RANCIÈRE, JACQUES, *Disagreement: Politics and Philosophy*, trans. by Julie Rose (Minneapolis: University of Minnesota Press, 1999)

—— 'The Politics of Literature', in *Dissensus: On Politics and Aesthetics*, ed. and trans. by Steven Corcoran (London: Continuum, 2010), pp. 160–76

—— 'Ten Theses on Politics', in *Dissensus: On Politics and Aesthetics*, ed. and trans. by Steven Corcoran (London: Continuum, 2010), pp. 35–52

—— 'Who is the Subject of the Rights of Man?', in *Dissensus: On Politics and Aesthetics*, ed. and trans. by Steven Corcoran (London: Continuum, 2010), pp. 70–83

RICHARDSON, MICHAEL, *Gestures of Testimony: Torture, Trauma and Affect in Literature* (London: Bloomsbury, 2016)

ROBERTS, GEORGE, 'The Uganda–Tanzania War, the Fall of Idi Amin, and the Failure of African Diplomacy, 1978–1979', *Journal of Eastern African Studies*, 4 (2014), 692–709

RÖMHILD, REGINA, 'Beyond the Bounds of the Ethnic: For Postmigrant Cultural and Social Research', *Journal of Aesthetics and Culture*, 9 (2017), 69–75

ROHI, POONEH, *Araben* (Stockholm: Ordfront, 2015)

ROSTEN, MONIKA GRØNLI, 'Territoriell stigmatisering og gutter som "leker getto" i Groruddalen', *Norsk sosiologisk tidsskrift*, 1 (2017), 53–70

RYAN, MARIE-LAURE, KENNETH E. FOOTE, and MAOZ AZARYAHU, *Narrating Space/Spatializing Narrative: Where Narrative Theory and Geography Meet* (Columbus: Ohio State University Press, 2016)

SAID, EDWARD, 'Reflections on Exile', in *Reflections on Exile and Other Literary and Cultural Essays* (London: Granta, 2012), pp. 173–86

—— *The World, the Text, and the Critic* (New York: Vintage Books, 1991)

SAINSBURY, DIANE, *Welfare States and Immigrant Rights: The Politics of Inclusion and Exclusion* (Oxford: Oxford University Press, 2012)

SCARRY, ELAINE, *The Body in Pain: The Making and Unmaking of the World* (Oxford: Oxford University Press, 1985)

SCHRAMM, MORITZ, 'Ironischer Realismus: Selbstdifferenz und Wirklichkeitsnähe bei Abbas Khider', in *Neue Realismen in der Gegenwartsliteratur*, ed. by Søren R. Fauth and Rolf Parr (Munich: Fink, 2016), pp. 71–84

—— 'Jenseits der binären Logik', in *Postmigrantische Perspektiven: Ordnungssysteme, Repräsentationen, Kritik*, ed. by Naika Foroutan and others (Frankfurt a.M.: Campus, 2018), pp. 83–96

SEYHAN, AZADE, *Writing Outside the Nation* (Princeton: Princeton University Press, 2001)

SHAKAR, ZESHAN, *Tante Ulrikkes vei* (Oslo: Gyldendal, 2017)

SHARMA, DEVIKA, 'Doing Good, Feeling Bad: Humanitarian Emotion in Crisis', *Journal of Aesthetics and Culture*, 9 (2017), 1–12

SILVERMAN, MAXIM, *Palimpsestic Memory: The Holocaust and Colonialism in French and Francophone Fiction and Film* (New York: Berghahn, 2015)

SMITH-PREI, CARRIE, 'Affect, Aesthetics, Biopower, and Technology: Political Interventions into Transnationalism', in *Transnationalism in Contemporary German-Language Literature*, ed. by Elisabeth Herrmann and others (Rochester: Camden House, 2015), pp. 65–85

SOGUK, NEVZAT, 'Border's Capture: Insurrectional Politics, Border-Crossing Humans, and the New Political', in *Borderscapes: Hidden Geographies and Politics at Territory's Edge*, ed. by Prem Kumar Rajaram and Carl Grundy-Warr (Minneapolis: University of Minnesota Press, 2007), pp. 283–308

SPERL, MARKUS, 'Fortress Europe and the Iraqi "Intruders": Iraqi Asylum-Seekers and the EU, 2003–2007', *New Issues in Refugee Research*, research paper 144, UNHCR (2007), pp. 1–19

SPIELHAUS, RIEM, 'Studien in der postmigrantischen Gesellschaft: Eine kritische Auseinandersetzung', in *Kongressdokumentation 4. Bundesfachkongress Interkultur, Hamburg 2012*, ed. by Marius Koniarczyck and others (Hamburg: Kulturbehörde der Freien und Hansestadt Hamburg, 2014), pp. 96–100

SPINOZA, BENEDICT DE, *Ethics*, ed. and trans. by Edwin Curley (London: Penguin, 1996)

SQUIRE, VICKI, *The Exclusionary Politics of Asylum* (Basingstoke: Palgrave Macmillan, 2009)

STEELE, SHELBY, 'White Guilt', *American Scholar*, 59 (1990), 497–506

'Svennebanan', in *Slangopedia* <http://www.slangopedia.se/ordlista/?ord=svennebanan> [accessed 15 August 2018]

THORUP, KIRSTEN, *The God of Chance*, trans. by Janet Garton (London: Norvik Press, 2013)

——— *Tilfældets gud* (Copenhagen: Gyldendal, 2011)

TOMSKY, TERRI, 'From Sarajevo to 9/11: Travelling Memory and the Trauma Economy', *Parallax*, 17 (2011), 49–60

'Torture', in *Oxford English Dictionary Online* (Oxford: Oxford University Press, June 2019) <http://www.oed.com/view/Entry/203700> [accessed 16 August 2019]

TRINH, T. MINH-HA, *Elsewhere, within Here: Immigration, Refugeeism and the Boundary Event* (London: Routledge, 2011)

TYGSTRUP, FREDERIK, 'Affective Spaces', in *Panic and Mourning: The Cultural Work of Trauma*, ed. by Daniela Agosthino and others (Berlin: De Gruyter, 2012), pp. 195–210

——— 'Notes on Affect', in *Literatura e espaços afetivos*, ed. by Heidru Krieger Olinto and Viveiro de Castro (Rio de Janeiro: 7 Letras, 2014), pp. 147–57

UN GENERAL ASSEMBLY, 'Universal Declaration of Human Rights', United Nations, 217 (III) A, art. 14 (1948) <http://www.un.org/en/universal-declaration-human-rights> [accessed 13 March 2017]

URRY, JOHN, *The Tourist Gaze* (London: Sage, 1990)

VARATHARAJAH, SENTHURAN, *Vor der Zunahme der Zeichen* (Frankfurt a.M.: Fischer, 2016)

VEISLAND, JØRGEN, 'A Mysterious Closeness: Africa and Europe in Kirsten Thorup's "The God of Chance"', *Forum for World Literature Studies*, 5 (2013), 276–88

VERTOVEC, STEVEN, *Transnationalism* (London: Routledge, 2008)

WACQUANT, LOÏC J. D., *Urban Outcasts: A Comparative Sociology of Advanced Marginality* (Cambridge: Polity Press, 2008)

WASSEN, STINA FREDRIKA, 'Where Does Securitisation Begin? The Institutionalised Securitisation of Illegal Immigration in Sweden: REVA and the ICFs', *Contemporary Voices: St Andrews Journal of International Relations*, 1 (2018), 78–103

WELZER, HARALD, 'Communicative Memory', in *A Companion to Cultural Memory Studies*, ed. by Astrid Erll and Ansgar Nünning (Berlin: De Gruyter, 2008), pp. 285–98

WEST, CORNEL, *Race Matters* (New York: Vintage Books, 1994)

YILDIZ, EROL, 'Ideen zum Postmigrantischen', in *Postmigrantische Perspektiven*, ed. by Naika Foroutan and others (Frankfurt a.M.: Campus, 2018), pp. 19–34

YILDIZ, EROL, and MARC HILL, 'In-between as Resistance: The Post-migrant Generation Between Discrimination and Transnationalization', *Transnational Social Review*, 7 (2017), 273–86

ŽIŽEK, SLAVOJ, *Violence* (London: Profile, 2008)

ZORAN, GABRIEL, 'Towards a Theory of Space in Narrative', *Poetics Today*, 5 (1984), 309–35

INDEX

❖

www.ingramcontent.com/pod-product-compliance
Lightning Source LLC
LaVergne TN
LVHW061305060426

835513LV00013B/1243